Desire and the female therapist

Desire and the Female Therapist is one of the first full-length explorations of the erotic transference and countertransference from the point of view of the female therapist. Particular attention is given to the female therapist/ male client relationship and the aesthetic effects of desire, made visible in art objects in analytical forms of psychotherapy. Drawing on psycho-analytic and aesthetic theory, particularly Lacan and Jung, the book offers a significant new approach to desire in therapy.

Following on from Joy Schaverien's innovative previous book *The Revealing Image, Desire and the Female Therapist* connects psycho-therapy and art therapy and offers a contribution to both. It is richly illustrated with pictures as well as clinical vignettes, and the drawings and paintings made by an anorexic man, combined with his own words, graphically illustrate many of the archetypal themes discussed.

Written primarily for psychotherapists, art therapists and analysts, this book will be essential reading for all those professionals who are affected by the erotic transference and countertransference in clinical practice, and all whose clients bring artworks to therapy.

Joy Schaverien is an analytical psychotherapist and art therapist in private practice. She is training as a Jungian analyst with the Society of Analytical Psychology in London.

Desire and the female therapist

Engendered gazes in psychotherapy and art therapy

Joy Schaverien

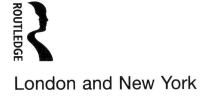

London and New York

First published 1995
by Routledge
11 New Fetter Lane, London EC4P 4EE

Simultaneously published in the USA and Canada
by Routledge
29 West 35th Street, New York, NY 10001

Typeset in Times by
J&L Composition Ltd, Filey, North Yorkshire
Printed and bound in Great Britain by
Biddles Ltd, Guildford and King's Lynn

British Library Cataloguing in Publication Data
A catalogue record for this book is available from the British Library

Library of Congress Cataloguing in Publication Data
A catalogue record for this book has been requested

ISBN 0–415–08700–7 (hbk)
ISBN 0–415–08701–5 (pbk)

For Peter

Contents

Illustrations

Chapter 5

Chapter 6

Chapter 7

Chapter 8

Chapter 9

Preface

The two main threads which run throughout this book are desire and the gaze. The book is an investigation of the erotic transference and countertransference explored through the female therapist/male patient dyad and through the aesthetic effects of desire, made visible, in art objects in analytical forms of art psychotherapy.

The book builds on ideas first developed in *The Revealing Image* (Schaverien 1991); this offered a new theoretical approach to considerations of art in analysis and psychotherapy as well as art therapy. In it I introduced the term analytical art psychotherapy and analysed the central role of art objects in the transference and countertransference relationship in clinical practice. *Desire and the Female Therapist* is intended as a further bridge between the disciplines of psychotherapy and art therapy. The interplay between these is constant throughout; in some chapters the main discussion is based on my present psychotherapy practice whilst, in others, it is developed from art therapy experience in psychiatry. I hope that there is a useful cross-over between these different experiences and that the links between the psychological states discussed transcend any particular therapeutic setting.

The desire of the female therapist is present throughout the book although not always explicitly. To some degree I have written about my own desire as therapist, client and artist, but the implications are wider than this would seem to imply. Beginning from my own experience, I have researched widely and attempted to demonstrate that the erotic is an essential element in the appreciation of art, as well as in psychotherapy. The emergence of eros, which is generated in the transference in psychotherapy or in relation to pictures, is purposeful. It is a sign of life and a move towards individuation for therapist as well as client. Many before me have indicated that it is the therapist's desire which comes first; in this sense we start from the countertransference.

Thus, as a way of introduction, it seems relevant to offer a little of my own background. I trained as an artist at the Slade, and then some years later became an art therapist. I worked as an art therapist in a number of different NHS psychiatric settings and in group and outpatient psycho-therapy. Then I became a Senior Lecturer in Art Therapy at the college of Art and Design at St Albans where I was course leader of the MA for a number of years. I exchanged this role for a private psychotherapy and analytical art psychotherapy practice and am currently training as a Jungian analyst with the Society of Analytical Psychology in London.

The book follows the path I have taken and so it is addressed to colleagues from all these different disciplines. It is written for experienced practitioners and trainees in art therapy, analytical forms of psychotherapy, Jungian analysis and psychoanalysis. However, I hope that it will also be of interest to artists, psychologists, occupational therapists, psychiatrists, art teachers and all who may be curious about the relation between art and psychoanalysis in theory as well as clinical practice.

As an artist originally, my starting point was art; it was this which led me to theoretical inquiry. Thus the pictures in this book play a very central role. They explain nothing but, as is the way with visual imagery, show a great deal; they animate the theoretical discourse. Most of us are familiar with this approach in books for young children where the written word is complemented by pictures. It could be considered to be similar with this book. Art therapists are familiar with pictorial imagery and often under-stand complicated conceptual ideas first through imagined pictures. Psy-chotherapists, on the other hand, may find it easier to think without pictorial imagery. The book uses words and pictures and it is hoped that they will complement each other and offer something useful to readers starting from either of these positions or, as is most likely, somewhere in between the two.

Many psychotherapists, particularly Jungians, regularly use art as part of the analytic process. However, other colleagues, unfamiliar with art as a medium, ask questions regarding how to respond when clients bring art-work to their sessions. Clients do not always limit themselves to expression in the medium which suits their therapist. They sometimes find it easier to make a picture of their feeling state than to speak of it. There is no substitute for art therapy training, but we do not restrain a client from using a medium which is useful to her or him just because it is unfamiliar to the therapist. Instead, acknowledging our limitations (at least internally), we follow the lead of the client. Sometimes clients who come for art therapy do not paint and the art therapist may feel de-skilled as a conse-quence. This is likely to be because she or he may feel unqualified to work without art objects. The psychotherapist may feel similarly de-skilled by a client who *does* bring pictures to psychotherapy sessions.

As a result of this, certain common misapprehensions regarding the meaning of art in psychotherapy may develop. For example, it is com-mon, for art therapists as well as psychotherapists, to claim that the aesthetic quality of pictures is irrelevant in therapy. I have argued

(Schaverien 1991) that this is to miss the point; the aesthetic element is a significant factor in the therapeutic encounter and this inevitably affects the viewer. Therefore an understanding gained from familiarity with art, one's own process and that of artists 'in the world', will influence the whole of the interaction. This is developed within the book in relation to the aesthetic countertransference and the gaze.

Another common response among psychotherapists is to interpret the act of bringing pictures to sessions as acting out. This may, at times, be a defensive response on the part of a therapist who feels uncomfortable with the unfamiliar medium. There are occasions when there is an element of acting out involved but, at other times, it may be a result of a need to show something that can find no other medium for expression. Thus although unconscious processes are one aspect of the motivation, art in therapy is rarely solely acting out. The meaning of any act in therapy is significant and much of the subtlety is missed if the artwork is seen merely as a form of unconscious behaviour. The transference implications of the *act* need to be distinguished from the effects of the *imagery*. When pictures are brought to a session, *both* the meaning of bringing the picture and that of the imagery within the relationship as a whole merit consideration. I hope that the book will offer an elucidation of the complexities of the intra- and interpersonal effects of pictorial and plastic imagery in therapy. It is my aim in discussing these processes to interest both art therapists and psychotherapists. I am attempting to bring word and image into conjunc- tion, in more ways than one, in the pages which follow.

One way of viewing the pictures shown in this book would be as illustrations of some of the psychoanalytic concepts discussed. The pic- tures in Chapter 4, for example, illustrate many of the themes and images discussed in Chapter 2. This is one facet of their role in the book but the significance of the pictures is beyond mere illustration of psychoanalytic concepts. The pictures, and the case study they illustrate, demonstrate the formative effects of art within a therapeutic relationship. They reveal the process of analytical differentiation and show that, through the effects of the pictures, separation from an undifferentiated or intransigent psycho- logical state may begin to take place. In this, I will argue, the artwork is central.

Joy Schaverien
South Luffenham
October 1994

Acknowledgements

Responsibility for all the ideas expressed is mine. However, many people have contributed to this book, most evidently, those who have given permission for me to tell fragments of their stories and to show their pictures; I am grateful to all of them. A very special debt of gratitude is owed to 'Carlos', whose pictures and words greatly enrich the book, and to his family.

Galia Wilson, Damien Wilson and Hymie Schaverien have contributed in many ways, both directly and indirectly. Peter Wilson's thoughtful comments and unceasing encouragement have played a significant part.

Whilst finishing the book I have been involved as a clinical trainee in seminars at the Society of Analytical Psychology in London. The discussion in the seminar groups has contributed to my thinking and extended its scope in many ways. I am grateful to the seminar leaders and to my colleagues in the group. Andrew Samuels merits special thanks; his insights have enabled me to write of that which has often felt unsayable. Edwina Welham and Tessa Dalley both read the manuscript at a crucial late stage and the text is greatly improved due to their comments. Gillian Hazlerigg read and commented on Chapter 2. The *British Journal of Psychotherapy* gave permission to publish Chapter 5, a version of which appeared in the *British Journal of Psychotherapy*, vol. 11 (1).

Definition of terms

'Patient' and 'client' are applied interchangeably in the text and this reflects my continued indecision regarding such terms.

The term 'picture' refers to artworks in general as well as pictures specifically. Thus, the term picture is very often applied as shorthand and includes art objects in other media.

'Art therapy' and 'art psychotherapy' as well as 'analytical art psychotherapy' are all terms I use in the text. Elsewhere I have discussed my relation to these terms in detail (Schaverien 1991, 1994c).

Chapter 1

Introduction

There is no analysis if the Other is not an Other who I love (with the corollary, whom I hate), through the good offices of 'that man/that woman without qualities' who is my analyst.

(Kristeva 1983: 14)

The erotic transference and countertransference as it manifests itself in the area in between the female therapist and male client is the main topic of this book. It will be argued that pictures which are viewed in the area in-between client and therapist may sometimes lure the viewers into a deeper relationship. Through the imagery and the medium of the gaze, they are drawn to each other. Thus the book is centrally about desire – countertransference and transference desire and desire embodied in artworks.

In this introduction I will give a brief overview of the book and a summary of some theories of sexual difference and female desire. This is my starting place. It is the therapist's desire which comes first (Stein 1974; Hillman 1977; Lacan 1977a). The therapist's desire is the initial motivation which brings her to be a therapist and without this there would be no therapy. Therefore the book begins with the countertransference, that of the female therapist.

DESIRE AND THE FEMALE THERAPIST

Since Freud first identified what he called 'transference love' (Freud 1912, 1915), the erotic transference has been understood to be a feature of any therapeutic relationship. Kristeva puts it thus: 'Sigmund Freud . . . thought of turning love into a cure. He went straight to the disorder that love reveals'(Kristeva 1983: 8). Frequently the love experienced in the transference is understood to be based in infantile experience and the corresponding countertransference is interpreted as maternal. This is especially the case with female therapists. However, this is only one facet of the dynamic and, it is argued that in all gender combinations, some of the

desire expressed in the transference and experienced in the countertransference is based in adult sexual feelings.

First, some explication of desire. Desire is not a fixed term and it could
be understood to have many facets and even meanings:

'To wish or long for, to crave . . . a wish, a longing, or a sexual appetite . . .
a person or thing that is desired' (*Collins Concise English Dictionary*).

'Unsatisfied appetite, longing, wish, craving, request, thing desired'
(*Concise Oxford Dictionary*).

Flower MacCannell (1992) traces the term back to its Christian uses:
'desire is "primitive" with the soul because it is a motive force which leads
the soul to God, linking things future (hope), things present (perception)
and things past (memory)' (Flower MacCannell 1992: 63–4).

In psychoanalysis, following Freud, the term desire has been associated
with Lacan. Sheridan (1977), who is Lacan's English translator, explains in
his note at the beginning of *Ecrits* (1977b), that Freud's French translators
used the term '*desir*' rather than '*voeu*' which corresponds to the original
German '*Wunsch*' which is rather more a wish. He points out that:

> The German and English words are limited to individual isolated acts of
> wishing, while the French has the much stronger implication of a
> continuous force. It is this implication that Lacan has elaborated and
> placed at the centre of his psychoanalytic theory, which is why I have
> rendered 'desir' by 'desire'. Furthermore, Lacan has linked the concept
> of 'desire' with 'need' (*besoin*) and 'demand' (*demande*).
>
> (Sheridan 1977: viii)

I quote this because, in the text, I shall be applying both Lacanian and
Jungian theory and so my use of the term may alter at times. Sometimes
one meaning of desire will predominate and then another. Furthermore, I
shall be applying the term in relation to artworks and this adds the element
of desire in the aesthetic appreciation of pictures.

Chapter 2, 'Desire and the female therapist', is about the erotic transference and countertransference experienced by the female therapist and
the male client. Here I apply the term mainly, but not exclusively, in
relation to sexual appetite. The desire to which I refer has to do with the
yearning for human contact and that is fuelled by eros. Theoretical issues
are discussed and examples are given from my private psychotherapy
practice. I should make it clear that I consider that the erotic transference
and countertransference serves a purpose. It is eros which is the connecting
link between the client and therapist. Eros forms the bond which enables
the relationship to survive the intensity of the extremes of positive and
negative emotion which may become manifest in the transference.

In Chapter 2, the literature is reviewed with particular attention to the
experience of the female therapist and male patient. Much has been written

about the mother/daughter dyad from the perspective of the feminist therapist; far less attention has been accorded the mother/son transference/countertransference. Male therapists write about the erotic transferences of their female patients and there are an increasing number of recorded cases of sexual abuse by male psychotherapists (Carotenuto 1982; Rutter 1989; Russell 1993; Jehu 1994). Although there is less evidence of acting out by female therapists there have been cases of female therapists breaching the boundaries when working with male and female patients (Russell 1994; McNamara 1994). Some female therapists suggest that the reason sexual abuse is less common is because they are not aroused by their patients, male or female. I challenge this claim; if there is less acting out from this dyad, it is not because there is no erotic countertransference.

Chapters 3, 4 and 5 follow on from this chapter and the focus is the male patient's transference. This is an exploration of desire and denial of desire in anorexia, through a case study of a male patient. This is unusual in several ways, first in that the patient discussed is male and eating disorders are predominantly suffered by women. In Chapter 3, I discuss the male anorexic, describe the clinical setting and introduce the patient. Chapter 4 is a detailed illustrated case study. The pictures reveal many of the images which are present, but unseen, in other forms of psychotherapy. Here desire is considered in relation to the initial denial of want, wishes and need in anorexia and the pictures demonstrate the emergence of desire (eros) in the transference. This case demonstrates the need for separation from the initial undifferentiated state. Desire presupposes a gap, a distance between the subject and its object and so, in the merged state, there is no desire. The coming to life of desire for an 'Other' brings differentiation. In this case there was, at first, a fused – a half-alive – state in which there was no separation. Later, through the formative effects of making pictures, showing them, and subsequently speaking of them, the undifferentiated state gave way to differentiation, symbolisation and, eventually, entry into language and the 'Symbolic order' (Lacan 1977b).

In Chapter 5, I introduce a new understanding of the significance and efficacy of art as a form of treatment in anorexia. I propose that the benefit to be gained from the art process is in its role as a 'transactional object'. The anorexic is relating to people and the world through a concrete medium – food. I suggest that art, which is also a concrete medium, may come to take the place of food. Pictures may become objects through which desire and need are channelled and the intensity of the obsession with food may then diminish.

The pictures are shown early in the book because I will draw on them for discussion throughout. These three linked chapters illustrate many of the themes which follow. The pictures reveal the developmental processes discussed in Chapter 2, as well as those described in the later chapters. The intention is to show the dynamic imagery which emerges between a female therapist and male patient. This chapter is drawn from my time as an art therapist working in a psychiatric hospital. The difference in the management of an erotic transference in psychiatry and psychotherapy accounts, in part, for a change in tempo between Chapter 2 and Chapter 4.

Chapters 6 and 7 are linked. In Chapter 6 the theme of desire widens to include discussion of cultural and aesthetic affects of pictures. I develop the aesthetic countertransference (a term introduced in an earlier work (Schaverien 1991)), in relation to desire in art and in psychoanalysis. In this chapter I draw on Bion and Kant, as well as Lacan, to elucidate the idea that pictures may have the power to seduce the therapist and that this may be a positive factor in therapy. In Chapter 7, the topic of infantile desires and the erotic transference/countertransference is illustrated by pictures which reveal the emergence of the child image. The case discussion of a female patient suffering from depression is central and the child image reveals the return of the repressed. Throughout these two chapters it is argued that the silence in psychotherapy is similar to the figure/ground relationships within pictures. Thus, it is argued, pictures may reveal that which is present in the silence in the interpersonal transference/counter-transference.

Chapters 8 and 9 are also linked. The seduction through the pictorial image is developed in Chapter 8, with an investigation of the lure of the image. Here desire is related to the surface attraction; there is discussion of reflections in mirrors and water and this leads to Narcissus. There are parallels here with the two-way relating of some patients in therapy. Chapter 9 continues the theme through exploration of the gaze. The three-way relating of the client–picture–therapist is developed in relation to the gaze of the picture, which is also the gaze of the client and of the unconscious. The gaze deepens the relationship of the transference and countertransference. Thus it deepens the artist's relationship to her/himself.

This is a book about desire in art and in psychotherapy. It is about the desire which manifests in the female therapist/male patient pairing and the desire which manifests in pictures. Thus some preliminary discussion of debates regarding sexual difference and female desire is germane.

SEX AND GENDER

In order to locate the discussion of gendered relations in psychotherapy, it is necessary to distinguish the terms sex and gender. Stoller (1968) restricts sex to biology; sex is determined by physical conditions, i.e.: chromosomes, genitalia, hormonal states and secondary sexual characteristics. The terms which apply to sex are male and female. Gender is different; it is psychological or cultural rather than biological. The terms for gender are masculinity and femininity. 'There are elements of both in many humans but the male has a preponderance of masculinity and the female has a preponderance of femininity' (Stoller 1968: 9). 'Gender identity' and 'gender role' are conditioned by both the above and develop, beginning at birth, into a 'core gender identity' (Stoller 1968: 29–30). Stoller argues, based on a wealth of clinical evidence, that the reinforcement of the environment establishes gender identity, irrespective of abnormalities in biological development. If parents are told their child is male or female at birth, the child develops an awareness that this is their identity (Stoller 1968, 1975). Thus, 'gender identity and gender role' are affected by both biological and environmental factors.

Oakley (1972) makes a similar distinction between sex and gender. On the basis of accumulated social and anthropological research data, she concludes that: 'The evidence of how people acquire their gender identities . . . suggests strongly that gender has no biological origin, that the connections between sex and gender are not really "natural" at all' (Oakley 1972: 188). This is not to deny differences but for these we have to look to the social and so, psychological, construction of gendered relations to attempt to understand some of the differences in the ways in which women and men experience themselves and each other (Oakley 1972).

The wider social construction of gender is explored by Cockburn through analysis of the gender relations surrounding technology. Through detailed exploration of the allocation of labour in relation to machines, she demonstrates the ways in which production, manufacture and use of technology, at work and in the home, are allocated according to gender role expectations. These reflect, and also contribute to, the social and economic status of women and men, respectively (Cockburn 1983, 1985; Cockburn & Ormrod 1993). She suggests that: 'genders should be seen as the product of history' [as is class] (Cockburn 1983: 7). Her thesis is relevant because it demonstrates how gender relations are constructed. She reveals the ways in which we are conditioned to accept certain states of being as inevitable, or even natural, when, in effect, they are a product of a system of beliefs or unquestioned assumptions.

These sociological views provide a reminder that inner worlds are also a product of outer worlds and that, when we discuss psychological processes, these cannot be divorced from the environment in which they develop. In this, psychoanalysis has a problematic heritage and numerous texts have been written with reference to Freud's original contributions, particularly with regard to female sexuality. His main works in this field are: 'Three essays on the theory of sexuality' (Freud 1905), 'The differences between the sexes' (Freud 1925), 'Female sexuality' (Freud 1931), 'Femininity' (Freud 1933). The extensive influence of these essays on his followers means that they contain many insights which are apposite today, even if we cannot agree with them all. However, in the context of debates regarding the biological or cultural origins of gender, his view was that women's 'nature is determined by their sexual function' (Freud 1933: 135). Following this, the traditional psychoanalytic standpoint is that we are determined by our biology.

Mitchell (1974) has done much to contextualise Freud's views and so make them applicable to our thinking today. In an introduction to the post-Freudian Lacanian school of psychoanalysis, Mitchell (1982) argues that, for psychoanalysts 'the unconscious and sexuality go hand in hand'. Thus psychoanalysts cannot subscribe to a view in which biology comes first and then is formed by culture (Mitchell 1982: 2).

> The ways in which psychosexuality and the unconscious are closely bound together are complex, but most obviously the unconscious contains wishes that cannot be satisfied and hence have been repressed. Predominant among such wishes are the tabooed incestuous desires of childhood.
>
> (Mitchell 1982: 2)

This traditional psychoanalytic view has generated much of the feminist discourse on the topic, as we shall see in Chapter 2.

DESIRE AND DIFFERENCE

One of the current debates in feminism centres on whether men and women are 'essentially', that is 'naturally' different. 'Essentialist theories' are those which consider that the experience of the world is determined by biology before culture (Brennan 1989: 7). The type of thinking which follows from this is that women are the weaker sex; that they are naturally more nurturant and intuitive than men. In the 1960s and 1970s feminism set out to challenge such beliefs:

> If it was allowed in any context that there was something fixed in sexual identity, then that argument was open to abuse: if women were naturally more nurturant, then by the same logic, women could be naturally incompetent. To admit even a positive argument from nature was to foreclose . . . on the belief in the ultimately social account of sexual difference; to rule out strategies for change directed against the social order as it stands.
>
> (Brennan 1989: 7)

French and Anglo-American feminists are at variance regarding sexual difference. Many French feminists argue that women are different and, accepting this, they attempt to establish the nature of the difference; seeing in it positive value. They challenge the 'phallocentric thinking and patriarchal structures of language' (Brennan 1989: 2). Conversely the writing of Anglo-American feminists 'is characterized by the insistence that women are equal, and its concern with the real world' (Brennan 1989: 2). Some express concern, perceiving a return to essentialist views from within the feminist movement itself and particularly from psychoanalytic views of mother–child relations (Doane & Hodges 1992). Lynne Segal (1987) is critical of many of the views of established feminism: 'There has always been a danger that in re-valuing our notions of the female and appealing to the experiences of women we are reinforcing the ideas of sexual polarity which feminism originally aimed to challenge' (Segal 1987: xii). What was once revolutionary offers a new kind of orthodoxy: 'we have come full circle with a fundamental and essentialist theory of gender difference' (Segal 1987: 142).

In writing about female therapists working with male patients I will be suggesting that difference in the experiences of women and men, culturally and socially, will affect their relationships in therapy. There may be discrepancies in the ways in which women view themselves and are viewed by their male clients. This may have a direct bearing on the therapy. Much of the feminist debate regarding sexual difference centres on the interpretation of the Lacanian Symbolic. The Symbolic is not about symbolism in the traditionally understood form but rather about the speaking subject. It is about the move towards the Other. It is about psychical organisation and is the condition of sanity. Without a symbolic law, human beings cannot function. 'The Symbolic places all human beings in relation to others, and gives them a sense of their place in the world, and the ability to speak and be understood by others' (Brennan 1989: 2). It does this by enabling them to distinguish themselves from others through establishing a relation to language. 'Outside the symbolic law there is psychosis' (Brennan 1989: 2–3). Sanity relies on the Symbolic because it offers a means of differentiation. The Symbolic enables separation and so, relationship.

Lacan developed his thinking from Freudian theory in which women are viewed as castrated because they do not have the phallus. Lacan considers that they are thus outside the symbolic order. The father is needed to bring separation from the state of identification with the mother. Much feminist discourse centres around Lacan's attribution of language to the father. Separation is the law of the father but 'For Lacan the actual father matters . . . less than his structural, symbolic position as an intervening third party' (Brennan 1989: 3). 'Generally, Lacanians insist that the symbolic is patriarchal because the woman is the primary care giver, the man is the intervening third party, occupying the position co-incident with language' (Brennan 1989: 3).

The Symbolic order appears to refer to a symbolic structure based on a 'linguistic model made up of chains of signifiers' (Benvenuto & Kennedy 1986: 102). It is the move from the speaking subject towards the Other which is the Symbolic order. The male possesses the visible sex organ and so it is he who makes the move towards the Other. The phallus, which is not the same as the actual penis, is the mark of lack; of difference in general and sexual difference in particular. It refers to the fact that the subject is not complete unto itself.

Ragland-Sullivan develops this in a more positive way and suggests that: 'Lacan's "lack" is a "lack-in-being", common to both sexes' (Ragland-Sullivan 1992: 423) and that:

> Although many feminists still think of the Symbolic order as masculinist, synonymous with the father's name or some phallic law, the crucial point for contemporary feminism is an ethical one. It needs to address the clinical issue of a mediative function of the Symbolic as that which separates the Imaginary from the Real, creates loss and forms the necessary distance from the other's jouissance. If the mother desires that her child be one with her, her desired object, that child, whether male or female, will lack the basis for exchange out of the family plot.
>
> (Ragland-Sullivan 1992: 423)

This is a crucial point, too, in the context of the discussion in this book. I am applying Lacanian theory clinically and this understanding of the lack accords with the way it manifests itself in pictures, as I will demonstrate in Chapters 4 and 7. I will suggest that there are times when pictures in therapy may reveal the lack. This reveals both the unconscious desire and its denial.

Furthermore, pictures may come to be experienced as Other in themselves. It is thus that the mediating function of pictures in the clinical setting offers an opportunity for differentiation. It separates the Imaginary from the Real and in this way creates loss, or brings the loss to consciousness. The Real is the fused state; the undifferentiated identification with the original state – with the maternal (Ragland-Sullivan 1992: 377). The Imaginary is linked to the 'mirror stage' which will be elaborated in Chapter 8. This is the stage in which the image of the self is confronted; it does not relate to either fantasy or to imagination in its traditional form. The Imaginary is described by Benvenuto & Kennedy (1986: 82) as being the area in which the subject may get lost without access to the Symbolic order. It may be as if, chasing his mirror image, he never separates sufficiently to enter the Symbolic. This is the area prior to language where non-verbal or pictorial forms may offer an opportunity for access to states which otherwise remain unseen.

Pictures in therapy sometimes reveal desire. Consequently, I am suggesting, that entry to the Symbolic may be achieved first through art and second through language. Using a rather different theoretical frame, in *The Revealing Image* (Schaverien 1991), I argued, basing the theory on the writings of the philosopher Cassirer, that it is through the objects we make that we come to know ourselves. 'Consciousness is mediated and transformed through symbolic forms. Like myth and language, art is one of the means through which the "I" comes to grips with the world' (Cassirer

1955b: 204, quoted in Schaverien 1991: 4). I have no wish to conflate very different theories. However, I find that my understanding of Lacan is aided by that of Cassirer. Cassirer's discussion of the movement from the undifferentiated state to one of separation in the cultural field can be related to a clinical understanding. The point is that there are different levels of consciousness – of knowing. Some of these ways of experiencing are inarticulable and cannot be expressed in conventional language. They are expressed in other forms such as myth, ritual and art but finally, language is needed to enable separation to take place. Language fixes meaning and leads to community.

The Symbolic order is a social order; it is one in which community can function. Thus Lacan's desire could be understood to be a desire for community. 'Desire is a perpetual effect of symbolic articulation' (Sheridan 1977: viii). This is language; but I will argue that the movement towards the Other, that which makes the 'difference', may take place through the making of marks outside of the self – through art. For woman or for man the paintbrush (a phallic object perhaps) and its resulting marks may offer movement towards the object. The Other in the clinical setting is sometimes the therapist and sometimes the art object.

Through the transference to person, or to art object, a significant movement towards separation begins. It is this which may herald entry to the differentiated state of the symbolic. Thus, although Lacan's symbolic order relates to language and the speaking subject, there may be some common factors with the painting subject. It is particularly so in therapy where the painting may be made for the therapist as witness. For Lacan the male is privileged because of his visibility; the picture offers a form of visibility but not in any necessarily phallic sense, rather as revealing the lack, uncovering loss and so embodying the desire. This is demonstrated in Chapter 7.

When, in the first paragraph of the Preface, I suggested that art is desire made visible, it was this which I intended. Art reveals experience which otherwise may go unsymbolised because it cannot enter into language. Thus, in psychotherapy, art plays a formative and significant role. This goes far beyond merely demonstrating psychoanalytic processes in operation; it effects a change in state from unconscious to conscious and from undifferentiated to differentiated.

FEMALE DESIRE

In a discussion of the female therapist it is necessary to consider, not only the experience of being a woman, but also the ways in which women are viewed by men. This is particularly the case when discussing the erotic aspects of the male patient's transference. The erotic countertransference is experienced with our female, as well as male, clients and very often it is accepted as 'normal' because it is understood to be maternal. Women are mothers and mothers are women, and so this is an implicit, as well as explicit, assumption. This may make it difficult to admit that we are also sometimes the object of sexual desire by both men and women. Furthermore, there are times when we may reciprocate these feelings, becoming sexually aroused. For a heterosexual woman it may be alarming to experience sexual fantasies about female as well as male clients. In this book the main focus is the male client because this is a neglected area in psychoanalytic literature. However, I acknowledge that sexual arousal in the female therapist is not exclusively limited to heterosexual male patients. Same sex and different gender combinations arouse many different kinds of feelings in the therapist and among these are sexual ones.

Irigaray (1974), a French difference feminist, begins her discourse from female experience and the body. She engages with Lacan's Symbolic order and argues from the perspective of female sexuality:

> Perhaps it is time to return to that repressed entity, the female imaginary. So woman does not have a sex organ? She has at least two of them, but they are not identifiable as ones. Indeed she has many more. Her sexuality, always at least double, goes even further: it is plural.
>
> (Irigaray 1977: 28)

This is not merely about female sexual experience, although this is an aspect of her discourse. We have seen that the Lacanian Symbolic is based on the idea, derived from Freud, that women experience themselves as castrated men. Without the visible penis, they cannot enter into language which is phallic. When she writes 'it is plural', she refers to the experience of living in a female sexed body; but the body is a metaphor for language:

> 'She' is indefinitely other in herself. This is doubtless why she is said to be whimsical, incomprehensible, agitated, capricious . . . not to mention her language, in which she sets off in all directions leaving 'him' unable to discern the coherence of any meaning. Hers are contradictory words, somewhat mad from the standpoint of reason, inaudible for whoever listens to them with ready-made grids, with a fully elaborated code in hand. For in what she says, too, at least when she dares, woman is constantly touching herself. She steps ever so slightly aside from herself with a murmur, an exclamation, a whisper, a sentence left unfinished.
>
> (Irigaray 1977: 29)

We see here that Irigaray's interest is in the difference between women and men and so some consider her to be an essentialist. However, her view is more subtle than this and relevant for discussion of the role of woman as therapist. She argues that the way women experience themselves is not linear, or direct, or phallic; but this is not nothing. Irigaray does not disagree with Lacan, that women are different from men, but she elaborates that difference and Whitford (1989) considers that those who claim that this is an essentialist thesis miss the point. Irigaray is not claiming that women are lacking and so less than, or framed by men (Whitford 1989: 110). It is the *symbolic* and not the *innate* which interests her. Women suffer from ' "drives without any possible representatives or representations" ' (Whitford 1989: 110) but this is not because of 'any immutable characteristics of women's nature [rather this is] an effect of women's position relative to the symbolic order . . . [women] are its residue, or its waste' (Whitford 1989: 110).

The mother/daughter relationship is unsymbolised, undifferentiated because of its sameness and this hinders women from having an identity in the symbolic order apart from the maternal function. Thus women remain 'residual', 'defective men', 'objects of exchange' and so on (Whitford 1989: 109). Irigaray accepts the clinical view that women have difficulty separating from their mothers, that they tend to form relationships where their identity is merged and in which self and other are not clear. However, she presents this as a result of women's position in the symbolic order. The girl–child 'exiles herself from a primary metaphorisation of her, female, desire in order to inscribe herself in that of the boy child, which is phallic' (Whitford 1989: 114). This is a *result* of exile not its *reason*.

This is a highly complex argument and not really the topic of this book. None the less it is apposite when considering the desire of the female therapist. She could be considered to be in a powerful position and here her role is, in part, that of the one who makes the difference. If this exiled position is the starting point, vestiges may remain of the sense that women are unsymbolised and so cannot enter the discourse of society. Then, when they are in powerful positions within the social order, such as when working as therapists, they may find it difficult to accept the reversed power imbalance of their situation.

This will have a bearing on the therapeutic relationship and it may be for this reason that the female therapist may conflate sexual/erotic feelings and maternal/erotic feelings. Women may turn first to the maternal for a frame of reference for their power. The female therapist may view her own sexual arousal as inadmissible and reframe it as maternal. Thus, she may interpret the transference as infantile and part object in preference to seeing the erotic in a whole-person sense. This is not to claim that there is not frequently an infantile element in the erotic transference, but this is not always the full story.

It may be subtly demeaning to constantly frame the discourse or sensations of an adult in the language of infancy. If female desire is plural, then she may have many and not merely one desire. This may mean her countertransference experience is complex and made up of both maternal and sexual erotic impulses and feelings. In addition to the nurturing and maternal role, she is the one who brings separation from an undifferentiated state. For the female therapist this may be rather different than for her male colleague.

There is an additional way in which we might conceive difference; we might view Irigaray's description of female sexuality as parallel to the art process. Art is not direct as is language; it is not, strictly speaking, a language at all, and yet it is a movement towards the Other. There are times when pictures offer a means of organisation, differentiation and a move towards relationship; but this is not a direct move, usually it is indirect and oblique. If sanity is dependent on the Symbolic, this implies that without the word there is no separation from the fused state. I am suggesting that art may offer a way of entering the Symbolic; it is not linear and apparently lacks coherence, and yet it is a form of differentiation. Whether we consider language to be the domain of the patriarchy, or not, it is helpful to think of the relation between art and the spoken word as a form of difference. Art plays its part at the cusp, the meeting place of conscious and unconscious. Through art we are sometimes poised on the borderline between madness and sanity and, through it, guided to the Symbolic.

THE GAZE

The gaze, and its relationship to desire, is the topic of Chapter 9, but it is an implicit theme throughout. It is through the act of painting and through the relationship to the artwork once it is finished that art has its effect. Thus, very often it is through the gazes, engendered through looking at the pictures, that their impact is experienced in the therapeutic relationship. The engendered gaze, of the title, refers to elements in the transference and countertransference when pictures are central; these are the gaze engendered through looking at pictures and that which is influenced by the gender of the artist.

The gaze is sometimes considered to be gendered and masculine but this is not my meaning. Grosz (1992: 447) explains that scopophilia, which is the drive to see, can be divided into active and passive forms. In the active 'the subject looks at an object' and, in the passive, the 'subject desires to be looked at'. This has been explored through analysis of the spectator's relation to film, in film theory. The male is associated with 'the active' looking and female with the 'passive' looked at. However, in this context, I would make the distinction that this is not my meaning. Further, I do not consider the gaze of the picture to be gendered. It is pointed out by Grosz (1992) that there is a difference between the gaze and the look and this distinction was made by Lacan, with reference to Sartre. Lacan argues that the gaze is not masculine; 'vision is not, cannot be, masculine . . . rather, certain ways of using vision (for example to objectify) may confirm and help produce patriarchal power relations' (Grosz 1992: 449). For Lacan the gaze is about seeing and being seen. 'The gaze is not an internal attribute, like a bodily perception; it is situated outside. By this Lacan means that, like the phallus, like desire itself, the gaze emanates from the field of the Other' (Grosz 1992: 449).

This is the point which I will attempt to draw out in Chapter 9. It is this which relates to my theme; the pictures made in therapy are sometimes experienced as the 'field of the Other'. In this they connect to the trans- ference, embody unconscious desire and offer hope in anticipation of the realisation of some desired state. Thus, the gaze could be considered to be one path through which desire is transmitted interpersonally. When pic- tures are the mediating object in between the people, they offer a particular channel for the gaze; interpersonal gazes may be mediated through the pictorial imagery. Sometimes such pictures offer a direct means of access to the self.

Moreover, when we look at pictures in the company of the artist, another effect of gender comes into play between female therapist and male client. When the imagery embodies the desired object, idealisation of the feminine is sometimes revealed, in depiction of women. The client's transference desire is then visible. The female therapist is more likely than her male colleague to experience herself as identified with that figure or imagined person. This will have an impact on the countertransference and may draw her into the client's inner world in a graphic sense. The gender of the 'Other' is influential in all therapeutic relationships but particularly so when the gaze becomes engaged through pictorial imagery.

The gaze is a channel similar to Gilligan's (1982) discussion of the voice. The voice is a powerful psychological instrument and channel, connecting inner and outer worlds (Gilligan 1993: xvi). Very often women's authentic voices are not heard. Gilligan observed that if a speaker expects to be heard there is a change in the voice. When speaking in an arena that is experienced as safe, we speak directly, unselfconsciously and in a voice which is connected to the 'core self'. When there is no resonance, or where the reverberations are frightening, the speaker tends 'to sound dead or flat'. Thus, 'speaking is an intensely relational act' (Gilligan 1993: xvi). In therapy the listener gives weight to the speaker's words. When the client (male or female) has felt unnoticed, careful listen- ing is a therapeutic act.

It is similar with pictures; they, too, mediate between inner and outer worlds and give expression to the authentic self. The gaze is a channel which, like the voice, activates the inner self and gives access to it. The therapeutic relationship offers a space to be heard and, when pictures are involved, seen. For those people who find it difficult to express themselves in words the first means of expression for the 'authentic self' may be art. The weight given to communication from the client, whether this is spoken or painted, is a significant form of affirmation. The serious attention of the therapist authenticates the expression. If what I show to you is taken seriously, I will take it more seriously myself. As it is with the spoken word in therapy, so too it is with the gaze which engages with pictures.

In concluding this introduction I quote Chodorow (1994), writing about the ways in which men and women form their sexualities:

> To understand how men and women love requires that we understand how any particular woman or man loves; to understand femininity and masculinity and the various forms of sexuality requires that we understand how any particular woman or man creates her or his own cultural and personal gender and sexuality.
>
> (Chodorow 1994: 92)

Female desire is not merely one thing but neither is male desire. Therefore, when I discuss the difference in working with female and male clients in the next chapter, I am also writing about different people and so individual sexualities. There are certain basic patterns which underlie our development but each of us lives these in particular ways. The male patient/female therapist dynamic is the explicit topic of the next chapter and the underlying theme of the rest of the book. The point here has been to begin by thinking a little about the ways in which sexual difference may affect the therapeutic relationship.

Desire and the female therapist

In this chapter I explore the erotic transference and countertransference from the point of view of the female therapist working with the male patient. In all therapeutic relationships, irrespective of gender, similar patterns emerge. None the less there are themes which may be attributable to the influence of the reality of the gender of the couple. Much has been written regarding the transference and countertransference which manifests between the male therapist and female patient and, in recent years, feminist psychotherapists have addressed some of the transference issues specific to the female therapist–female patient pairing (Eichenbaum & Orbach 1983; Chodorow 1978). Far less attention has been given to the transference and countertransference implications of the female therapist–male patient dyad. However, there is an increasing literature written by female analysts on this theme.

THE GENDER OF THE THERAPIST

It has been argued that the gender of the therapist does not influence the transference. The theory is that, if an affect is motivated by transference, it will emerge irrespective of the gender or personal qualities of the therapist. It is also generally accepted that mother–child, pre-oedipal and erotic–oedipal transferences will become manifest in any pairing. Homo-erotic, as well as hetero-erotic, elements will emerge in all analyses and so it may be considered controversial to attempt to make distinctions between male and female patients. However, the therapeutic relationship is affected by reality as well as the client's internal predispositions. Like the room in which therapy takes place, the gender of the therapist is part of the real relationship which is instantly identifiable. Inevitably, this produces an impression which, whether conscious or unconscious, will influence the transference.

In certain cases gender is an important element for the patient from the start. Some patients consciously choose their therapist on the basis of gender, preferring to work with a woman or a man (Spector Person

1983, 1985; Williams 1993). This could be understood to be a transference to the gender of the therapist which begins prior to the first personal encounter. In such a case it would be reasonable to assume that the gender is significant. Sometimes a referral is made by a colleague who may ask if the prospective patient would prefer to see a man or a woman and, whilst some do not have a view on this, others state a strong preference. Even in cases where little or no prior thought is given by the patient to the gender of the therapist, I propose that it is a factor which may, to a greater or lesser degree, have an influence on the process, and even sometimes the outcome, of therapy. The reality of the gender of the therapist may affect the sequence in which certain elements of the psyche constellate. In addition it must be acknowledged that the gender of the patient will make some sort of impression on the therapist. It follows that sometimes this will influence the countertransference.

The Women's Therapy Centre in London bases its work on the premise that women's problems are socially, as well as personally, determined. Women will therefore be likely to understand the problems encountered by each other in a patriarchal society (Orbach 1978; Ernst & Maguire 1987). Following the logic of this argument I have heard it suggested that men are more appropriate therapists for men and, indeed, certain feminist psychotherapists have refused to work with male patients. It is clear that there are times when women need separation from men in order to identify issues of specific relevance to women and, it may be, that there are times when men, too, need separation for similar reasons (Jukes 1993).

There is, however, much that can be gained from the cross-gender combination in psychotherapy which makes it easier to confront certain issues. Avoidance of a dynamic rarely resolves the problem; thus it is my intention to examine the interconnectedness of gender relations in analysis from the viewpoint of a female therapist. One thread of this enquiry regards sexual abuse and, although the research on this is not reviewed in this chapter, information can be obtained from the Prevention of Professional Abuse Network, which has a detailed list of published research in this area (see list of organisations on p. 218 for details). The incest taboo is most often violated by fathers who abuse their daughters. Similarly, it is more common to hear of the male therapist abusing his female patient by entering into a sexual relationship with her than it is to hear of the female therapist as an abuser. (Although it is less common, Welldon (1988) and Russell (1993) give examples of abuse of sons by their mothers and male patients by their female therapists.) Thus, we know that sexual acting out occurs in all forms of psychotherapy but it is more prevalent in the male therapist–female patient dyad.

After finishing writing this chapter I attended a conference entitled 'Feminism and Psychoanalysis' organised by the Freud museum in May

1994. The conference was convened to mark twenty years since the publication of Juliet Mitchell's book *Psychoanalysis and Feminism* (Mitchell 1974). I was surprised to find that, despite the depth and breadth of the topics discussed, the female therapist–male patient dyad was not mentioned at all. The female therapist–female patient received much attention and the significance of differences in the gender of the therapist were discussed briefly but no-one mentioned the male patient. Therefore this chapter may also be seen as a means of redressing what I perceive as a serious omission in psychoanalytic feminist theory.

Recently there have been a number of conference papers, followed by discussion, on topics of concern to female psychotherapists. Sinclair (1993) addressed some issues particular to the gender of the female psychotherapist. This was one of the themes at the conference entitled 'Contemporary Psychoanalysis and Contemporary Sexualities', which was organised by the Psychoanalytic Forum in London in June 1993. The male patient was discussed at this conference by Orbach and Spector Person and it was suggested that the reason that there is less sexual acting out in the female therapist–male patient dyad is because male patients rarely experience sustained erotic transferences. Another assertion by Orbach and Spector Person was that female therapists do not experience sexual arousal in the countertransference with either male or female patients.

Contrary to these views, I find sexual arousal to be common in all gender combinations including the female therapist–female patient dyad (see O'Connor & Ryan 1993). Men also experience long-term erotic transferences to female therapists (Kavaler-Adler 1992) and I have published an example of one such case (Schaverien 1991). Another is the subject of the next two chapters in this book. In it a number of the themes which are discussed in this chapter will be illustrated. However, it may be that for some men, initial resistance is stronger than is commonly the case with women.

SEXUAL ACTING OUT

Feminist therapists often claim an understanding of particular aspects of transference and countertransference of significance to women, and especially, the mother–daughter transference. What seems to be missing is discussion of sexuality as it relates to men. If, as women, we are to fully own our difference, we have also to admit to our sexuality within the therapeutic relationship. This includes owning impulses towards acting on erotic countertransferences. Despite protestations to the contrary, I consider that we are no more immune from the temptations of our desires than our male colleagues. Unless this is admitted, it remains split off and attributed as merely an aberration of the male.

Samuels (1985a) and Rutter (1989) have both written about encounters which brought them close to transgressing the boundaries of the therapeutic relationship. Both tell us that it was the shock to their ethical sensibility and integrity that caused them to reflect more deeply on these phenomena. Greenson discusses the problems of resisting the sexual advances of a female patient (Greenson 1967). Many of the female therapists whom I will quote in this chapter have written about erotic transferences and countertransferences with their male patients. I suspect that underlying their papers are similar ethical dilemmas to those described by Rutter and Samuels, but I am not aware of many written accounts by female therapists of the temptation to breach the boundaries with regard to sexual acting out. It seems to me that it is time to admit that this is possible. If sexual abuse of patients by female therapists is less common, then we need to explore why that might be but we can only do so if we first acknowledge that it is not because we are not tempted.

One reason why there is reticence to make disclosures regarding the countertransference in such cases is that there is a degree of professional guilt. There is a concern that one is being exhibitionistic and revealing one's own neediness and seductiveness. Furthermore, when I have attempted to communicate these ideas in professional papers, I have found that some colleagues insist that the whole-person level, which so often feels appropriate when mutual sexual excitement is being focused upon, cannot constitute 'real analysis'. I think that what might be termed the 'pre-oedipalisation' of such material is sometimes a defensive view, occasioned by the kind of professional guilt to which I refer, rather than an accurate assessment of the situation; to assume that the analyst's desire originates, exclusively, in the patient can constitute a form of abuse in itself. Desire may be pushed back into the patient and this is then justified as it is considered a form of projective identification of an early, infantile part-object state or process. Despite the value of such views and the usefulness of such criticisms, it is important to open out debate in this area. There is clearly a need to separate 'manic, shadow activity', leading to sexual misconduct, from a professionally conducted, sexually inflected, analytic dialogue. In a new work *The Wounded Healer: Countertransference from a Jungian Perspective*, Sedgwick (1994) gives a very considered account of this type of work from the male analyst's point of view.

Over the years I have written a number of papers and a book about transference and countertransference issues in analytical forms of art psychotherapy (Schaverien 1982, 1987b, 1990, 1991). Although it has been implicit in much of my previous work, I have not explicitly discussed the source of my interest in the topic of this chapter. It is only after much consideration, exploring it in my own analysis and talking to female colleagues over many years that I have come to address publicly the topic of desire, as well as potential acting out by female therapists.

I began my psychotherapy career more than twenty years ago in a therapeutic community. The boundaries are rather differently established in such a unit than in individual psychotherapy. In this day hospital staff and patients met in various groups throughout the day and also spent much time together in the community between the groups. The boundaries therefore seemed to extend to the whole environment. A male patient with whom I was working developed an intense erotic transference to me and I experienced a reciprocal countertransference. Although it was not spoken of, the attachment between us was communicated through an awareness of each other that was only partly conscious. On one occasion, at the community Christmas party when the boundaries were more relaxed than usual, he kissed me. I was surprised to find that, within myself, there was a powerful barrier to responding to this kiss, despite the fact that I was intensely attracted to him.

In retrospect I think that it was probably the taboo against incest and an awareness of his fragility which intuitively made me stop him, but I did not understand this at the time. I was surprised by the power of my resistance. It was as if I summoned resources from within of which I was unaware. He took a step back, but not because I pushed him physically, nor because I said anything; it was the quality of my gaze which caused him to draw back. The point is that intuitively I knew that this touch, this physical contact, was inappropriate. This was not a thought, it was a preconscious response. There was an intuitive understanding that to have engaged in sexual activity would not have satisfied the desire for either of us. Nor would it have furthered the therapeutic aim. Instead it would have destroyed the quality of the engagement. Even this kiss altered something.

Transference love is one of many frail and slender threads which connect the present to the past. The connection to the past is also a way to the future if it is carefully respected. In concretising such a desire by acting on it, the impossibility of satisfaction becomes even more evident than it was before. The link to the self through the 'Other' is severed. Bodies might meet but the inner need which existed in that area 'in-between' remains untouched. This causes a depression which adds to, even exacerbates, the original loss, deprivation or abuse. In this case the fact that he and I both intensely desired physical contact does not alter this fact. Freud made the point on many occasions that no human desires can ever be satisfied solely by biological means.

As therapists we are in a privileged position; we make intimate relationships a part of our everyday work and these must be honoured. The love I felt for this man had evolved from a therapeutic relationship and so needed to be protected; it existed in an area set apart. In a social situation a relationship with me would have become like any other of the numerous difficult relationships this man had had with women. The only hope for him was in not acting on this powerful transference and permitting it to develop and to come to conscious awareness. It is through abstinence from acting on the desire that transformation takes place. This has been elucidated many times since Freud first wrote about the transference (Freud 1912, 1915).

I emphasise that this incident took place many years ago when I was inexperienced. Since then, and in common with other therapists, I have experienced many similarly intense erotic countertransferences in response to the transferences of male patients. As a woman of heterosexual orientation there has been a difference in the experience of erotic transference with men and with women. I have fantasised a physical relationship with female patients, too, but for me with women, the countertransference desire has, up to now, lacked the intensity which would tempt me to act out. Thus, I consider that the sexual orientation and the reality of gender make a significant difference.

In this case I came near to acting on the sexual feelings which were evoked in relation to a male patient. This was formative for me; it was an initiation into the meanings and power of 'transference love' (Freud 1915). Today I find that I am still angered when female patients tell me about the sexual engagement into which they have entered with their (usually male) teachers, ministers, doctors, psychologists, counsellors, psychotherapists, psychoanalysts, and Jungian analysts. I see the confusion which results from this betrayal of trust. Yet I know that this anger is, in part, driven by the shadow because I am only too aware of how easy it would be for me, similarly, to breach the trust which is invested in me by my patients – female or male.

Furthermore, in private discussions with female colleagues, I have become aware that, at some time, usually early in their careers, many of them have also been confronted with a testing situation of this nature. One of the most telling ways that we come genuinely to understand the need for abstinence in the therapeutic encounter is when we ourselves are confronted with the temptation to act out. Theory is most useful when it is backed up by experience in practice and it is no less the case when it comes to the topic of sexual abstinence. In reviewing the literature I have come to suspect that many of the analysts who have written about the specific issues of women working with male patients have had to confront similarly charged situations. If sexual abuse of patients by female analysts is less common than by men, then we need to explore why that might be but we can only do so if we first acknowledge that it is not because we are not, occasionally, tempted.

There is a particular dynamic for women as therapists which is rather different from the experience of men. Sexual abuse is, of its nature, abuse of a less powerful person by one who is in a dominant position. As women we may view some male patients as powerful in relation to us and forget the power imbalance of the clinical situation. We are especially vulnerable to this if we have been raised in a generation which expected males to be dominant and women passive in initiating sex. We may mistakenly assume that the man can look after himself if he claims to want sexual engagement. But, like some women, certain men live sexually active lives, needing to prove themselves sexually as a substitute for other forms of relating. The appeal of the male patient may be his vulnerability and his sensitivity as well as his sexuality. We female therapists need to admit our own desire before we can analyse the desire of our male patients and we can only do so if we are not ashamed to admit all aspects of the countertransference. Sexual wishes of female therapists and their male patients need to be recognised as multi-layered and not assumed to be based solely in infantile sectors of the unconscious (see Samuels 1995).

Many of these issues are illustrated by a recently published book which documents the alleged sexual exploitation of a male patient by a female psychiatrist/psychoanalyst in the USA (McNamara 1994). In this book McNamara gives a vivid and disturbing account of a psychotherapy that went tragically wrong and ended in the psychotic breakdown and subsequent suicide of a male medical student. It is claimed that the psychiatrist became overinvolved with her patient. Whether or not she had sex with the patient remains unknown but it is claimed that sexually explicit writings, in her own hand, indicate that she had, at the very least, shared her sexual fantasies with him, encouraging an intense, eroticised regression. It is alleged that she permitted him to think that she was his mother and in enacting this role, she wrote him stories and gave him gifts. This went beyond the boundaries of any usual therapeutic contract; she was available for him at all times of day and even when she was on vacation.

Whatever the truth of this case, the point is that this therapist experienced sexual arousal which was mixed up with a maternal countertransference. Rather than working with this countertransference as a multi-layered phenomenon, she took it as exclusively maternal, thereby becoming entangled with her patient (positioned as an infant) by expressing her fantasies to him (positioning herself as mother).

McNamara writes of the furore which was raised in the press when the case came to court. The public response was outrage. She contrasts this reaction with other cases of sexual abuse by psychiatrists in the same area of Boston in recent years. There were several and all the other cases involved male therapists and female patients. Some of them were more senior than the female analyst and one case involved multiple counts of sexual abuse; a prominent male psychiatrist had sex with five of his patients. What is notable is that when this came to light it was quickly dealt with and the matter settled. None of these cases led to resignations and none received the type of publicity that the case of sexual misconduct by a female analyst attracted. Admittedly the patient here committed suicide, and that may have been a publicity-attracting factor, but feminists were quick to point out the discrepancy in the treatment of male and female practitioners. It seems that when women do sexually abuse their patients, the public outrage is greater than that when the therapist is male.

This case demonstrates several interesting points for the topic of this book. First, it is evident that it is quite possible for the maternal transference/countertransference dynamic to overwhelm the reality and implications of sexual feelings. It also shows that it is possible for female therapists to seriously abuse their male patients.

In addition to acting out there are other, more subtle forms of sexual abuse between female therapists and their male patients, just as there are between mothers and sons. These include unconscious incestuous demands which make it impossible for the son to leave his mother and make relationships with other women (Chasseguet-Smirgel 1984a). The son–lover myth, as expounded by Jung (1956, CW 5) and Neumann (1954), is the mythical parallel of this psychological state. This incestuous atmosphere may be repeated in the transference and engage the therapist in an unconscious erotic countertransference. It is possible for this to become subtly abusive. The unconscious state may be repeated in the therapist's disregarding the adult aspects and so keeping the patient to herself rather than fostering his ability to make relationships with others.

I propose that fear of the intensity of such incestuous engagement may result in premature termination of their analysis by male patients. I will give examples of three men, all of whom reached a crisis point which, I suggest, was linked to sexual arousal and/or power–dependency issues. The first illustrates the difficulties sometimes encountered in the power dynamic in the male patient–female therapist dyad; the second, a dependent infantile erotic transference; and the third, a sustained long-term erotic transference with elements of infantile and adult sexuality.

THE EROTIC TRANSFERENCE

Freud and Jung had rather different understandings of the developmental role of sexuality. For Freud the significance of eros in the transference was that it led back to actual childhood and to the incestuous desires of the oedipal stage. Jung related eros to the wider cultural context; for him incestuous desires in the transference indicated a need to return to an earlier psychological state from which to grow forward (1956, CW 5). Eros expresses a need for renewal, its meaning 'is to be sought not in its historical antecedents but in its purpose' (Jung 1959a, CW 8: 74). Sexual desire, as it manifests in the transference, is a symbol for patterns of relatedness (Jung 1956, CW 5: 7–11). The very nature of the unconscious means that it is inaccessible without the help of an 'other' and it is the analyst who holds the conscious attitude which the patient seeks. It is this which binds the patient to the therapist. Thus, the purpose of the apparently infantile erotic connection is a desire for individuation; for a state of consciousness (Jung 1956, CW 5, 8 and 16).

Jung's major work on the transference is *The Psychology of the Transference* (Jung 1946, CW 16). In it he wrote about the desires experienced in the transference and countertransference and linked this 'unconscious mix' to the alchemical process. In both these situations two people open themselves to a process by which both are transformed. Jung further develops this through the researches of Layard (quoted in Jung 1946, CW 16) into 'kinship libido'. Here, incest is prevented through a complicated system of physical boundaries and the cross-cousin marriage. This, Jung likens to the conscious–unconscious mix between patient and therapist. Thus Jung both acknowledges the incestuous longings and establishes them as a central element in the transference and countertransference. Stein (1974) has extended this, in relation to incest in the therapeutic interaction, and Samuels (1989) has pointed out how Jung's application of alchemy can be understood as a metaphor for the interpersonal transference and counter-transference relationship. Schwartz-Salant (1989) has discussed this in relation to projective identification. In 1991 I wrote a detailed case study and illustrated it with pictures made by a male patient in analytical art psychotherapy with a female therapist. The imagery this patient produced reveals the processes which Jung discusses and furthermore illustrates some of the added dimension when the therapist is female and the patient male.

In post-Freudian theory, distinctions are made between transference neurosis and delusional transference and the related erotic and eroticised transference. The difference is characterised by the presence or absence of the symbolic function. The erotic transference is a form of 'transference neurosis' and is a common and necessary phase in psychotherapy. It is a simple form of transference love which reveals past patterns of relating and mobilises the potential for growth.

The eroticised transference is rather different because it is a form of delusional transference. Symbolisation is absent and so the transference is experienced as a concrete, material, reality. There is no imaginal space and no 'as if', so feelings of love or of persecution are overtly and sometimes terrifyingly present. The therapeutic alliance may be replaced by a constant and conscious obsession with the therapist characterised by a demand for gratification. This is understood to be a form of acting out against becoming conscious (Blum 1973). Eroticisation is a form of resistance and there is a loss of the learning potential of the transference (Blum 1971: 522). The resistance may be against a dependent transference (Rappaport 1956: 515) or pregenital issues (Kulish 1986). Whatever underlies them 'these are not ordinary reactions of transference love, and these patients can resemble intractable love addicts' (Blum 1973: 64). It follows that the type of patients who form eroticised rather than erotic transferences are usually the borderline or more disturbed patients (Kulish 1986). This type of erotic transference is the extreme but elements of such a transference may emerge at some time in many analyses.

When erotic transference is a resistance, the therapist rarely experiences a reciprocal countertransference. Zinkin (1969) gives an example where, despite his patient's persistent declarations of love, he felt unmoved. He suggests that if there is no arousal in the analyst despite the patient's erotic feelings, this may indicate that there is denial of some other impulse – possibly hate. Therefore a distinction is needed between the beneficial emergence of eros in the transference and those times when it is resistance.

Female therapists working with male patients may frequently encounter such resistance. This might account for the dearth of reports of such transferences by female therapists. Greenson writes that 'All cases of eroticized transference that I have heard of have been women patients in analysis with men' (Greenson 1967: 339). It is, however, noted that erotic and eroticised transferences do occur in female analyst–male patient pairs (Goldberger & Evans 1985). They also occur in female analyst–female patient pairs (Lester 1990) but less has been written about them and we can only speculate about why this may be. It is possible that male patients terminate before, or when, the erotic transference begins. It also seems that female therapists may find it more acceptable to remain within the frame of the maternal rather than to confront the sexual transference.

MATERNAL AND PATERNAL TRANSFERENCE

Mother–child imagery often predates sexualised imagery and Guttman (1984) suggests that this may be because it is easier for the male patient to express regressed feelings than sexual ones. Whilst the patient's re-experiencing of early identification with the mother through the manifestation of the maternal transference is an important phase in analysis, problems arise if the transference is viewed solely in terms of infantile dependency. Lester (1985) suggests that there may be a subtle, socio-cultural pressure on the female therapist to minimise manifestations of erotic transference and to accept some unclear responsibility for departing from a strictly maternal, nurturing stance. The female therapist may find it more acceptable to understand pre-oedipal transferences, than to confront erotic feelings that may be aroused by the oedipal wishes of the patient (Lester 1985). The problem then arises that the erotic transference may be interpreted in maternal terms.

It is the commonly held view that the analyst's masculinity facilitates separation; it enables the analysand to identify with the father and separate from the mother. Irrespective of the reality of the gender of the analyst, there is a traditional view, that some form of interruption to the symbiotic mother–child transference is needed. Persistent interpretations of the infantile nature of the transference may give an implicit message that the patient is forbidden to invest in people other than the analyst (Chasseguet-Smirgel 1986) and this may make it difficult for him to make relationships outside the analytic frame. The limits of the maternal attitude are to be found in the analyst's masculinity, 'whether the analyst is a man or a woman. This enables the child to cut his tie with the mother and turn towards reality' (Chasseguet-Smirgel 1986). The male patient, working with a female analyst, will be able to separate if he can find the masculinity in her attitude. Chasseguet-Smirgel (1984b) does not regard the analyst's gender as limiting the potential transference and she considers that male analysts evoke maternal transferences through the analytic attitude and similarly, paternal transferences may be aroused in relation to female analysts.

It is argued that paternal transferences to female analysts (Goldberger & Evans 1985) are 'phallic mother' transferences (Karme 1979). This is originally a Freudian concept and according to Rycroft (1968: 117), possibly a hermaphroditic figure. This leads one to speculate that it may have the potential for transformation of the trickster archetype in Jungian terms. 'The phallic mother is a pre-Oedipal fantasy of an omnipotent and absolutely powerful, sexually neutral figure' (Grosz 1992: 314). She is the object of desire and also the subject who desires the child as her object (Grosz 1992: 315). Although this is attributed to the mother by both sexes, it is the boy who will associate the phallic mother with possession of the male genital organ. The phallic mother is an image which can become persecutory intrusive and potentially penetrating (Grosz 1992).

We have seen that the significance of debates regarding maternal and paternal transferences rests on the premise that the primary symbiosis of the infant–mother bond needs to be severed. It is the role of the father to effect this rupture, to come between mother and child and establish the child as a viable person in the outer world. This traditional view is no longer universally accepted and recent additions to theory offer alternative understandings of early developmental experience.

Benjamin (1988) challenges the priority of primary symbiosis of the mother–infant undifferentiated state and instead proposes 'intersubjectivity'. She suggests that, from the start, there is always a relationship of two people – a mother and a child – who interact. Therefore separation grows out of mutual regard and is a gradual developmental process which does not need to be disrupted (Benjamin 1988). 'Intersubjectivity' means that the infant grows, not simply through what is taken in from the outside, but also what she/he brings to the interaction from the start (Benjamin 1988: 125). Development takes place 'between and within'. Benjamin is influenced by the work of Stern (1985) in this regard. Her view seems to accord with more recent researches by Piontelli (1993) and, although it comes from a very different theoretical base, Fordham's (1971) view of the 'primary self' gives an account of mother and child as two individuals from the start. His work predates these feminist views and is, like them, based on close observation of what actually happens between mothers and their infants.

Parallel to these views the role of the father is also being put in question. The idea that the father's main task is to separate the symbiotic mother/child union is redundant if there is a recognition of mutuality and difference from the start. Samuels's (1985a, 1989, 1995) view of the father as centrally involved in the psychological development of his children follows from an acceptance of the child's autonomy. He proposes that what is necessary to psychological health is a form of 'erotic' and 'aggressive playback' with their fathers. While 'erotic playback' is of prime importance for the daughter's development and 'aggressive playback' for that of the son, all children need elements of both types of engagement (Samuels 1989, 1993). Growth of the personality is fostered by the intense interest the parent and child have in each other. Following Jung, he emphasises that the purpose of the incestuous desire is not primarily a need for sexual gratification but for psychological growth (Samuels 1995).

If the female therapist working with a male patient understands the sexual feelings expressed by her patient to be based in mother–child transference dynamics, she may interpret in a way which will foster regression. There are times when this is totally appropriate, but when there is a strong sexual atmosphere, this merits attention in its own right. It may be a form of abuse of power by female therapists to reduce all the drives experienced by a male patient to the desires of infancy; this may be an affront to the adult man.

In the real relationship with a male patient whose erotic transference is based in infantile love for his mother, there is something of a paradox which is at best confusing and even, in some cases, humiliating. At the same time as wishing for gratification of pregenital desires, the male patient may have adult sexual feelings and bodily sensations. Although the demands on the therapist are infantile and often related to early experience, there may be awareness of the fact that the couple are an adult man and woman. The intimate pattern originating in infancy is expressed as a desire in the present. He demands, but also fears, her reciprocation of his sexual wishes. The infantile base of the transference means that there needs to be acknowledgement of the adult who desires sexual intimacy at the same time as enabling the expression of the regression.

This raises the issue of professional guilt to which I alluded earlier. I emphasise that I am not objecting to reductive analysis on the grounds that it humbles the man. I am objecting to a de-sexualised reductive analysis on the grounds that it de-potentiates the child. Below, I will quote Searles (1959) who writes about the reciprocal nature of the erotic element in work at the oedipal phase. He clearly differentiates between the countertransference experienced when the patient is at the pre-oedipal stage and when, in the oedipal phase, there is an appreciation of the child as a viable sexual person. He makes the point that this is a necessary developmental phase. Thus, I am attempting to examine the transference which very often contains infantile sexual demands and the transference which contains elements of real adult feelings. Very often both are operating simultaneously and this is my point; it is this which produces a particular type of conflict for the male patient and very often for the female therapist. This is where it is so essential to be able to interpret both and not to be caught in the 'avoidance shadow'. We need to be able to move fluidly between the infantile and the adult and not merely relate to one.

Olivier (1980) discusses the countertransference from the viewpoint of Jocasta, the mother of Oedipus. She argues that the son, unlike the daughter, is desired because he is 'Other' for his mother. Thus, infantile desires of the patient in the transference evoke the incestuous love of the mother for her son in the countertransference. When a seductive mother–son dynamic is activated in the transference, the countertransference may powerfully affect the therapist. This is complicated when the patient is an adult man because a sexual union would be possible. However, the infantile nature of the origins of this transference offers an opportunity for reliving the oedipal phase with a new and more positive outcome. If successfully transformed to conscious understanding, the transference love will be the catalyst which liberates the patient from the attachment to the past.

In view of this we must not take too literally ideas regarding maternal and paternal transference. Transferences to women which may be considered to be paternal or phallic mother could be understood as a pattern of relating which is evoked through the regression of the transference. Thus, the pattern father may be evoked in relation to a female therapist just as the pattern mother occurs with male therapists. Sometimes this pattern has an archetypal intensity and then such images as 'Phallic Mother' or the 'Great Mother' are evoked (Jung 1959b; Neumann 1955) or 'Ideal Lover'. Colman (1993) gives examples of married couples and shows how the marriage partner may be the carrier of similar projections. It is this projection which leads the patient out of the undifferentiated state towards a more separate or individuated way of being. Thus if, for example, the paternal transference is seen as a vestige, a pattern, an archetypal theme, it will emerge regardless of the actual gender of the therapist. I am suggesting, however, that the order, priority and intensity of engagement with such imagery may be affected by the reality of the gender of the couple.

GENDER AND POWER

There are social and cultural, as well as psychological, influences in any gender combination in analysis. Psychoanalytic insights cannot be separated from those of the culture in which the therapy takes place. Relationships between people, of whatever gender, will inevitably be influenced by the individual's experience of the predominating culture of the wider society. In addition, the psychology of the individual is affected by the smaller culture of the family or institution in which she or he has grown to maturity. Thus, whether conscious or not, there are implicit themes which enter the relations between women and men. These include sexual and power dynamics (Spector Person 1985).

It has been pointed out by Woods (1976) that latent, or even overt, male chauvinist attitudes are frequently ignored in psychotherapy because such attitudes are 'ego-syntonic and parallel cultural bias'. The therapist needs to be alert to the defensive nature of demonstrations of male power, which may take the form of dominant behaviour or subtle denigration of the therapist. These need to be confronted empathically but firmly and Woods (1976) encourages female therapists to monitor their own unconscious sexist attitudes which may collude with the patient's defence against dependency. In the early stages of a therapeutic relationship the patient may experience a significant power struggle because the therapeutic relationship conflicts with his self-image. It may feel shameful to admit dependency.

The power imbalance of the therapeutic relationship evokes the memory of past relationships and, especially, those of early childhood. The reviving, and so releasing, of these is in the nature of the transference. When the therapist is a woman and the patient a man, there is an apparent paradox. Women as mothers are powerful in the early years of a child's life. It is the mother or primary care taker, usually female, who is the first object of desire. This means she is the focus of all the ambivalent emotions associated with dependence; in the first years the child's experience is of a form of matriarchy. In adult society this is reversed: it is men who hold most of the power. When men bring their vulnerability to a female therapist, conflicted feelings, associated with the power of their mothers, may surface. Some men become defenceless, even awed by the perceived power of the therapist, while others defend fiercely against any form of dependent transference. Often men use their social skills to divert attention from their dependency needs. Power issues related to his sexuality were evident in the case of Mr A.

Mr A, a business man in his early fifties, was referred for psychotherapy because he had been experiencing physical symptoms which could be traced to no physical cause. He was married, successful in his work and related as a powerful, sociable and outgoing personality. In his relationships he was amusing and also fiercely autonomous; everyone depended on him and he bore his business and personal worries alone. In the first session the power dynamic became evident when Mr A attempted to negotiate a lower fee for cash. Immediately there was power play in this bargaining, as if this was a transaction between business associates. Each session began in a similar way. He made jokes to dispel his initial discomfort. His humour was infectious and flirtatious. It was certainly sexist but none the less there was a strong temptation to laugh with him, partly to relieve the tension. It was the realisation that his outgoing humour covered up a very deep unhappiness which prevented the therapist from joining him and laughing at his jokes. This could be understood in Fordham's terms as a 'defence of the self' (Fordham 1963, 1971). The jokes had become a decoy from the really distressed and vulnerable self which usually remained hidden.

As Mr A recounted his history, it became apparent that his symptoms were connected to unresolved grief. When he reported the memory of the deaths of his parents, he was clearly moved. Both his parents had died when he was a young adult. He was now in middle age but he had never really grieved. He was distressed to contact great sadness as he came to realise that he felt disconnected from his past by their premature deaths. This painful acknowledgement was a relief and during the following weeks, the physical symptoms abated. In each session he began by attempting to get the therapist to join him in his jokes and then, when the defensiveness of the jokes was pointed out, he began to express his feelings and struggled to hold back his tears. He admitted that it was a relief to talk and to recognise his distress. None the less, he struggled against revealing his weakness and vulnerability. After six months, he decided to terminate his therapy and we discussed the reasons he might wish to leave. He consciously acknowledged the loss connected with his decision and that he could not accept the dependency it evoked in him. It could be said that Mr A had gained what he had come for; the symptoms were understood to have meaning and so they had lost some of their intensity. We could speculate that, by leaving when he did, he was repeating the rupture he experienced when his parents died.

However, the purpose of this case illustration here relates to power and the erotic transference and countertransference. There was no evidence of an erotic transference with Mr A and it is possible that he terminated to avoid the development, or acknowledgement, of this deepening of the therapeutic relationship. His early childhood remained an area which was relatively untouched by the therapy. It is likely that his fear of dependency was significant and possibly connected to the dual nature of this aspect of the therapeutic relationship – the infantile and the erotic. Mr A was a dominant man who, initially, attempted to redress the power imbalance. He was relieved to confront his vulnerability but none the less, this remained difficult for him. For a man who is generally outgoing and successful it can seem shameful to reveal his weakness and perhaps this is particularly difficult in the company of a woman. For the female therapist it can sometimes feel taboo to directly challenge male power.

It takes an imaginal leap to view the adult in the consulting room as a child. With a patient like Mr A, in the early stages of therapy, the man–woman dynamic is foremost. Even though there was no evident sexual arousal there was certainly an awareness of its potential. The power play could be understood in sexual terms and the point is that this was not primarily a mother–child interaction. If Mr A had stayed in therapy for longer, it is likely that this would have modified over time and the mother–child dynamic may have come to the surface and so have needed interpretation. However, my point here is that there are times when interpretation of adult feelings in infantile terms is a defence for the female therapist against consciousness of sexual arousal. It may also be a way of maintaining her tenuous power in a challenging relationship.

Furthermore, and considering this case in the context of this chapter, I wonder whether, if I had interpreted not the infantile but the sexual component in the relationship at this stage, it might have enabled Mr A to engage in a deeper way. It would have meant challenging his power as a dominant sexual man. It is possible that I unconsciously colluded with the traditional man–woman dynamic and so did not manage to bring to consciousness the sexual dynamic between us.

COUNTERTRANSFERENCE

> The analyst is within love from the start, and if he forgets it he dooms himself not to perform an analysis. . . . The analyst occupies that place of the Other; he is a subject who is supposed to know – and know how to love – and as a consequence he will, in the cure, become the supreme loved one and first-class victim.
>
> (Kristeva 1983: 13)

Countertransference is complex and love is far from the only emotion that is experienced. There may be hate, fear, boredom and many other affective states which contribute to countertransference phenomena. However, paradoxically, it is often love which causes the most problems. As already stated, many female analysts claim that they do not experience erotic countertransferences with either male or female patients (Spector Person 1983, 1993). Similarly, in the psychoanalytic papers which discuss the female therapist–male patient dyad, the question repeatedly arises of why so little has been written regarding the erotic transference from this pairing. In contrast with 'the common story of the female patient falling "deeply in love" with her male analyst or into a "wildly unmanageable erotic transference", there are virtually no published reports of strongly sustained erotic transferences of male patients towards female analysts' (Kulish 1986). We know that erotic countertransferences are more likely to be overtly acted out by male analysts (Feldman-Summers & Jones 1984). Chesler (1972) and Rutter (1989) provide many incidents of female patients who have been sexually exploited by male therapists. It is more common for male analysts to discuss the problems of the erotic transference, than to admit the patient's reciprocal power over them by writing about the erotic countertransference. Guttman (1984) suggests that female therapists are more ready to discuss their own erotic countertransference than their male colleagues. She points out that the first papers to draw attention to the importance of countertransference responses of the analyst, as a guide to understanding the transference, were written by women. Heimann (1950), Little (1950) and Tower (1956) were influential in this regard.

Tower (1956) discusses erotic countertransference experienced by female analysts working with male patients. She writes: 'various forms of erotic fantasy and erotic countertransference phenomena . . . are . . . ubiquitous and presumably normal' (Tower 1956: 232). She suggests that these are aim-inhibited – that is without impulse towards action – and also separated in time from the erotic transference (Tower 1956: 232). Many analysts today would agree that such countertransferences are common, and certainly normal, but not with the view that they are aim-inhibited. The erotic countertransference is usually evoked by, and so present at the same time as, the erotic transference. Clearly such impulses would be less problematic if they were aim-inhibited and we do inhibit them, but in order to understand their meaning not because this is their prime characteristic. In this way they are admitted to consciousness and so transformed instead of being acted out or denied.

'Falling in love' is a transference phenomenon which is at the borderline between that which can be understood psychologically and that which 'is biological' or 'hereditary' (Tower 1956). We might understand this to be a description of an archetypally determined state. She compares the cases of two men. For one, analysis had a successful outcome, whilst for the other it was unsuccessful. This she attributes to the difference in the countertransference. Although she liked both men initially, during the treatment she came to feel 'intensely connected' to the first man. At times this was 'extremely testing', but she felt he was aware of and able to accept her affection for him. This she stresses was non-sexual and was communicated unconsciously between them. This type of attachment is one of the curative factors of psychotherapy which we cannot predict nor precipitate. Clearly, it helps if there is a genuine affection between the therapist and patient. It may be a phase which passes or it may last throughout the therapeutic relationship. We can ask questions about why it occurs in some cases and not others but, as Tower seems to indicate, it is not always possible to answer such a question.

Searles (1959) quotes Tower (1956) in his paper 'Oedipal love in the countertransference'. When this paper was published, countertransference was still considered, in the main, to represent underanalysed elements in the psyche of the analyst. Searles openly discusses his own countertransferences and confesses that when he first experienced erotic countertransference arousals with his patients, male and female, he feared it was due to his own unresolved oedipus complex (Searles 1959: 285). However, he came to understand these as important indicators of the state of the transference.

The erotic countertransference is related to developmental phases in analysis which echo stages in the parental relationship to the child (Searles 1959). Through descriptions of falling in love with patients who, in reality, would have made the most unlikely partners, Searles demonstrates how this love could be understood to be a natural response to the oedipal phase. Searles distinguishes this 'Oedipal love' from countertransferences experienced when the analysand is at a more infantile phase of development. During this regressed phase the countertransference may be more that of 'a loving and protective parent' (Searles 1959: 286). Thus, Searles distinguishes between two aspects of countertransference love which may be evoked in relation to the same patient at different times in an analysis.

It is part of normal development that the parent experiences an appreciation of the child, during the oedipal phase, as a potential partner. The renunciation of the parent's incestuous desires is a result of recognition of their separateness. When this is successfully negotiated there is a deeply felt acknowledgement of mutual love and respect which leads to the capacity to feel loved but unbound. Within an analysis the recognition of the capacity for being loved, when not helpless and dependent, forecasts the seeking of a new adult love object outside of the analysis (Searles 1959: 289).

The erotic transference is made up of infantile, pre-oedipal and oedipal desires. These are experienced as very real affective states in the present of the therapeutic relationship. There is not always an intense transference but when there is, it is unmistakable and totally engaging for both people. Peters (1991) gives a graphic account of the difference. Sometimes the analyst may actually fall in love in response to the patient's love. More often there may only be elements of love or non-sexual liking, which are less troubling for the analyst. Occasionally there is no response in the countertransference despite declarations of love from the patient. The understanding of this love is crucial for the wellbeing of the patient and for the professional survival of the therapist. There is a difference between the recognition of eros and sexual activity. The devastating effects of the damage done when these two are confused is becoming increasingly evident. The point is that eros may lead to sexual activity but this is not necessarily its only purpose nor its only outcome (Jung 1946, CW 16; 1960, CW 8).

INCEST TABOO – MOTHERS AND SONS

The intimate nature of the therapeutic relationship means that it is inevitable that incest constellations are evoked. Transference and countertransference offer the theatre for regression to an earlier psychological state. Thus, at some time in a regressed transference, the incest motif will emerge irrespective of the gender of the therapeutic couple. It will become manifest in same sex, as well as cross-gender pairs, and regardless of the reality of the dominant sexual orientation of the couple. The incest motif is likely to evoke an erotic atmosphere but constrained by the taboo associated with prohibition. This may dominate the therapeutic relationship, for a time. It may cause either person to unconsciously withdraw or both to become intensely involved with each other. Kulish (1986) suggests the taboo nature of the feelings aroused in the countertransference may account for the female therapist's reticence in reporting her experiences to colleagues by writing about them. None the less, most writers agree that regression to incestuous erotic feelings is a significant part of an analysis. Jung (1946, CW 16) relates the transference–countertransference to the kinship libido, the cross-cousin marriage. I have referred to this in relation to long-term work with a male patient whose erotic transference is evident in the pictures he made (Schaverien 1991: 189–95).

There is some discordance in the literature, regarding differences in the incest taboo, and in which pairing its effects are most inhibiting. Samuels (1985b) considers that, as a result of the close relationship a mother has with her son in infancy, the mother is less likely to be anxious about her oedipal impulses than the father. Fathers tend to be more worried about erotic involvement with their daughters and so may distance themselves, with the resulting damage to the self-esteem of the daughter (Samuels 1985b).

Kulish (1986) expresses the widely held view that the incest taboo operates more strongly against mother–son than father–daughter incest. Searles (1959) cites Barry & Johnson (1957) who claim that, in contrast to father–daughter incest, there is less evidence of transgression of the mother–son incest taboo. This is because the mother–son incest barrier is universally and rigorously present in all cultures. Rich (1979) confirms that: 'Despite the very high incidence of actual father–daughter and brother–sister rape, it is mother–son incest which has been most consistently taboo in every culture' (Rich 1979: 186). She considers that this taboo expresses an inherent male fear which links woman with fear of death. Rich's sociological view is similar to that expressed by many psychoanalysts as we will see below.

It was Horney (1932) who first drew attention to the 'Dread of Woman'. She suggested that male fear of women, and particularly the vagina, was the source of much idealisation of the feminine. In this she was the first to challenge Freud's notion of castration anxiety. When this material constellates in the transference, the countertransference may be uncomfortably affected for the female therapist. It brings her person and her body into the subject matter of the session in a very intimate way. This is why an understanding of the symbolic nature of the transference is so helpful. It can be a relief to the patient to understand that the origins of his interest in the therapist's body are connected to early developmental phases and it can also be helpful to the therapist to understand it in this way. However, problems arise when this understanding is used as an avoidance of the reality of the feelings in the present. It is often the unconscious fear of woman which underlies an intense idealisation which may occur in the transference; the negative may be split off. Alternatively, there may be a persistent denigration expressed towards women in general and the therapist in particular, and it is likely that in this case the positive feelings are denied. The fear of women may also underlie the apparently detached attitude of some male patients to their therapy.

Chodorow's (1978) feminist object-relations analysis has been extremely influential in feminist thinking. (Recently Chodorow has been criticised as essentialist and also for appearing to blame mothers for the psychological ills of their children. The subtleties of such debates are not the topic of this chapter, however, they are of note (Segal 1987; Doane & Hodges 1992).) Chodorow compares differences in the development of boys and girls. The girl is the same as her mother and so she experiences continuity in her 'gender and gender role identification' (Chodorow 1978: 182). It is normal for both girls and boys to repudiate the mother during the oedipal phase because: 'Mothers represent regression and lack of autonomy'. Girls and boys go through a phase where they become hostile but there is a difference in the nature and outcome of this hostility. In the girl her hostility to her mother becomes a form of self-deprecation because, like the mother, she, too, is female. For a period of time during adolescence this attitude dominates but eventually, for the girl, the '"normal" outcome entails acceptance of her own femininity and identification with the mother' (Chodorow 1978: 182).

The boy's negative attitude is contempt. During the oedipal stage the boy gives up his oedipal and pre-oedipal attachment to his mother, as well as his primary identification with her (Chodorow 1978: 174). To feel himself adequately masculine, he has to differentiate himself, he 'must categorise himself as someone apart', a consequence of which is that 'boys come to deny and repress relation and connection in the process of growing up' (Chodorow 1978: 174). The girl is more likely to have difficulty in separating and the boy to have problems with connectedness. For a boy, elements of devaluation of the feminine remain; especially if he feels that his masculinity is threatened by his primary identification with the mother. 'Dependence on his mother, attachment to her, identification with her, represent that which is not masculine: a boy must reject dependence and deny attachment and identification' (Chodorow 1978: 182).

Thus, the boy is likely to repress qualities that he views as feminine in himself, and simultaneously reject and devalue women (Chodorow 1978: 181). In the therapeutic relationship elements of these differences become apparent. This repudiation of the mother underlies the sometimes powerful idealisation and denigration of the female therapist by patients of both sexes. It is particularly with male patients that idealisation of the feminine seems to be linked to an unconscious association with death. Some of the difficulties male patients experience in therapy with a woman are related to a deep and primitive fear for their survival.

Chasseguet-Smirgel (1984a) considers that the difference in pregenital and early oedipal sexuality in girls and boys is in their awareness of their reproductive possibilities. The girl knows her body is not yet developed; there is no visible evidence that she is like her mother; she does not yet have breasts so she knows that she will have to wait to bear children. The boy may have fantasies that he could be an effective partner for his mother, i.e.: make babies (Chasseguet-Smirgel 1984a: 91). In this the seductive mother may give reassurance of the little boy's potency. If the father is absent this type of unconscious conspiracy between mother and son can damage the son's ability to make viable relationships with other women. He tends to remain arrested at the pregenital stage and it can often be this which underlies the formation of a certain type of incestuous transference–countertransference dynamic.

The fear of death associated with the son's desire for the mother is developed by Chasseguet-Smirgel (1984b). The little boy's realisation that the woman 'possesses an organ which allows access to her body' is terrifying. His pregenital impulses are projected; he fears that which he also desires; thus his intense desire for connection with the mother is experienced as her desire. He fears that he will be sucked back into the womb, absorbed and so annihilated (Chasseguet-Smirgel 1984b: 171). Referring to Stoller (1968), she points out that the fear of femininity, and so close identification with the mother, is, for men, linked to a fear of loss of their sexual identity. In the beginning of his life the young male is 'plunged into his mother's femaleness' [but] 'This primary symbiosis must be undone so that masculine identity can be developed by separating from the maternal identity' (Chasseguet-Smirgel 1984a). For this difference to be made, for this separation to take place, the father is required.

In the transference there is often a regression to this early incestuous confusion. The type of premature and false sexuality described above may manifest in intensely seductive, dependent, angry and sexualised behaviours. This form of incestuous conspiracy maintains a bond between the inner world mother and the grown man. This is often reproduced in therapy, especially with a woman. The impulses derived from the infantile–erotic or oedipal stage may be experienced in the transference as idealisation, flattery, seductive behaviour – even love. There may be an unconscious desire for merger with a pre-oedipal mother/lover and simultaneously a terror of what that would mean. Frequently this over-valuation of the female therapist is a sign that potential denigration and hate are being split off and denied. The terror, withdrawal or denial of the transference experienced with the female psychotherapist must be understood and spoken of. We have seen in the case of Mr A that very often the male patient will start discussing termination at the point at which dependency becomes an issue. A further example is Mr B, whose dependent erotic transference was evident from the start of therapy.

INFANTILE EROTIC TRANSFERENCE

Mr B, in his early thirties, still lived with his mother and father. He was a middle child in an unusually large family and so he had received very little individual attention during his early years. Now most of his siblings had left home and he felt lonely. He could not leave his mother as he felt she needed him to look after her. She was dependent on alcohol and had several related physical problems. Mr B had been impotent since his late teens. He had girlfriends but never a sexual relationship. He always left them when this began to become an issue. For a number of years after leaving school he was unemployed and suffered a bout of depression which remained untreated. He now had a job and his problems had intensified when he had recently tried to leave home. He found accommodation but before he could move in, he was overwhelmed by extreme anxiety in the form of panic attacks. This threw him back to the parental shelter. He was referred for psychotherapy and quickly engaged, attending twice a week.

From the beginning there was an intensely infantile/erotic atmosphere in the transference. He was experienced by the therapist as seductive and heavily dependent. He became increasingly unable to do without the therapy but, at the same time as reporting his need for the sessions and his difficulty in managing between them, he described thoughts of running away to another part of the country and never returning. He imagined leaving both his mother and the therapist and never returning. He did, in fact, drive to the other end of the country telling the therapist that he would be away for a week. He drove all day and night and, exhausted, he stayed in a bed-and-breakfast place where he became overwhelmed with loneliness. He returned the next day and phoned; he needed to make contact immediately.

When, within a few months of Mr B beginning therapy his mother unexpectedly and suddenly died, he was deeply upset but also relieved. He felt responsible because he had been with a woman friend at the time. He felt that if he had stayed at home he might have saved his mother from the accident which was the cause of her death. Three days after the death of his mother, Mr B had his first sexual experience with this same woman friend. This developed into a regular relationship and he was frightened of the demands of his woman friend but also liberated. He was aware that there must be some link between the two events and curious about it. Very soon after this he terminated his therapy without warning.

We might speculate about the reasons he terminated so abruptly. On the positive side perhaps it was helpful that he was able to leave the therapist as he had been unable to leave his mother. It is likely that the relationship with his woman friend was, in part, the reason that he left. He may have transferred his dependency needs to her. However, it may also be that the therapist was unconsciously identified with the mother, from whom he could not separate, so, in order to continue the sexual relationship, he had to leave his therapy. He may have experienced the therapist as a burden – like his mother. It follows that a fear, but also unconscious wish, that the mother/therapist would die may have been part of the motivation for this sudden termination.

There are other possible understandings which relate to the theme of this chapter. Mr B was desperately needy and entered into a regressed trans-ference. From the start of his psychotherapy the intensity of the incestuous atmosphere was pronounced. The termination was sudden and premature and perhaps an unconscious avoidance of a much deeper dependency. In the countertransference I felt abandoned and could not believe that he would not return. His neediness and erotic dependency had considerable appeal. I did not want him to leave, I wanted to keep him. I felt I had more to offer him than his woman friend. None of this was communicated to him consciously. But it can be seen that, in the countertransference, it is likely that I was becoming the embodiment of the mother from whom he had to escape.

In addition, we have seen that in the past Mr B always left his girlfriends when sex became an issue and it is possible that this was repeated in the transference. Mr B's infantile neediness and sexual desires were confused and mixed up. In the session before he terminated he had discussed his sexual fantasies about his schoolteachers – he wondered if they recipro-cated his sexual wishes. This seemed to relate to the transference and it is likely that he experienced sexual arousal in relation to the therapist. It is likely that this arousal was also projected – the therapist being experienced as both needy and seductive. We see from the countertransference that this was to some degree the case, and I suggest that this was an 'embodied countertransference' (Samuels 1985a) in that this was an embodiment of his mother's feelings in relation to him. In addition, his fear of the extent of his own projected dependency would mean that the therapist may have become associated with engulfment. He may have left because he feared merger which would, as we have seen, be unconsciously associated with death and annihilation.

The link between mother and death was strongly present in this therapeutic relationship. Mr B could not leave his mother and this was acted out in his inability to engage in sexual intercourse. When she separated from him by death, he was able to feel some sexual arousal and then to act on it for the first time. Kristeva (1989) writes that:

> For man and for woman the loss of the mother is a biological and psychic necessity, the first step on the way to becoming autonomous. Matricide is our vital necessity, the sine-qua-non condition of our individuation, provided that it takes place under optimal circumstances and can be eroticized.
>
> (Kristeva 1989: 27–8)

There is love and sexuality in this separation. The desire for the mother must be killed off and another object outside the familial tribe must be found. The eroticisation of the object and its transfer from the mother to an 'Other' is the aim of this matricidal impulse. In the case of Mr B this happened, almost literally, in that his mother actually died, but before he was conscious of his negative wishes, and so before he was able to separate from her. The matricidal impulses remained unconscious and were subsequently acted out in relation to the therapy. He terminated prematurely, leaving his therapist, as his mother had left him.

Once again I think that if I had interpreted his sexual desires and also fears in relation to the transference, he might have been able to stay. His sexual and infantile needs were very mixed up. But at this stage I think that the sexual impulse needed acknowledgement prior to the infantile.

SEXUAL THEMES IN THE TRANSFERENCE

Sexual themes, linked to particular imagery, may be evoked in the male patient by his transference to a female therapist. Guttman (1984) lists the affects of archetypal themes which commonly emerge in the male patient–female analyst dyad. (Although she is a Freudian analyst she uses the term archetypal.) She differentiates between asexual and sexual imagery; both involve the female therapist as an object of positive and negative regard. Like other contrasting elements, these may be present simultaneously or they may become manifest at different times. For example, the therapist may be experienced as a good, nurturing mother but this might alter to fears of being engulfed and smothered. The therapist may be viewed as idealised or sexually desirable, and this may shift to the negative, sexual, image of vamp or whore. Furthermore, images which are apparently maternal often have a sexual element, whilst overtly sexual images may be related to the maternal.

In the transference, particularly in the grip of an archetypal constellation, the therapist may be experienced as terrifying, sexually powerful, tantalising or potentially dangerous in some other way. Both patient and therapist may collude in resisting this type of transference. Expressing sexual feelings directly to a woman may seem very dangerous to a male patient and, similarly, the female therapist may resist conscious recognition of the male patient's sexual wishes. She may unconsciously deny them as well as her own erotic countertransference (Guttman 1984). There may be unconscious taboos, for analyst as well as for patient, on articulating feelings associated with culturally unacceptable images, particularly those relating to violence and sexuality. An extreme negative transference may affect the analyst's awareness of herself as a woman and a positive sexual transference may be problematic because women are often afraid of being seen as blatantly sexy.

Within the transference the therapist is often experienced as the perpetrator of past failures and abuses; she may be viewed as all powerful, as persecutor, as well as object of love and much else besides. This may be problematic if she comes to identify with these images or if she finds it difficult to accept the powerful position in which the male patient's projections place her. The countertransference may also be affected by socially stereotyped images of men which the female therapist, as a woman, brings to the encounter. The therapist may deal with her discomfort by viewing the male patient as a needy child. This may be more acceptable to her than confronting the sexual arousal which might follow acknowledgement that he is desirable as a man.

Guttman points out that it is relatively easy for the therapist to react positively to a patient of the opposite sex who is clearly attracted to her (Guttman 1984: 190). She considers that, even if it is not consciously admitted, much of the reciprocal countertransference will be communicated non-verbally in gestures and body language. The analyst needs to be aware of the effects of such a countertransference. If it is handled consciously and appropriately, such an attraction can have a positive effect on the patient. It may enable him to express feelings he may not easily share. Guttman (1984) suggests that a well-handled attraction to the patient may actually facilitate his feelings of self-worth.

An example of an unusually conscious understanding of this was given by Covington (1993). She describes a patient who stated, in the beginning of his analysis, that it would only work if he could fall in love with her and she with him. She considers that it is probably necessary for this to happen with patients of both sexes. Samuels (1995) suggests that, contrary to avoiding the erotic nature of the therapeutic situation, it might be import-ant to address the question: 'Why is this person not lovable?' or 'Why am I not aroused by this person?' (male or female). Asking this question may reveal the problem which has brought the person into analysis in the first place.

Countertransference problems arise when the therapist's need to be loved, the 'desire to feel special to another person, are unfulfilled. There can be a temptation to seek validation and acceptance through the power of being an analyst' (Sniderman 1980: 306). In such a situation, as with male therapists and female patients, there is always the potential for abuse. The distinction must always be between observing the affect and acting upon it. The important thing, as in all analysis, is for the therapist to be conscious of the countertransference and, when the time is right, to interpret the trans-ference.

Resistance in the female therapist may be exacerbated when the male patient's oedipal feelings are linked to images in which the woman is sexually degraded (Lester 1985). This may arouse a negative countertrans-ference which is exactly what the male patient fears. It is often this that makes him refrain from disclosing negative images to a female analyst. It is less inhibiting to discuss negative female stereotypes with other men as this is the norm in social interaction. What is unusual in this therapeutic relationship is that the 'witness is a woman' (Guttman 1984). 'The male patient will be careful in expressing his sexual feelings lest he be consid-ered dangerous' (Guttman 1984: 191). Men are commonly troubled about being seen as potential rapists and they fear that expression of such impulses is tantamount to acting on them. This was the case with Mr C.

Mr C, a divorced man in his mid-forties, described himself as auto-erotic. He had been in psychotherapy twice a week for several months when he missed several sessions. Eventually he contacted the therapist by phone and admitted that he was unable to come to his sessions because he had begun to experience intense sexual arousal accompanied by violent fantasies. It became clear that he was confused by his feelings and frightened by the intensity of them. He returned and explained that he feared that he might attack or rape the therapist; he became very aware that we were alone in the building. He said: 'What do you do if you fancy your therapist?' He felt that this was both inadmissible and needed some action from him. He became acutely aware of the limits of the boundaries of the therapy room – would they hold? He desired, but also feared, that the therapist would permit a sexual relationship with him.

Once we began to speak of this he was able to recognise the pre-oedipal, infantile aspect of his feelings. He linked it to his previous relationships with women where he would get close and then withdraw in terror. He desired a sexual relationship but he had always felt he needed something first without understanding what it might be. It began to become evident that he desired maternal holding before he could experience himself as sexual in relationship. Once he had admitted what he felt he was able to contact his dependent, erotic and sadistic, violent fantasies. These included an interest in newspaper reports of men who had murdered their girlfriends and dreams which revealed his murderous impulses towards his mother, his sister and the therapist. Through talking about, and so normalising these feelings, they began to be less fearsome for him. Once the violent feelings were acknowledged, the erotic transference intensified and the relationship deepened.

This is the purpose of the erotic connection; it deepens the patient's capacity for relatedness. Mr C was frightened when he began to experience sexual fantasies associated with violent imagery. Like Mr A and Mr B, his first impulse was to run away but he was able to make contact with the therapist and then to return and discuss his feelings. We both survived and this transformed the feelings, admitted them to consciousness and, because his desire was no longer split off, the relationship deepened and became rewarding for us both.

There was a significant infantile element in this transference. However, he was also a grown man with adult sexual desires as well. In the counter-transference I was deeply involved and sometimes sexually aroused by Mr C. From the very beginning of his therapy he engaged with an intensity which was hard to resist. I found myself looking forward to seeing him, as one might a lover. I missed him if he stayed away and, sometimes, I found it difficult to end the session because I wanted to be with him for longer. I could imagine walking with him and being together in bed and sometimes, during a session, the impulse to touch him was very strong. (I should make it clear that, despite the intensity of these feelings, each session ended on time and there was no physical contact.)

I came to understand my impulses to be closely linked to the transference. Within the frame of the therapy room I came to be experienced by Mr C as every woman who had ever been important to him. This was seductive but it was also a useful way of getting to understand his communications. I began to trust that if I felt a wish to hold him, it was probably counter-transference and that it was likely that he was experiencing such a desire. If, on the other hand, I felt disconnected, it was usually because he was angry or in the grip of some other intense emotion and so cutting himself off from me. This was similar to his taking himself away from the therapy when he began to be sexually aroused. The difference was that now he was able to stay in the room and only cut off emotionally. Eventually he needed to do that less and less and would recognise it in himself and comment on it.

The point is that here the sexual element in the transference, which was a mixture of infantile impulses and adult desires, was openly discussed between us. With Mr C it was possible to acknowledge his infantile needs and to link them to his sexuality. Further, it was through the acknowledgement of the multitude of facets of the therapeutic relationship that he began to develop the capacity to communicate with the people in his outer life in a more appropriate way than he had previously. Mr C was often difficult to be with and rejecting of me and yet, despite exasperation and other more extreme negative countertransference feelings, my work with him was always sustained by the affection I felt for him. Like Tower (1956), Guttman (1984) and Covington (1993) quoted above, this was communicated in such a way that he eventually became able to trust my affection for him and gradually learn to trust others.

CONCLUSION

There is a flux from idealisation to denigration in many transference/countertransference relationships. Originating in the mother–child dyad the desire for unity, and the need for the establishment of a separate identity, is a central theme in all analyses. This has a particular character when the therapist is a woman and the patient a man. (The three illustrations that I have given are of men who were predominantly heterosexual. It remains a question, for further exploration, whether there is a difference if therapist, patient or both are homosexual.) I have suggested that, when erotic dependency issues emerge in the transference, a crisis may occur and the male patient may terminate prematurely. It seems to me that this may, in part, account for the assertions that sustained erotic transferences do not occur between female therapists and their male patients. If this crisis can be overcome, a sustained erotic transference may develop which may enable the male patient to make a deeper relationship to himself and eventually to others. Surviving this crisis may be a significant point in the therapy with a male patient.

It has been my intention to demonstrate that female therapists are not immune from the temptations which beset male colleagues. It is clear that it is quite possible for the female therapist to abuse her power in a number of ways, including sexual acting out. If as the evidence indicates there is less incidence of acting out by female therapists, it is not because of the absence of eros from the situation. Desire of many kinds is a common and necessary part of the transference and the difference lies in the response. This is eloquently expressed by Kristeva who writes: 'During treatment, the analyst interprets his desire and his love, and that sets him apart from the perverse position of the seducer' (Kristeva 1983: 30). This is our aim in all therapeutic interactions and the erotic transference and countertransference between female therapists and male patients highlights the challenge that this sometimes poses.

In this chapter I have established the groundwork for the book. The cases discussed in this chapter were based on my current analytical psychotherapy practice. In the three chapters which follow I will explore the transference of the male patient through a case study of one man who was suffering from anorexia. This is a rather different approach, based as it was in a psychiatric hospital. None the less the principle is the same and psychological states revealed in the pictures correspond to those discussed in this chapter. Further, the pictures graphically reveal the imagery which is so often present in the male patient–female therapist dyad. It is the desire and the denial of desire in anorexia which gives this study a particular significance in this context.

Chapter 3

Desire and the male patient: anorexia

The pictures which illustrate this, and the following chapter, exemplify many of the themes of the book. This is a case study of anorexia in a male patient. However, although this is an important aspect of the story, it is not all. In Chapter 2 I discussed some of the developmental theories relating to the mother/son transference as it manifests between female therapist and male patient. In that chapter the focus was the desire of the female therapist. In this chapter the theme is the desire of the male patient.

The theme of desire is complex in this regard; anorexia is essentially denial of desire and yet I am showing this case study as an example of the desire of the male patient. There are a number of reasons for showing this case study in this context. The client was male and this is itself unusual as most anorexics are female. The erotic transference and countertransference engagement centred in the pictures and was to some degree worked through in them. Furthermore, this case study reveals that there is a significant purpose in the desire which emerges in an erotic transference. It is the desire, which sometimes takes the form of a love for the therapist, which leads to consciousness and a way out of the undifferentiated state to separation and differentiation.

In the pictures made by the patient, whom I shall call Carlos, many of the themes which were discussed in Chapter 2 can be seen to appear spontaneously. The transference which commonly arises in other forms of psychotherapy is revealed. We see that this transference is not simply a desire for the therapist in any particular guise. Rather the symbolic free-floating nature of the transference becomes evident as the imagery moves from one phase to another. The transference may be seen as a quest which, in this case, finds expression through imagery. It is the unspecific and multi-faceted desire for connectedness which is generated by means of the therapeutic relationship.

Thus, the implications of presenting this case study are intended to be wider than both anorexia and analytical art psychotherapy. Carlos's story is offered here as a vivid illustration of the transference desire of the male patient; as evidence of the embodiment of that desire in pictures; and as a record of the treatment of anorexia through the medium of an analytical form of art psychotherapy. This took place within a psychiatric hospital context but it reveals psychological processes which are common in psychotherapy. Moreover, the evident aesthetic quality of the pictures means that they illuminate many of the themes which will be discussed in subsequent chapters. Later in the book I shall draw on this case study to elaborate other aspects of theory such as the lure of the image in Chapter 8 and the gaze in Chapter 9.

The pictures illustrate the battles and internal conflicts which Carlos had to confront during the course of his therapy. However, I wish to make it clear that my intention is not merely to show that these images arise; this has been demonstrated adequately in the many case studies that have been published over the years. Jung (1959a, CW-8; 1959b, CW-9; 1946, CW-16), Baynes (1940), Adler (1948) and more recently, Kay (1985), Edinger (1990) and Rosen (1993) are among the Jungian analysts who have presented case material illustrated by the patient's pictures. Thus, we know that art releases potent imagery. My interest is in extending this to an understanding of the aesthetic effects of such imagery on the transference and countertransference.

We have seen that it is not easy to admit to the erotic transference and countertransference between the female therapist and male patient. In 1991 (Chapter 8) I published an illustrated case study of a male patient working with a female therapist. In this case I did not comment on the gender of the patient/therapist pairing directly and, although I wrote a good deal about the incestuous connection, I did not refer directly to the erotic arousals in the therapeutic relationship. It was clear from the imagery that the gender dynamic was a significant factor. The incestuous, erotic transference was evident in the imagery but I did not write explicitly about the erotic coutertransference. My affection for the patient was implicit in the study but not directly addressed. This indicates the difficulty in openly admitting to this element of the countertransference. In Chapter 2, I have shown that this is a common factor in the writings of other female therapists.

In a recent valuable contribution to the art therapy literature Dalley *et al.* (1993) show the process of art therapy through a detailed illustrated case study. They devote each chapter to a single picture and this gives a very detailed and clear exposition of the role of art in the therapeutic relationship. Each picture is discussed from the viewpoints of the client, the therapist and an external observer – the 'supervisory voice' or 'overview'. The client and therapist give individual accounts of their memory of the emergence of the picture and then, both therapist and the 'overview', comment on the theoretical implications. The theoretical base is drawn from the self-psychology of Kohut (1971), object relations and art therapy theory. This gives a vivid account of the process of art therapy as well as drawing out important general theoretical points.

In the case they describe the client was male and the therapist female. There was evidently an intense involvement, on the part of the client, but here too there is no discussion of an erotic element in the transference or countertransference. I suspect that this would have been a factor for two reasons. First, the intensity of the engagement of the client in his therapy suggests to me that his desire was, for a time, focused on the therapist. It would seem likely that this played a part in the evident transformation in his state. Secondly, the fact that the therapist was moved to write the story of the therapy indicates her continuing interest; she was clearly affected by this client. We have seen, in Chapter 2, that eros is certainly not an aspect of every therapeutic engagement and so it is possible that it did not feature in this one. However, I suspect that it may have been an element.

In the chapter entitled 'The relationship with the therapist' the picture discussed is a portrait of the therapist. The client makes reference to the fact that the therapist was a woman and he found it easier to talk to her than to his first, male, therapist (Dalley *et al.* 1993: 129). This is acknowledged by the therapist, who considers that it was less intimidating for him that she was a woman (Dalley *et al.* 1993: 134). It seems to me, with regard to this picture in particular, that it is likely that there was some form of erotic transference. Clearly there was, for a time, an intense involvement for both people and the therapist recognises the idealised element of the picture. She observes that the picture marks the beginning of the relinquishing of his idealisation of her and an engagement in a more 'interactive process' (Dalley *et al.* 1993: 137).

It was certainly art that engaged this client in the therapy but the writers clearly demonstrate that the relationship to the therapist played a significant part. My point here is that whether or not there was an erotic element in this case, there seems to be a common reticence in women to write of this aspect of the therapeutic relationship. This echoes a reluctance in speaking of the erotic countertransference directly and, even sometimes, in taking it to supervision.

In the case study which follows there was an erotic engagement. This is again evident in the pictures, which reveal infantile, incestuous imagery; and this was echoed in the transference. Maternal and erotic feelings contributed to the affection which developed in the countertransference, but here too it was not easy to admit to it. I worked with this patient within a psychiatric team which is very different from the boundaried setting of the analytical psychotherapy, described in Chapter 2. In that chapter the explicit, as well as the implicit, sexual transference and countertransference was admitted; it was, when appropriate, openly discussed during the course of the therapy.

In inpatient psychiatry the situation is much less clear, and it may not be possible to interpret the transference. When a team is involved it is not always possible to ascertain where and, in whom, the transference is located.

There is potential for conflict when some of the staff are working with a behavioural model and others within a psychotherapeutic frame. It is important not to confuse the client with conflicting approaches and so everyone has to adapt and this may limit transference interpretations. Furthermore, in this case the actual family was still actively involved and this real situation makes the transference unclear. The pictures revealed it; they 'bared the phenomenon' and so it was there to be seen as a form of visual interpretation (Schaverien 1991: 107–10). Although it was not always interpreted to the patient, I will link the pictures to the transference and countertransference throughout the text.

ANOREXIA IN THE MALE PATIENT

This case study records the process of art therapy with a young man who was suffering from anorexia nervosa. This is an eating disorder in which the vast majority of sufferers are female and Carlos was one of the small percentage of men who suffer from this problem.

It is generally accepted that anorexia is, in varying ways, a defence against growing up and becoming an adult woman. It is generally characterised by a refusal to eat anything but extremely small amounts of selected foods, even in some cases nothing at all. This leads to weight loss, dehydration, poor circulation and other symptoms of starvation. Psychologically, anorexia is considered to be a denial of the changes that the body undergoes at menarchy and the cessation of menstruation is a key factor. It has been suggested that diagnosis of male anorexia is more complex because without the cessation of menstruation as a symptom it is more difficult to identify. Consequently, there may be males who go undiagnosed as anorexics (Crisp 1980; Palmer 1980). Certainly all the literature concurs that male anorexics are rare in comparison with the many females who suffer from it; the estimated percentages vary but it is agreed that they are a distinct minority. Palmer indicates that diagnosis of anorexia in the male may be missed because it is comparatively rare, but: 'in the definite case the subject's low weight, odd eating and his attitude to both will be enough to make a clinical diagnosis possible' (Palmer 1980: 39). Further, he suggests that 'investigation can reveal similar patterns of hormonal change to that which underlies the amenorrhoea in the female' (Palmer 1980: 39).

Dally and Gomez (1979) review the literature and give evidence of anorexia in males as long ago as Whytt (1767). They quote Ryle (1939) as having collected fifty-one cases, of which five were men, indicating that there have always been a proportion of male sufferers. Bruch writing in 1974 considered that the few boys who suffered from anorexia did so before puberty and did not develop sexually until after they had recovered. Recently (1993) the *Eating Disorders Association Newsletter* has started a regular column to address, what they consider to be, the increasing number of male anorexics. Crisp (Crisp & Burns 1990: 77) questions the claim that there is an increase in anorexia in males. He finds that the 10 per cent of male anorexics display very similar symptoms to the females who develop anorexia. This paper is one in a recent collection of papers on *Males with Eating Disorders* edited by Andersen (1990).

In feminist writing men with anorexia are frequently dismissed as an irrelevent minority. There are considered to be too few to merit serious study, and the male is not central to the theme of women and society which has preoccupied feminist writers on eating disorders. Chernin in *The Hungry Self* writes that: 'As yet we know very little about the 8 percent of anorexics who are male. It is possible that they are men who carry a strong identification with their mother' (Chernin 1985: 57). She comments that some therapists of her acquaintance see men who are preoccupied with food. This she views as a part of 'the contemporary male effort to reclaim and develop in themselves the qualities of feeling, sensitivity, and tenderness they have been taught to associate with women' (Chernin 1985: 57). This is a thought-provoking couple of paragraphs but it is also seriously inadequate as an explanation and it leaves many questions unanswered. Male anorexics have received little attention from those writers who take a non-medical model approach.

Differences in the understanding of the aetiology of anorexia are important because they generate different attitudes to treatment. So, although I do not aim to give an overview of the literature, it is relevent to acknowledge some of the accepted approaches. These range from the administration of resistance-suppressing and appetite-enhancing medication to behavioural regimes, controlled diets, systemic approaches to the family (Palazoli 1974; Minuchin *et al.* 1978), feminist psychotherapy (Orbach 1986; Chernin 1981, 1985), traditonal psychotherapy and psychoanalysis (McCleod 1981; Shorter 1985).

In psychiatric journals research is usually an attempt to establish, on the basis of objectively assembled data, common factors in the aetiology of the disease as well as prognosis and diverse approaches to treatment. It often seems that these writers attempt to understand the problem from a scientific position. Their frame of reference places them outside the problem. The opposite pole is written, as it were, from the inside. Many of the feminists who write about eating problems explain that they have themselves suffered from some form of eating problem. Their theories regarding the causes are based on gender role and relationship. They discuss child development with regard to sociological theory and the relationship to the parents, particularly the mother. They analyse the mother's relationship to society, society's expectations of women, female sexuality, desire and power. Treatment is usually psychotherapy with a female therapist and this work has been pioneered at the Women's Therapy Centre in London (see Orbach (1978, 1986), Lawrence (1984, 1987) and Dana & Lawrence (1988)). There are some similarities between these and feminist approaches in the USA (Woodman 1982; Chernin 1981, 1985; and Spignesi 1983).

I concur with the view that there is probably little difference in the aetiology and treatment of the male and female anorexic. However, in discussing male desire, it might be worth considering some possible implications of developmental differences. Of course the manifestation and origins will be different in each case but one of the commonly accepted explanations for the onset of anorexia is that it is a fear of becoming an adult. For the girl this means becoming a woman *like* her mother, menstruating and becoming capable of bearing children. It means leaving her mother to become like her, to compete with her, possibly to oppose her during the oedipal phase and to become her rival (Chernin 1985). The daughter may desire a union with her father and so unconsciously fear rivalry with her mother. She may fear separation and leaving the state of dependency and to avoid this confrontation the anorexic becomes instead regressed and exists in a state of limbo (Spignesi 1983). She becomes totally dependent on her mother and also, paradoxically, she controls her. The result is that mother and daughter are bound together in fear of separation. The potential healthy aspects of aggression are split off and denied.

A similar process may be operating for the male anorexic. However, the difference would be in the effects of his regression. Because he is other than his mother, his regression may be linked to his sexuality more directly than it is for the daughter. To grow up and leave mother the man must leave his dependent state. He must relinquish his incestuous desire for the mother. He must oppose the mother, not to become like her but to become different, to enter the world of men, the world of the father. If this is not successfully negotiated, then his regression will remain linked to a desire for the mother. This desire is, at a conscious level, for her nurturing and protective power but it may also include an unconscious desire for her as the idealised sexual partner. Thus, the son's conflict will be bound to his sexuality in a rather different way than the daughter's. His need to remain a child may be a need to oppose and even to supplant the father. This he does by attaching himself to his mother as an infant but with the additional appeal of his sexuality. I submit that the male anorexic is likely to be in the grip of a peculiarly strong and confusing, unconscious incest battle within his own psyche.

It is the incest dimension which I suggest highlights a difference in the understanding of the state of the male and female anorexic. The regression in both may involve elements of a wish to return to the maternal shelter to be a child and protected. For the male child regression is complicated by the fact that he is other for his mother and, as we saw in Chapter 2, the regression then takes on a more intensely sexual nature. The focus of discussion here is anorexia but male dependency issues are more general than this and we have already seen in the last chapter that such an incestuous desire may be a feature of other forms of disturbance in men.

This may become amenable to change if the figures of the inner world, which have developed out of the original parental relationships, can be admitted to consciousness. The patient needs to develop an understanding of them in order that separation may take place. One way for such archaic patterns to be mediated is for them to come live into the transference. The danger for the anorexic, as for patients with other borderline disturbances, is that to admit these archetypal contents to consciousness is to risk being engulfed by them. Pictures offer a way of mediating such elements. Through them it is possible for these elements to come live into the transference but to be held in the picture. In this way powerful, archetypal images may be viewed but 'held' at a distance. They are witnessed and so, gradually, admitted to consciousness.

THE TREATMENT

The combination of medical model, behavioural, family therapy and psychodynamic approaches which was offered to Carlos seems to be common in psychiatric hospitals where a multi-disciplinary team is involved (Crisp 1980; Palmer 1980; Bruch 1974, 1978). The method by which anorexic patients were treated on the ward where Carlos was admitted was uniform. Prior to admission interviews with the consultant psychiatrist, senior nurse and social worker determined the patient's preparedness to work on the problem. Thus, prior to admission the patient had to admit that all was not well. For anorexic patients this is no small advance, as they are often convinced that they have never felt better, and vehemently deny that their body weight is dangerously low. A target weight was agreed as a condition of treatment and once a low average was agreed a chart was drawn up to record the weight gains and losses.

Medication was not used. Although appetite-enhancing or resistance-lowering methods of treatment, such as tranquillisers or insulin treatment, reduce symptoms in the short term, i.e. they bring about more rapid increase in weight, they do little to alleviate the underlying causes of the anorexia. Therefore the patient is susceptible to a recurrence of the symptoms, or to loss of control, leading to bulimia or excessive weight gain. Most anorexics fear bingeing on cream cakes and other 'goodies' to excess and so, taking into account this very real fear, the treatment aimed at a slow increase in weight. A firm boundaried environment permits the patient to temporarily relax control, relinquishing responsibility for food intake. There were no special diets in this treatment and no eating except at mealtimes. The anorexic patient was expected to eat the same food as others and at the appropriate times. Many are vegetarian and this was respected. Families and friends who liked to bring in treats for the patient were discouraged from doing so. Thus, the boundaries were established and maintained. The patient, who will inevitably complain about the unfairness of the control, can none the less rely on this structure.

The family, if there is one that is involved, is asked to participate in the treatment. Carlos's family attended monthly meetings with the patient and various staff involved with him. This is because anorexia is regarded as, in part, a family problem. It can be helpful for the other members of the family to be involved in attempting to understand what the anorexic member may be expressing in the context of the family dynamic.

CARLOS

Carlos was admitted as an inpatient to the psychiatric hospital where I was the art therapist one January. He was 23 years old and looked younger. This was partly due to his emaciated condition. He weighed less than 6 stone and was approximately 5 ft 9 in in height. Gradually during the past four years he had virtually stopped eating and had withdrawn from all his previous activities. Prior to his admission his condition had deteriorated to such a degree that he had become totally dependent on his mother. Unable to let her out of his sight he had taken to following her from room to room and would not permit her to leave him alone. In common with other anorexics he complained of feeling empty, becoming introverted and he described himself as very, very far away from happiness. He was preoccupied with food, felt huge if he ate and hated his flesh. When he could see and feel his ribs, he felt his body to be right.

Carlos was the eldest of six children. He was born in a South American country and his mother had moved to this country to marry when he was 2 years old. At the start of his treatment he was unaware of this because, although the man his mother married was not his natural father, he adopted him. The first two years of his life had been spent in the home of his maternal grandparents where he lived with his mother and her sisters. Thus, his first years were spent in a predominantly female environment. His natural father was known to him throughout his childhood as a friend of the family who came to this country periodically to visit. This man always took a special interest in him and, in his adolescence, he interpreted this as a homosexual interest.

Until his brother was born, when Carlos was 12, he was the eldest child and the only boy in the family, his mother's only son. This was a doubly special position, and it is likely that he didn't feel challenged for this position by his sisters. The birth of his brother coincided with the beginning of Carlos's adolescence so it is quite likely that he felt jealous and even ousted from the special position in relation to his mother. Until this time he had, according to his parents, been 'good' but at the age of 13 he entered what he described as a 'rebellious' phase and this, too, may have been a reaction to being displaced. Carlos left school with no qualifications and then drifted through a series of jobs. He was sexually ambivalent; he had had a girlfriend for several years but he did not want her sexually. His sexual fantasies were always related to men. He described himself as homosexual but, although he had found sex with men quite enjoyable, he had never found someone to be close with emotionally.

The family relationships are vividly illustrated in the picture, Plate 1. This picture was made in response to being asked to portray his family. He described the figures in the picture as his mother, in white, and the father, in black. His sisters, too, are clothed in white robes and, like his father his brother, peering out from the protection of the mother's robe, also wears black. The father stands slightly behind and with his daughters. It is notable that Carlos is crouched beside his mother on the ground so that he is equal in stature with his younger brother. He said he chose to colour himself both white and black because of his confusion about his sexual identity. The family is clothed in rather religious-looking garb which suggests that they are all nuns or priests. They are covered up so that they have no sexual attributes nor does the mother have facial features. The parents' wings suggest some kind of rather idealised angels.

When asked where he would like to be in the picture, he said he would prefer to be at the back with his sister who has left home. The sister who is looking down at him he described as liking to feed the family with cakes, which are in the foreground. There was some competition here because Carlos was trying to see that the family stayed healthy by eating salads. The attempts to control the eating of family members is typical of anorexics. The sister with outstretched arms was going through a rebellious time behaving, he said, rather as Carlos himself had done at her age.

The rays of the sun shine all around but, Carlos pointed out, they emanate from the mother. It is she who holds the key he said. This he explained was because he had discovered the truth about his natural father; his mother had told him during a family therapy session. However, she had asked him not to tell his sisters in case they would think badly of her. The effect of this was to increase the incestuous bond. He was tied to his mother by this secret. Later, he took this picture to a session with the family to explain how he felt.

What is said about pictures is often the conscious meaning but this is not all. Like a dream, all the elements in a picture may be seen as unconsciously representing aspects of the artist's inner world. So that we might see that, as well as representing members of his family, these figures all represent some aspect of Carlos. Thus, the sister who has left home may be an aspect of him which wishes to do the same, while the little brother may represent the part of him that wishes to remain beside his mother.

It is relevant here to describe a psychodrama which was enacted by Carlos towards the end of his treatment. He portrayed his predicament in forming relationships by showing how, when he begins to get involved with a girl, it is as if he is held on a piece of elastic which is attached to his mother and this pulls him back to her immediately. He also described always being aware of her presence in a room and how he had to make a conscious effort to keep separate from her. So we see that his libido, his sexual drive and life energy was very much attached to his mother. This is a manifestation of an inner-world incestuous connection which Jung saw as purposeful:

> The basis of the 'incestuous desire' is not cohabitation but as every sun myth shows the strange idea of becoming a child again, returning to the parental shelter, and entering into the mother to be reborn through her. But the way to this goal lies through incest, i.e., the necessity of finding some way into the mother's body.
>
> (Jung 1956, CW 5: 223, 1976 edn)

This refers to a symbolic rather than literal state of affairs. However, if we remember how Carlos had become totally dependent on his mother prior to his admission, we see that it had a very serious outer-world manifestation.

In keeping with the treatment policy, Carlos was given a small room on the ward. This room contained a bed, a cupboard, a sink and a television and he was confined there until his target weight was attained. At first he was resistant to eating and tried various methods to escape from taking in food. The nursing staff were responsible for monitoring his food intake and, although they did not sit with him at all times as is sometimes the case in treatment for anorexia, they did watch him closely. The role of the nurses is caring but, unlike the mother, they are not emotionally involved. Consequently, they are better able to observe the situation and remain firm despite the many exasperating and devious tricks which anorexic patients devise to dispose of food. Carlos was not permitted to leave the room for any reason. This, as well as the control of the food intake, was part of the contract which was negotiated and agreed with the patient prior to admission. The patient was weighed several times a week and his weight gain or loss was marked on the wallchart.

Although it could not be predicted on admission, it was to take ten months before Carlos was to leave the room and eleven months before he would be discharged.[1] This confinement may be seen as symbolic, especially for someone in a very regressed state. It could be understood as parallel to confinement in the womb and if we regard Figure 4.4 (p. 71) as indicative of his regressed state at the commencement of treatment, this certainly makes sense. Figure 4.4 shows an emaciated skeletal figure held in a bubble which is like his room in the hospital. The womblike aspect of the room is affirmed by the apparently circular container of the bubble. (This picture will be discussed in detail in Chapter 4.) The point of referring to it here is because it reveals the pathologically regressed state he was in at the time of his admission. At first Carlos spent much of his time, particularly when he was feeling distressed, curled up in a foetal position on his bed. This continued for the first few weeks and he returned to it later at times of stress.

ART THERAPY

Art therapy was part of an integrated approach to treatment and the art therapist worked as a member of the multi-disciplinary staff team. Art materials were offered to all anorexic patients on their admission. Sometimes they would need to have an explanation of how to use them but at others there would be little need for this. Carlos needed little encouragement and every time I visited him he had something new to show. There was a momentum to the production of his artwork which I have noted with certain other patients (Schaverien 1991: 222). It seems to come from an urgent need to externalise and to find a form for powerful inner images.

It will be noted that Carlos's pictures are, almost without exception, very carefully executed and it was not until quite late in his treatment that I found out that he was making little sketches and plans before drawing or painting. In this way he was able to censor their content and exclude any random marks. Although the imagery was powerful, it was not spontaneously executed. In common with other anorexics his need to be meticulous and in control was embodied in his pictures. The room, which was very small, may have contributed to this by limiting the size of gestures he was able to make. The last few pictures in the series were made in the art room, after he attained his target weight, and these pictures have a notably more free-flowing feel to them. This may have been due to the amelioration of his symptoms but it may also have been influenced by the space available.

The care Carlos took may reflect the need to have boundaries to contain the images which were released in the pictures. Powerful archetypal material, such as that which emerged in many of these pictures, can feel overwhelming. The unconscious breaking through into consciousness could have made the bounds of the paper feel like an insufficient container, so that, at first, he may have wished to rehearse the pictures on a small scale. This is confirmed by the change in technique when he permits some of the underlying conflicts to become conscious.

PICTURES AS A GIFT: THE TALISMAN

The art therapist's role as regards the pictures was to provide the materials, to witness and acknowledge the imagery which was surfacing in them. This valuing of the pictures is a symbolic valuing of the person. Carlos's first pictures were mostly small, executed on A4 paper, and he was gladly giving them away to his friends, family and to nurses who admired them. I intervened and explained that it was important for him to keep them for the time he was in the hospital. However, he found it difficult to refuse a request and so, as a compromise, he decided to give photocopies and keep the originals. Later, when he was more able to assert himself, he did not need to give them away in this form either and subsequently keeping them became very important for him. Here the art therapist intervenes, values the pictures and so affirms a purpose for them. The patient may be unable to do so for a number of reasons; it may be that he does not recognise their therapeutic value or he may not feel entitled to keep them. In affirming this purposeful nature, of something that might otherwise be viewed as recreational, the therapist values the investment he makes in the pictures and so she values the person. Later, as in Carlos's case, he is able to take responsibility for this himself. This is similar to any other psychotherapeutic transaction where the therapist may be understood to hold aspects of the transference until they can be reintegrated.

Among the pictures which Carlos made at this time was Plate 2 (The name picture). I have written about this picture elsewhere (Schaverien 1982, 1987b: 104–7). It was made as a gift for the art therapist only a few weeks after his admission. Rather idealised elements are assembled to construct my name: a tree makes the J, the sun in the centre is an O and a crescent moon and stars combine to make the Y. All is set in a blue sky with four small clouds. Made before the family picture (Plate 1), the sun in this picture emanates from the central letter of my name. In the family picture the sun's rays emanated from his mother's face. Thus it seems to me, looking at this in retrospect, that this picture reveals that, even at this early stage, there was a transference developing whereby the therapist was invested with similar attributes to the mother. He told me that he had given similar pictures to his mother and his aunt, and so it seems I was included in the same category. At the time I was confused by this; he had only been in the hospital for a few weeks and I felt that I hardly knew him. It seemed a rather inappropriate gift but I accepted it and kept it in the art room. In countertransference terms it was not easy to accept this gift, I was a little embarrassed. But it was important to understand that it was not given personally, to me, but to what I represented at the time. Gradually I was to become drawn in and feel a great deal for Carlos. At this early stage it was as if he were trusting me with something very precious and, in response, I became immediately engaged with him.

It was only later that I came to realise the significance of this picture as an embodiment of the transference. This is an additional facet of the transference; the making of the image is one aspect of the transference and the gift of it to the therapist another. I realise now that he had invested me, along with his mother and aunt, with his positive attributes. At this early stage he was reproducing, in the transference, the pattern of his relationships with women. This reveals the free-floating nature of the transference and its inner-world constellation which could be understood to be searching for an outer-world manifestation.

It seems that while he experienced himself as depressed and near to death, he invested his life force in the mother/therapist. In contrast to the other black-and-white drawings made at this time, this picture is colourful and even celebratory. In retrospect, reviewing all his pictures together, the unconscious meaning of this gift becomes evident. If we regard Plate 11 (The sun), which was one of the last pictures he made when he was in hospital, we see that it contains many of the elements which were to be seen in Plate 2. The difference is that this picture was not a gift for anyone. It was his own picture. In this image, which is flooded with sunlight, I think he was reclaiming the aspects he had temporarily invested in the mother/therapist and owning them for himself. Thus, it seems that this picture, made as a gift, reveals the twin aspects of the transference in analytical art psychotherapy – the scapegoat transference, embodied in the picture, and the erotic, maternal transference evoked by the therapist as a person.

This demonstrates why it is so important for the therapist to keep all the pictures safe for the duration of the therapy. She guards them all as potential talismans which may be magically invested with aspects of the therapeutic relationship. The unconscious meaning of such gifts is not always clear to either person at the time they are made but, what is clear is that if they are given away, some of the potential for understanding their meaning is also given away. Carlos kept his pictures and displayed most of them on the wall of his room, adding to them almost daily. Over the weeks the pictures built up to a retrospective exhibition which Carlos could live with and contemplate, gradually becoming familiar with their content.[2] Thus, the stages of familiarisation, acknowledgement and assimilation were gradually affected in relation to the series of pictures. The pictures were also viewed and admired by visitors to his room but they no longer took them away with them. This worked as self-affirmation and it permitted him to own, and to keep, the good things he made rather than feeling obliged to give them away. This became part of the therapeutic process.

There were a few pictures which he kept hidden under his bed and shared only with the art therapist. These were too painful to exhibit publicly. Only three times during our work together did I ask him to make a picture on a predetermined theme. Each of these pictures was of powerful significance for Carlos; in each some element of his relationship to his inner world was subtly changed. Through each of these pictures something which had been repressed, or previously unconscious, was admitted to consciousness. Two of these remained under the bed. The first was the family picture, Plate 1, made some months into his treatment. The second will be discussed later in the series Figure 4.9.

The third picture, elicited in this way, was so important for Carlos that he couldn't bear to keep it and eventually he destroyed it. This was a picture of an incident which took place in his childhood. He had been asked to make a picture of his earliest memory and initially the memory evoked was of a happy time with his grandparents, in the country of his birth, when he was very young. However, the picture was marred by a cloud in the sky which at first he could not understand. After associating to the picture he remembered a long-buried memory which caused him so much pain that he could say very little about it at the time. He did not keep this picture on the wall but stored it under his bed. Some time later he confessed that he had destroyed the picture in order to be rid of the memory again. I have discussed this incident in more detail elsewhere (Schaverien 1991: 112–13).

CARLOS'S ART THERAPY STUDY

Two years after he was discharged from the hospital Carlos took an A level examination in art. For his special study he chose to write about art therapy. Part of the essay is theoretical but he also wrote about his own art therapy pictures to illustrate the process. He called this study *Painting and Drawing as Therapy* and in the section on his own work entitled 'A Personal Insight', he describes the insight that he gained into his problems through his pictures. In addition, he made notes, shortly after he left hospital, on the reverse side of some of the pictures and these indicate something of their meaning for him at the time. In the next chapter I include these comments and this section of his study. In this way the reader will have Carlos's comments alongside my own. Where I quote from him I acknowledge it and his words are written in a different typeface to separate them from mine.

Carlos had written to me asking for references of books to read about art therapy but he did not discuss the content of his study with me. I did not see this work until some years after it had been completed. I make this point because the significance that Carlos made of his pictures is very similar to the sense that I made of them, quite separately when I was no longer in contact with him. I, too, wrote about them at the time we finished working together and, although I have updated this, it forms the foundation of my comments on his pictures. Carlos knew that I was writing it but he did not see my study. Despite this, the similarity in our interpretation of the meaning of the pictures is marked. There is nothing provable in such an observation but I do think that it offers a phenomenological view of a process which is useful to consider. We did talk about the pictures at the time but much of the process was non-verbal. Thus this case study may contribute to an understanding of how art psychotherapy facilitates communication, within a transference and countertransference relationship, without necessarily speaking directly of the meaning.

Sometimes we talked about the pictures and at others we did not. On many occasions Carlos would merely show me his pictures and we would regard them together and so acknowledge their content. Often this was evidently very painful for him and it did not at the time need additional words although I might offer a comment. At other times he would be eager to tell me what he had discovered in his imagery. In common with other anorexics, he was a very private person. By accepting his pictures without demanding explanation, I respected his privacy and this gave him the confidence to reveal his inner world without the fear of intrusion.

This may be helpful in developing an understanding of art psychotherapy as treatment in anorexia and other borderline conditions. It implies that art offers a means of communication in which the patient may maintain their privacy and then admit the therapist gradually. Carlos's pictures, with his own words, make an eloquent case for art therapy as a form of pre-psychotherapy with anorexic patients.

SYMBOLS OF TRANSFORMATION

I have already referred to a previous work in which I wrote a detailed case study of analytical art psychotherapy with a male patient whom I called Harry. In this I drew extensively on *The Psychology of the Transference* (Jung 1946, CW 16) as a theoretical base. The reason for this was that, in Jung's discussion of the incestuous coniunctio of the transference and countertransference, linked to alchemy, I found a correspondence with the images made by Harry. This furthered my understanding, at the time we were working together, of the intense involvement which engaged both patient and therapist.

In writing about Carlos I did not seek a different text. It was rather that, as I had found *The Psychology of the Transference* (1946, CW 16) when I was working with Harry, so I came upon *Symbols of Transformation* (1956, CW 5) when I was working with Carlos some years later. The Hero's journey, as discussed by Jung, seemed to express the process that appeared to engage Carlos. Many of the images which spontaneously emerged in his pictures correspond to those discussed by Jung and sometimes *Symbols of Transformation* (Jung, CW 5) seemed to articulate the process of Carlos's inner journey. Thus, I shall quote Jung when it seems relevant.

In *Symbols of Transformation* Jung marked his break from Freud. It was in this work that Jung established his view of the purposeful nature of sexuality and, particularly the incest motif, in the transference. Despite the fact that the book is about the fantasies of a woman, a Miss Miller, it is the son's journey to free himself from the dominance of the mother archetype which is the subject matter. It is this which corresponds to the journey of Carlos.

In the context of current discussions regarding the limitations of Jung's attitude to gender, we can no longer apply his work uncritically. There are a number of theorists who are attempting to review Jung's work in the context of current debates. Certain writers question the premise of gender difference which informs Jung's theory of opposites. The hero motif, as a way of understanding masculinity, is generally considered outmoded (Samuels 1985b; Hopcke 1989; Tatham 1992). Carlos's sexual orientation was primarily homosexual and so Hopcke's (1989) discussion is relevant. He finds many contradictions in Jung's writing on the subject of homosexuality and shows that the major part of what Jung wrote on the topic was negative but not all. He quotes Neumann's (1954) discussion of the hero myth where 'the ego aligns itself with the principle of heroic masculinity in order to free itself from the dominance of the matriarchy' (Hopcke 1989: 71). Hopcke points out that this is then extended to pathologise homosexuality as an immature state of development. It is important to acknowledge these arguments when presenting a case such as that which follows. In it the struggle to separate from a real situation in which there is a powerful connection to a mother, did evoke imagery such as that suggested by Jung and Neumann. Further, the sense I make of the imagery is derived from the hero myth. However, I make the point that I do not present this case as an *explanation* of homosexuality nor of all male psychology. It is merely an example of one person's journey shown in the images which emerged spontaneously in his treatment. It could be discussed in other language such as that of the Freudian theorists whose work is reviewed in Chapter 2. Indeed, Lacanian theory is also applied in discussion of the case study but it is the imagery which seems so directly to lead to Jung.

Hopcke (1989) suggests that we might 'conceive of sexual orientation as a multi-faceted archetypal phenomenon' (Hopcke 1989: 187). Sexual orientation could be understood to be the result of a 'personal and archetypal confluence of the masculine, feminine, and androgyne'. In which case 'bisexual men and women are . . . individuals whose masculine, feminine and androgynous energies flow in a particular individual pattern in response to certain archetypal and personal experiences'. He suggests that such a theory permits an understanding of how an individual's sexuality might change over the course of a lifetime (Hopcke 1989: 187).

Wehr (1987) finds Jung's idealising of 'the feminine' anima has a shadow side, which shows in the denigration of 'women', particularly in discussion of animus in his texts. She, too, salvages something positive: 'my criticism of sexist elements in Jung's thought is not meant to disparage his very real contribution to human self-understanding' (Wehr 1987: 124). She considers that Jung's lack of understanding of female experience is evident but on the positive side his contribution is in understanding of the 'inner world of the male and its projections' (Wehr 1987: 126). Young-Eisendrath (1992) considers anima and animus are most useful clinically when they apply to Jung's theory of contrasexuality which 'invites a psychological analysis of the other arising in one's own subjectivity. This is extremely useful in clarifying gender differences . . . providing . . . we revise our theory of gender so that it is relative and contextualised' (Young-Eisendrath 1992: 175–6). She argues that there is no self-evident or neutral truth about gender: 'gender has no ahistorical, universal meanings. This means that I do not privilege either the structure or the function of the human reproductive organs as grounds for self-evident gender meanings' (Young-Eisendrath 1992: 159).

The case study which follows may place us at the centre of such debates. It is undoubtedly relevant to apply Jungian theory when discussing such evidently archetypal material as that of the pictures I shall show. However, my understanding of these images is not intended to bind us, through limited interpretations, to any normative notion of gender role or sexuality. These images are discussed as they present themselves, in the context of the series of pictures and in the context of the story of the therapeutic relationship out of which they emerged.

An additional potential pitfall in cases such as this is in being thought to blame the mother. That is not my intention either. Psychology is generated in the family but there is a further aspect which the individual brings to their life. Thus, in demonstrating an inner-world struggle, we must bear in mind the combination of factors which may lead to certain types of disturbance. When archetypal material emerges, with the intensity shown in the pictures made by Carlos, the struggle to separate from the internalised mother, or mother image, is clearly demonstrated. Whether this is understood as an outer-world problem or battle of opposition within the psyche is for interpretation. I suggest that, what we see in these pictures, is a combination of both and that they are complementary and therefore inseparable. For our discussion what is important is the role these pictures played in freeing the artist. They enabled him to begin to differentiate aspects of his inner world and to strengthen his relationship to himself. Furthermore, the symptoms of anorexia diminished.

In the next chapter I shall discuss the pictures in detail but first I would make the point that, when I write about them, it is with the benefit of hindsight. When they were made, I did not understand them as I do now, and this is because I have been able to study them in retrospect. Thus, I am now privileged to know the direction the series was to take in a way neither Carlos nor I knew at the time. Pictures do not have fixed meanings; their meanings are always multiple. The viewer will inevitably have their own associations to pictures. To avoid the pictures being subject to multiple diverse interpretations, there is a way of limiting the potential meanings and this is to attend to the context. In this case there are two such contexts. First, there is the context of the therapeutic relationship within which the picture is created, and second, it is viewed within the context of the series of pictures. In this way the series may be considered to be the whole and the individual picture has meaning as a part of that whole. I would hope that the pictures will be viewed in this way.

When analysts and psychotherapists write about their work they make word pictures for their readers. Their clients also contact such imagery and with their words they attempt to convey the power of the affect generated in association with this material. The difference here is that the imagery can be seen. The implications of the points I am making are more extensive than analytical art psychotherapy and psychiatry; these pictures reveal processes which emerge in other forms of analytical psychotherapy. Here, we have the benefit of seeing many of the images which are evoked in the transference in other forms of psychotherapy. Moreover, it is possible to reconstruct an element of the sessions and, by viewing the pictures, the feeling tone of the time they were made comes live into the present. It is so for the therapist writing about such a case and I hope it will be so for the reader.

Chapter 4

The pictures

Anorexia is an extreme form of denial of desire. The desire for food and so nourishment of the body is transformed, through a supreme effort of self-control, into abstinence. Desire pre-supposes an Other towards whom there is a movement; thus, it is to do with relationship. Anorexia is a turning away from the Other and, through a false sense of power, it is a movement away from life and towards death. In the case of Carlos this will become evident in the pictures he made during the process of his treatment.

The pictures which illustrate this chapter are both black and white and colour reproductions. The black-and-white pictures are integrated in the text and referred to as Figures prefaced with the chapter number and then the number of the picture. The colour pictures are referred to as Plates and these are assembled together between pp. 64–65. In addition, the pictures are numbered in their sequence in the whole series; this includes those not shown. This number is indicated in brackets and followed by the title and the date the picture was made and finally the size of paper and the medium. Thus, Figure 4.1 (1) is the first picture shown in Chapter 4 and it is number 1 in the entire series.

A PERSONAL INSIGHT

Perhaps the best way I can explain the process and benefit of art therapy is to discuss briefly a series of my own drawings. The fact that they are drawings, and not paintings, relates directly to my illness – a yearning for neatness, order and often meticulous detail. Painting would have been too messy and the 'safe' control of drawing had with it a sense of security. I was admitted to hospital, with anorexia nervosa and confined to a small room for ten months. My only source of release during that time was through my art. These are my drawings.   *(Carlos 1983)*

Already, in this written statement, we see that anorexia is a denial of desire of mess and risk. The yearning for neatness, order and detail is a form of control of passion.

FIGURE 4.1 (1) FIRST PICTURE. DATED 29 JANUARY. PENCIL DRAWING ON A4 PAPER

I'm amid all those bubbles
Yet somewhere lies a good world
of trees and light something better than this world.

Figure 4.1 First picture

The first picture by Carlos was a pencil drawing (Figure 4.1), made two days after his admission. In the foreground are numerous bubbles which he described as symbolising his problems. These, and the precipice with trees growing out of it, are recurring images. The sun is in the distance on the right side, often considered to be the side of consciousness. Later in the series, we will see its position change.

PLATE 3 THE CRUCIFIX (2) UNDATED COLLAGE: NEWSPAPER AND MAGAZINE PICTURES ON SUGAR PAPER

Carlos's second picture was a collage. One day, soon after his admission, I went to see Carlos and found him busy on the floor of his room with newspapers and glue. It was obvious that he did not want to be disturbed and within two days he had completed this picture. In the photograph we can see the collage pinned to the wall of his room and his other pictures can be seen displayed beside it. In the foreground is the corner of the bed and this gives an idea of the dimension of the room in which he spent his inpatient phase.

As a technique, collage is a way of making a picture out of found imagery and so, unlike paint, it offers control and distance. Despite this, and because of the scale of it, Carlos was literally in the midst of the images when he was creating it. He was totally engaged and his attention was such that no interruptions were tolerated until the picture was completed. Once finished, this stood as a graphic statement of his condition for all who entered his room to see.

The crucifix was significant as a Christian symbol which alludes, I suggest, to his spiritual aspirations which later became a part of the recovery process. It is also the rack on which he was currently feeling tortured. This picture expresses many of the dilemmas facing Carlos in common with other anorexics. The figure on the cross, recognisably Carlos, is made up completely of coloured magazine images of food. In the head of the figure is a tiny embryonic foetus and above this another embryo is part of the cross. The black-and-white newspaper headlines which make up the crucifix all refer directly to his problems with words which are very relevant. Among them: 'Power', 'He bites the hand that feeds him', 'Kill yourself', 'crack up', 'graveyard', 'why', 'trapped', 'not all power corrupts', 'frozen', 'fear', 'isolated', 'lonely', 'pocketful of rye' and, under one of the foetuses, above the head of the figure, is written 'Beauty and the Beast'. Each phrase vividly expresses the conflicts which assail the anorexic. The choice between life and death with which he is confronted is embodied in this image. The words form an integrated part of this embodiment. For example, the word 'power' – anorexia is often understood to be a misguided bid for personal power through the attempt to control the body

Plate 1 The family picture

Plate 2 The name picture

Plate 3 The crucifix

Plate 4 The precipice

Plate 5 The room

Plate 6 The battle

Plate 7 Death of the child

Plate 8 Confusion

Plate 9 The dragon

Plate 10 The hero

Plate 11 The sun

by starvation (McCleod 1981). 'Frozen' is the term Spignesi (1983) uses in describing the anorexic condition.

'He bites the hand that feeds him' is a potent phrase in this context. As stated earlier, prior to his admission Carlos was totally dependent on his mother. There are a number of ways to view such dependency and one would be to see it as passive aggression which would fit with 'biting the hand that feeds'. Klein views infantile aggression as an impulse to devour, destroy, scoop out and consume the breast. Such hunger is experienced as endangering the loved object and so the desire is experienced as unacceptable (Klein 1937: 306–43).

In this regard it is also worth considering the following passage by Meltzer:

> there is possessive jealousy which would appear to be a primitive, highly oral and part-object form of love. It is two body and yet it is not really envy; it might seem to be included in Melanie Klein's description of envy of the-breast-that-feeds-itself. It is seen with such intensity in the autistic children and in children whose drive to maturity is very low, so that they wish either to remain infantile or to die.
>
> (Meltzer 1967: 15)

Carlos was no longer a child and yet this description seems very much in accord with the state he was in on his admission. Further, the words used by Meltzer offer an interesting slant on those used by Carlos in his crucifix picture. 'The breast-that-feeds-itself' is an object of envy; the desire here is understood as mixed up with the envy of the breast that is felt to have all the goodies. In addition, the drive to maturity was very low in Carlos and, as we have already seen, he was regressed to the point that he spent most of the day curled up in a foetal position on his bed. Meltzer continues: 'This means in their unconscious to return-to-sleep-inside-mother. It is this form of possessive jealousy which plays an important role in perpetuating massive projective identification of this peculiar withdrawn, sleep sort' (Meltzer 1967: 15). Meltzer is discussing a manifestation of such a state in the one-to-one transference. In the case of Carlos, who was an inpatient in hospital, this could be acted out with regard to the institution as a whole, so that his sleep could actually take place within the confines of the room where he was safely held. If we look at Figure 4.4 (p. 71), we can see that this deathly, skeletal figure could well fit the description of an attempt to 'return-to-sleep-within-the-mother' and, for an adult, this is a deathly state.

Here we see that Carlos was turning away from life and his picture is technically executed in a manner which keeps his expression in control and his desires at bay. In terms of the transference to the therapist, we have seen that his wish for a connection has already been shown in the gift of the picture, Plate 2, incorporating her name, but she was also kept at a distance. Thus the early stage of the transference was simultaneously a movement towards the therapist and a need to keep her at a distance. In response, the countertransference was complex. First, here was a new patient who had already made a mark by the gift of a picture and so it was clear that I was not 'nobody' to him. Secondly, he was engaging in the art process with considerable intensity and revealing creative ability. Through his picture he was communicating the desperation of his state. There was an interest in his engagement with the art process. Moreover, there was an interest in

Figure 4.2 The badger

him. He was an attractive young man who was friendly and outgoing on the one hand and painfully regressed on the other. Again this had appeal.

FIGURE 4.2 (4) THE BADGER. DATED 2 FEBRUARY. PENCIL DRAWING ON A4 PAPER

This picture was done when I first came into hospital it signifies my trepidation and weariness; my fear of what was yet to come.

This picture seems to refer to a much reproduced painting by Holman Hunt called *The Light of the World.* In the Holman Hunt picture it is Christ who is knocking on a door without a handle. The meaning of this is that the door must be opened from the inside to let him in. Its similarity to that picture leads me to assume that it is a conscious reference. However, we did not discuss it, and it is possible that it was unconscious. Like the crucifix collage, here too, Carlos is identified with Christ.

The picture seems to depict night and the unconscious perhaps. The badger is a creature of night-time habit and here he is watched by three sets of eyes. The feel of this picture is of expectancy but it has a childlike quality in the style of execution and in the clothes of the badger. The five toadstools – three topped with candles – are reminiscent of the cakes in Plate 1 and perhaps Carlos's five siblings. The light the badger holds is also a candle as is the lantern behind him, perhaps bringing light to an unconscious state.

It could also be understood to reflect the state of the transference; the timid figure knocking on the door is a potentially dangerous animal. Its dangerous aspect is disguised as it is clothed in domestic garb. This means that the outer covering suggests that he presents no threat, he is tame. It could unconsciously reveal his tentative engagement with his therapist. He was, at this stage, tentatively making contact – making pictures with the therapist in mind – and interpersonally conveying the impression of an unthreatening, asexual, childlike, male.

FIGURE 4.3 (5) THE MUM TREE. DATED 4 FEBRUARY. PENCIL DRAWING ON A4 PAPER

On the back of the picture:
I am the ball, the tree is my mum.
From Carlos's study:
Upon drawing this I was totally puzzled as to its meaning. Only months later did I realise that the tree was my mother, and the sphere was my embryonic self.

Here is one of the pictures where our memories are different. I remembered him calling this 'the mum tree' when he made it and explaining to me that,

Figure 4.3 The mum tree

within the branches, it was possible to discern the words 'Mum'. His realisation of this months later may be explained by its becoming more clearly conscious.

The tree appears thorny but strong and, in its upright position, it might be viewed as phallic. At the centre is a circle, the 'sphere', which is similar to the bubbles already seen in Figure 4.1. It would be possible to see this circle as a moon or the womb of the tree. The tree is often an image of the self (Jung 1959a, CW 8). In view of later pictures I would draw the reader's attention to the creeper around the trunk of the tree. It appears to grow upwards and in a spiral and is made of tiny flowers all drawn with great care and attention to detail. Later we will see a creeper detaching itself from a tree (Figure 4.15). The ground is strewn with neatly drawn flowers which form a path which winds into the distance between mountains. To the right another path leads straight to the edge of the picture and to the left there is a division as if between one field and another. The tree seems to stand on the place where paths meet.

The archetypal element in this material is affirmed by the following quote from Jung who refers to the 'mother tree':

> As a serpent he [the hero] is to be 'lifted up' on the cross. That is to say as a man with merely human thoughts and desires who is ever striving back to childhood and the mother, he must die on the 'mother tree', his gaze fixed on the past. . . . This formulation is not to be taken as anything more than a psychological interpretation of the crucifixion symbol, which because of its long lasting effects over the centuries must somehow be an idea that accords with the nature of the human soul.
>
> (Jung 1956, CW 5: 367)

Jung emphasises that he is not making a theological point but merely pointing out the psychological significance of such material in unconscious processes. He links the 'mother tree' to a psychological interpretation of the crucifixion. This accords remarkably with the process in which Carlos was engaged. Thus, we might understand that, although the 'mum tree', on the one hand refers to Carlos's relationship with his real mother, it also resonates with the state of his inner world.

Jung states that interpretation in terms of parents is a 'manner of speaking'. What the parents stand for, or are symbols of, is the wider male and female principles of the universe (Jung 1959b, CW 9, Pt 1). He demonstrates that over the centuries, people from different cultures and diverse parts of the world repeat the same, or very similar, images and these have an archetypal or 'typical' base. The psychological aspects of these transcend the material and so interpretation in terms of parents is figurative. The whole drama may be viewed as taking place within the individual's own psyche where parents are not parents any more but only their residual images.

Recently this understanding has been developed by Samuels (1991a) who argues that the presentation of the parental images in therapy can be understood as messengers for psychological contents. He notes that the way the parents are presented appears to change during the course of an analysis. Rather than seeing these descriptions as accurate or truthful representations of the actual parents, he suggests that we might understand the ways the parents figure as being aspects of the inner world of the patient in the present. Thus, the changes are in the patient's relationship to these aspects of the self.

In the case of Carlos there is clearly a real family who are enmeshed in the patient's illness and because he was still living in the parental home, the real parents did feature in his treatment. Moreover, no one would suggest that anorexia is merely a psychic problem. Its manifestation is very material leading, as it sometimes does, to starvation to the point of death. However, I suggest that an important part of the struggle was taking place within Carlos's own psyche. In order for him to integrate the unconsciously projected aspects of his personality, he needed to become conscious. From his story and the pictures that we have seen so far we know that he was battling with his actual incestuous strivings. The conflict seems to originate in the family experience but it is now internalised in a personal manner and is beginning to be expressed in his pictures.

This image also reveals very clearly the merged state. As yet unborn, some aspect of him–self is held within the mother. As we have seen, anorexia is often considered to be a manifestation of an inability to separate from the maternal imago if not from the real mother. Here we could understand, in Lacanian terms, Carlos to be trapped in the 'Real', merged and unable to differentiate self from other, he cannot enter the Symbolic. There is no differentiation and this reveals the borderline element of which anorexia is a manifestation. Furthermore, it is likely that the desire for this fused state was beginning to manifest itself in the transference. The desire for oneness was revealed in the pictures and related to his idealised and beloved mother. It is likely that in the transference this idealisation was also located in the therapist. As we discussed the pictures an intimacy began to develop which drew the therapist into his world.

FIGURE 4.4 (6) THE BUBBLE. DATED 6 FEBRUARY. PENCIL DRAWING ON A4 PAPER

Written on the back of the picture:
First picture in hospital. I feel like I'm trapped in a bubble; I'm cut off from everyone. Two things pull at my mind. One leads to the world and life; the other leads . . .?
I feel very embryo/babylike, yet very old and deathly.
From Carlos's study:
I drew this with no intention other than to alleviate my boredom and frustration. The bubble encloses me, traps me, alienating me from the world. At first I thought the figure represented my depressed, deathlike state. After many months I realised that the figure and bubble represented the embryo. The psychiatrists told me that I was unable to face up to the responsibilities of adulthood and that my illness was a yearning to be

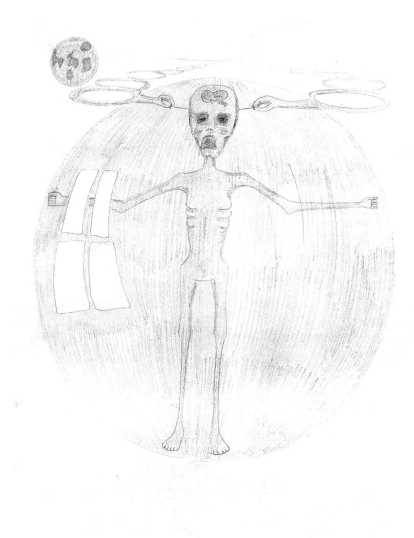

Figure 4.4 The bubble

childlike and secure once again. Such advice meant little to me, until I
saw it confirmed by this picture.

In his study Carlos states that this is his first picture. The date which is
written on it reveals that it came a little later than he suggests. However, it

significantly demonstrates his state on admission and graphically links to the first weeks of his stay in hospital. For him it is his first picture.

This picture reveals his regression at the time of his admission. A bubble reflects the light from the window of the little hospital room and also makes the shape of a cross. Within the bubble is a deathly figure and within the death's head mask is a tiny embryo. This could perhaps be seen as an aspect of him which is yet to be born. Pincers with hands seem to control or torture the head of the figure. An orb, which might be the world, at the top left of the picture appears far away. As well as being emaciated and deathly, this figure is without sexual characteristics. The regression, which is revealed in this picture, is not a healthy one but rather a deathly state. If this is a return to the womb then it is very dangerous. Jung writes:

> The incest motif is bound to arise because when the regressing libido is introverted for internal or external reasons it always reactivates the parental imagos and thus apparently re-establishes the infantile relationship. But this relationship cannot be re-established because the libido is an adult libido which is already bound to sexuality and inevitably imports an incompatible, incestuous character into the reactivated relationship to the parents. It is this sexual character that now gives rise to the incest symbolism. Since incest must be avoided at all costs, the result is either the death of the son–lover or his self castration as a punishment for the incest he has committed, or else the sacrifice of instinctuality, and especially of sexuality, as a means of preventing or expiating the incestuous longing.
>
> (Jung 1956 (1976 edn), CW 5: 204)

Carlos had certainly sacrificed instinctuality, anorexia is ultimately all about the control, denial or sacrifice of instincts. Jung suggests that avoidance or punishment for incest is either the death of the son–lover or his self-castration. We could understand Carlos's conflicted behavior to contain elements of both. Self-starvation could be seen as suicidal and the lack of sex organs in the figure within the bubble could be understood as a form of self-castration.

Furthermore, Carlos had regressed to a dependent infantile state in which his mother and food were the sole preoccupations of his existence. We can see from this drawing that his regression was life threatening and as a consequence his mother had become trapped. Her concern for him meant that she was constantly worried about him and his intake of food and so she was forced to play the mother to his infant role. This is common in cases of anorexia, the mother's anxiety about her child's food intake reverts to that of a much earlier time. The transference at this stage was as much to the hospital, as a whole, as to any individual. Thus, the hospital and the nurses who cared for him took on the role of the mother. His regression, which in the outside world could not be accommodated, was permitted within the bounds of the hospital.

In relation to Lacanian theory I propose that this picture reveals the 'lack'. In the introduction to this book I referred to the 'lack-in-being', quoting Ragland-Sullivan's (1992) discussion of Lacan. The 'lack', based on the Freudian view of woman as castrated, is often attributed to the feminine position. However, she suggests that we might understand the 'lack-in-being' as having a wider application as a state which is experienced by women and men. This would accord with my view that it is this state which is revealed in this picture. Carlos was in a state of merger with his internalised mother and so unable to enter the Symbolic.

This picture shows a castrated, trapped figure with no means of entering the world. Held within the maternal realm, he is unable to separate and what is missing is the phallus, or in this case, the actual penis. However, I consider this to be a rather literal reading of the situation; what is revealed in this picture is the 'lack-in-being', the loss. In this state of atrophy he is alone, without another and devoid of desire. Desire could be understood to be the life force, and at this early stage it is turned inwards. What is needed is the engagement with an Other to lead him out of this trapped state. In the very absence of desire its purpose is revealed. Some form of desire is essential to life, without it there is no future, no hope.

The therapist's response to this picture was one of concern. Carlos was dangerously regressed. The concern was, at one level, a genuine response to the situation. However, already the therapist was engaged with a familial intensity, which suggests that there was a countertransference element operating. Furthermore, it can be seen from his comments that, in transference terms, the drawing process is permitting Carlos to feel separate from the therapist and so able to make his discoveries by himself. There is an omnipotence in this and for the anorexic, this privacy within a relationship is essential in the early stages. This is where art offers a real possibility; Carlos begins to understand himself but without having to admit to his involvement with the therapist in the transference. Transference interpretations were not at this stage useful.

FIGURE 4.5 (7) THE CANDLE. DATED 9 FEBRUARY. PENCIL DRAWING ON A4 PAPER

The human figure in this drawing is recognisable as Carlos. However, he has portrayed himself as very small and childlike – a sort of boy–doll. A prickly hedgehog with closed eyes sits demurely on a hamburger/pin cushion. In this are stuck a needle and a pin, both of giant proportions. Behind the hedgehog is a candle, alight with a flame and from the top of which a cobweb or net seems to mask the face of the figure. Perhaps his feelings of immaturity are encapsulated in the childlike aspects of this

Figure 4.5 The candle

picture. The candle has light-giving properties and its erect stance may indicate his awe of masculinity. We might see the candle as the phallus of the 'father' or the light of consciousness dimmed by the cobwebs which have covered them over. Perhaps here he is beginning to look at his desire but like the badger, any danger from his own phallic power is disguised by his doll-like appearance.

FIGURE 4.6 (8) THE SQUIRREL. DATED 12 FEBRUARY. PENCIL DRAWING ON A4 PAPER

From the back of picture:
I started to eat 'properly' again. This signifies – me, conquering my starvation bat.

Figure 4.6 The squirrel

This picture seems to relate to the previous one. The same little hedgehog or squirrel figure, now with open eyes, appears to be born from monstrous food. He carries aloft a cherry, in which the window of the room appears to be reflected. This is also reminiscent of the bubble from Figure 4.4. A glass with liquid in it and two straws complete the picture of children's party food. Perhaps these were the cakes and sweet drink which he craved and yet feared. The rotund figure of the hedgehog may be related to a fear of how he would appear if he indulged himself. It seems significant that the cakes have a breastlike quality. This may again imply that he is held within the maternal/therapist's body.

It might be worth commenting on the aesthetic quality of this picture. Both this picture and the previous picture (Figure 4.5) are drawn in a similar way. They are aesthetically quite pretty pictures with a formal picture-book quality. In Chapter 6, I will be discussing the countertransference effects of such imagery. I suggest that the rather pretty picture-book appearance of these pictures offers a surface message that everything is all right. They are even quite humorous. This, in common with other aspects of anorexia, keeps the therapist at a distance. The countertransference appeal of such imagery is limited. This contrasts with the next picture (see Plate 4), which communicates directly and violently with the therapist-viewer and evokes considerable anxiety in relation to his state.

PLATE 4 (9) THE PRECIPICE. DATED 14 FEBRUARY. CRAYON AND FELT-TIP PEN ON WHITE PAPER

From the back of the picture:
There must be a road back to goodness, however
I'm not on my way to that goodness,
I'm on the very edge of life and death.
From Carlos's study:
I felt extremely close to the edge of life – my thoughts were suicidal. The sun told me that there had to be life . . . somewhere. I wonder now, if the splintering path is symbolic of the pedestal which I had subconsciously placed myself upon. Anorexia falsely made me feel very powerful – because I was ill I was able to 'use' the sympathy of people close to me.

A figure lies on the edge of an abyss, collapsed and dangerously near the edge. This precipice is the top of a huge cliff made of ice or glass with bits chipping off and falling in bloody fragments. The figure appears to be drained of life. His blood appears to seep away in the direction of a deep and irregular hole in the middle of this cliff. There is apparently no escape because there is no other land, only the sun at the furthest end. The figure is trapped whichever way he turns. There is an alternative view of this which would suggest the possibility that this image is also about birth. The figure could have come from this hole in the centre. Whichever way it is viewed it seems that, like the bubble picture (Figure 4.4), this, too, reveals the edge between life and death on which Carlos was at this time poised.

The sun is very far away, too far to touch the figure. The sun might be viewed as symbolising the libido or the life energy and, in terms of hero myths, it is regarded as the male principle of the psyche. It might be seen as offering hope but it is very distant. Carlos himself describes the sun as offering the hope of life somewhere. The cliff/path leads to the sun and pierces it. In several later pictures a similar path emerges and we have already seen it in Figure 4.1. This picture, as Carlos's own words indicate, conveys his desperate state. The figure is black and defeated and seems to have no energy for life. The connection Carlos makes about the pedestal on which he had placed himself is of great significance in terms of anorexia. In order to understand what underlies the need for such control, it is first necessary to relinquish that control; this may then be seen as a positive first step.

Despite its rather stylish execution, this picture graphically embodies profound despair, and as an embodied image, it could be understood to be a scapegoat. It reveals, and also probably carries, the suicidal impulse and so enables the artist to view the impulse as if from a distance. The depth of the hopelessness of the situation is revealed here in a way that could not be put into words. Of course when someone is admitted to hospital in an emaciated state this is a very successful way of non-verbally communicating despair. However, the underlying feeling may be unconscious. Pictures have the advantage of revealing the inner world and bringing it to consciousness. Once pictured, such an image can never again be denied. It mediates between the inner world and the outer environment, in this case between Carlos's undifferentiated inner state and his viewer-self and also between Carlos and the art therapist.

When this picture was first shown to me, I did not offer an interpretation. Carlos and I merely regarded it together and in this way it was possible to acknowledge how he felt. When a patient is as clearly in touch with his feelings as this picture indicates, it is important not to interfere with the process. If the patient is identified with the image, this will be evident to the therapist in the atmosphere. It is this connectedness that we stay with and it is this which offers potential for change. It is this non-verbal acknowledgement which is also an intimate form of meeting and, paradoxically, because it is wordless, it connects at a deeper level through the image. The gaze of both people meet in the picture and both are affected by this meeting and the transference and countertransference are deepened. (This will be developed in Chapter 9.)

In terms of desire, and so life, I would suggest that despite the desperation of his plight this picture begins to suggest an element of desire. In a dream all the elements are recognised as aspects of the dreamer's inner world. In a picture it is similar; all the aspects of the imagery belong to the painter. Thus, we might see the sun as the introduction of hope and the beginning of some element of desire or a move towards an 'other'. We saw in Plate 2 that the therapist was identified with the sun, which was at the centre of her name, and so we might consider that, at some probably unconscious level, the movement is towards her as holding the hope of

Figure 4.7 The castle

transformation. Thus we may understand the very first stages of the Lacanian Symbolic to be revealed here.

FIGURE 4.7 (10) THE CASTLE. 16 FEBRUARY. PENCIL DRAWING ON A4 PAPER

From the back of the picture:
After a few weeks in this room with this illness this is how I feel.

'The castle shares the symbolism of the enclosure, the walled city and represents the difficult to obtain. It usually holds some treasure or imprisoned person' (Cooper 1978). Here in Figure 4.7 there is a clifflike path, but it is circular. This could be a close up of the hole in the centre of the preceding picture, Plate 4 (the precipice). The path surrounds a castle with a moat and there is a portcullis to defend it against entry or exit. Similarly, the drawbridge does not quite reach the path. The towers of the castle are pointed and phallic in shape and their windows are dark. The tower on the left has two crosses at the top of it, as does the smaller one next to it. The castle itself is draped in cobwebs, suggesting that it is a place which has not been entered for a long time.

Viewing this picture in retrospect, it is possible to see it as indicating the deeper layers of the journey on which Carlos was embarked. It seems that the castle stands for some aspect that remained unconscious and it was a place he had to find a way into to explore. The conscious element appears to be held from outside by the sun in the distance. In terms of a male–female split, we might see this as a deepening of his relation to the feminine in that he is now facing it, looking into it, and this is aided by the masculine element held in the sun.

Alternatively, in the transference, it may be that he can now stand back and look at the maternal shelter as an imprisoning castle. In this he is aided by the therapeutic relationship. The sun is, metaphorically, in the position to be outside – the observer – but it is also in the picture. Thus perhaps this element represents the therapist. The aesthetic quality of the picture is also significant. Here something is suggested which is not shown; the picture does not indicate 'chocolate box' normality. Again we shall see, in Chapter 6, the difference between the pretty picture, which does not alter anything, and the more mysterious image such as this, which affects the viewer. The countertransference is affected by this aesthetic quality; there is a potential seduction in an image such as this; the viewer is curious and wishes to know more. Thus, she is drawn into the inner world of the artist in a profound manner; her desire begins to be evoked. This is not necessarily a sexual appetite but desire in the form of interest. The therapist becomes an interested viewer and this begins to draw her into the client's inner world.

FIGURE 4.8 (11) THE LOG. DATED 3 MARCH. PENCIL ON WHITE A4 PAPER

A log floats downstream and a hand clutches on to it suggesting a person in great danger of drowning. The submersion in water suggests submersion in the unconscious and this poses unavoidable risks as well as potential loss of

Figure 4.8 The log

control or drowning. Some positive elements in the picture seem to be that the water appears to flow and that there are signs of life. The old gnarled tree has new growth and young shoots. In the sky is a faintly drawn Christlike figure which is hardly discernible as it has been erased. There is a similar feel of desperation as there is in Plate 4 and the hope, in the shape of the growth on the river bank, seems very difficult to reach, rather as the sun does in Plate 4. There seems to be a suggestion in the new growth and in the Christ figure of resurrection and rebirth.

FIGURE 4.9 (12) MOTHER. DATED 9 MARCH. PENCIL ON WHITE PAPER

From the back of the picture:
Mother . . . dear mother
From Carlos's study:
The art therapist asked me to draw my mother. I realised after drawing this picture how much I idealised my mother. I had never realised this pre-viously, but my unconscious mind regarded her as more perfect than was truly possible. This picture told me what I knew in my unconscious mind but did not know in my conscious mind.

I had asked Carlos to make a picture of his mother because she seemed to feature prominently in his material. When we discussed this picture he described this figure as 'my mum and virginal'. The figure with its rather evident madonna quality is asexual, as was the boy–doll in Figure 4.5. This seems to indicate that he was repressing any knowledge of himself or his mother as sexual beings. Here the madonna figure's appeal seems to be as a remote figure of worship. Even as an inner image of woman/mother, this picture offers an impossibly idealised vision – all real women must fail beside it as mere mortals. The cobwebs in the background of the picture suggest that this is an area that has been left untouched for a long while. Spiders and their webs are frequently associated with the mother image.

There is again a religious reference. His identification with the Christ figure might lead one to speculate that unconsciously he identified with the virgin birth. His real father was not consciously known to him at this time and he was his mother's firstborn. This would mean that he could deny his mother's sexuality. Previously the Christian references have been to the male, but this is the female aspect. Numerous candles in the foreground indicate that this is an object of worship. The idealisation seems to suggest a denial of his fear of female sexuality and power, a defence against negative feelings in the transference as well as towards his real mother.

This picture was received and not commented on. Transference inter-pretations were not made and this was because it was not possible to make them. The therapist was both idealised and to a degree controlled, kept at a distance as this figure would indicate. However, by now she was also centrally engaged with Carlos and the repressed or unconscious erotic element of the transference was an aspect of this involvement. It is likely that because she held some of the idealisation, he was able to begin to dare to risk seeing his relationship with his mother. The shock with which

Figure 4.9 Mother

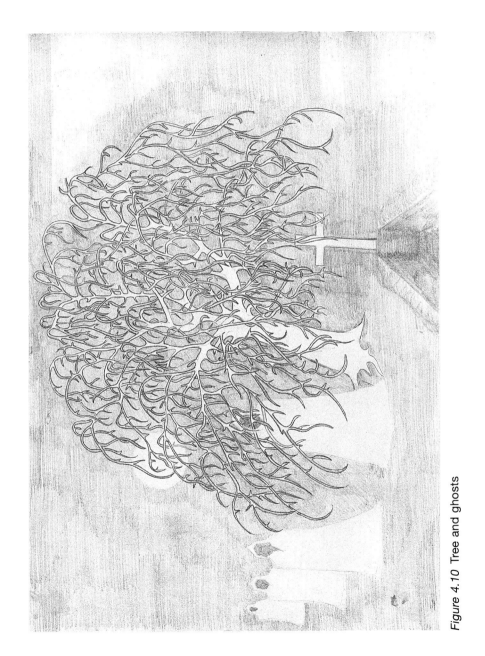

Figure 4.10 Tree and ghosts

Carlos recognised the idealisation in this image seems to suggest that an unconscious element came to light through this picture.

FIGURE 4.10 (13) TREE AND GHOSTS. DATED 10 MARCH. PENCIL ON A4 PAPER

From the back of the picture:
I am the tree,
my grave awaits me
my ghosts await me
life, death, grave, ghost . . .?

He related this picture to a fear/fantasy which he experienced on bad days when he was alone in his room. A tree in the centre of the picture is without leaves – a dormant or winter tree – it leans to the right of the picture and overhangs an open grave. A dark, faceless ghostlike figure in white robes stands under the tree, partly concealed. To the left of the tree three similarly attired figures stand receding into the distance. The open grave in the foreground is topped by a cross which seems to become part of the tree. At this time he was adjusting to life in the little room but he confessed to feeling very depressed and frightened to be left alone. He experienced these figures as present in the room with him and he feared them.

By externalising such a feared image in a drawing he was facing these inner-world ghosts. His fears were transferred to the picture and so it became a scapegoat in the positive sense of providing an outlet for such imagery. He was then able to show the therapist what he feared and discuss it. Thus, the feared imagery began to become familiar and so less frightening. Carlos's discussion of this vulnerability and fear again offered an intimate connection and the therapist was centrally engaged and concerned about him.

FIGURE 4.11 (14) THE WINDOW. UNDATED. PAINT ON GREEN/GREY SUGAR PAPER. 20 × 16 INCHES

When spring came he was still in his little room, gradually gaining weight. Through the open door he could see a large window which let in the sun. He was less regressed at this time and he started to react against his confinement. The room, which had initially offered a sanctuary, was now experienced with frustration. He wanted to be outside, so his motivation to gain weight increased a little.

This picture (Figure 4.11) was the first large painting he made; all his previous pictures, except the crucifix, had been on A4 white paper. It shows the window which he could see from his room; the panes of glass divide the picture into six separate and equal compartments. This is a subtly painted

Figure 4.11 The window

picture with the orange and yellows of the sky graded to form clouds. The sun is bright yellow and, although it is partly shaded by a cloud, it is very close to the viewer/artist. At the lower left-hand corner of the picture is a delicately painted bush with pink flowers and leaves. The whole seems to suggest growth and spring. In the lower right-hand side of the picture a pane of glass appears to shatter as a grey ball or a bubble passes through it. Technically the ball is painted, cut out and then pasted on so that it stands away from the paper, casting a shadow.

The sun and the ball are on different sides of the window but echo one another in shape. There is some aggression in the breaking window pane and we might consider that this indicates the beginning of separation. The violence needed in order to be born or to gain a place in the world is suggested in this image. It seems that this picture marks an important stage.

Figure 4.12 The crossroads

Through the image-making process and the sequence of images which have embodied his feelings, Carlos has begun to be able to contact his negative emotions. This may be the beginning of the relinquishing of the idealisation, shown by real flowers and real aggression. The transference to the institution as a whole probably fostered this by enabling him to be angry about being held back in the room. The need to separate from his child–self begins through this frustration with his room. It may implicate the therapist in the transference. He was beginning to accept that whatever he expressed was accepted and this enabled him to begin to experience his frustrations.

FIGURE 4.12 (15) THE CROSSROADS. DATED 26 APRIL. PENCIL DRAWING ON WHITE PAPER

From the back of the picture:
My weight is piling on now, and I feel as if huge bulges of flesh are hanging from all parts of my body. The crossroads are how I feel – which direction?
From Carlos's study:
After gaining two stones in weight this is how I felt about my body. I couldn't see it at the time, but many months later I realised how anorexia had completely distorted my view of reality.

Figure 4.12 shows that Carlos was now gaining weight and he experienced his body as really heavy. When his arms were at his sides he could no longer feel his ribs and he hated the feel of his flesh. He was indeed at a crossroads, he feared gaining weight but he also feared going back. He was in fact still very thin, his ribs were still clearly visible, and it was to be four months before he attained his agreed target weight. None the less, Carlos experienced himself as huge.

The crossroads appears to be like the cross of the crucifix. He is standing on it and so perhaps the figure depicted in Plate 3 has risen but is still weighed down by the burden of the body. As with so many of Carlos's pictures, his physical conflict seems to be echoed by a spiritual quest, a struggle for the meaning of his existence. We might also see the crossroads as the split-off aspects of his personality beginning to converge.

PLATE 1 (16) THE FAMILY PICTURE. UNDATED. PAINT ON SUGAR PAPER. 20 × 16 INCHES

The family picture which was discussed in detail in Chapter 3 was made at this time. It was kept hidden under his bed, while all the other pictures were displayed around his room. Three weeks after we had originally discussed this picture, I asked to see it again. After regarding it in silence for some time Carlos said, 'These aren't rays of sun, they are bars and I can see where the key is' and he pointed to his mother's face.

In a recent family meeting his parents had told him the truth about his birth and his natural father. Immediately this had made sense to him. He felt that, at some level, he had known this all along and so it was a great relief to him. He immediately wanted to tell his sisters but this his mother would not allow. She feared that her daughters would think less of her for having had a child before she was married. So, although the truth was no longer hidden from Carlos, it still had to remain a secret and thus continued to bind him to his mother.

The strong feelings that Carlos had about this, which emerged in relation to his picture, were expressed to his family in a further family meeting. It was decided that a period of separation from the family would be good for him and so it was agreed that the family would not visit him for six weeks. It was proposed by the social worker that the family treat it as if he were going away on a journey. They would wave him goodbye and return to see him again six weeks later. To begin with, Carlos was overcome with panic and fear at this proposal. He had never been away from them before. However, he soon developed a new sense of freedom and this became evident in the pictures he made at this time.

The separation from his actual outer-world real family made it possible for him to deal with the inner-world images which, while he was still in contact with them, could not be clearly identified. Thus, he began to be able to separate the internalised representations from the people to which they were attached. This intensified the transference to the institution and to the therapist. The pictures which follow on from this enabled him to work through some almost intolerable feelings. When the negative elements have been split off for so long the force with which they emerge can be almost elemental and terrifying.

FIGURE 4.13 (17) BIRTH. UNDATED. PENCIL DRAWING ON A4 PAPER

From the back of the picture:
The hospital stopped me seeing my mum for 6 weeks.
I thought/felt she'd abandoned me.
This is how I felt towards her.
From Carlos's study:
Whilst in hospital I wasn't allowed to see my mother, or family, for 6 weeks; this is how I felt towards my mother. Subconsciously I drew her figure above my own, symbolising her dominance over me. Because I had continued to be so dependent on my mother since childhood, my subconscious mind felt dominated by her. Because of this picture I was able to see why I was unable to be self-reliant and self-confident.

Like the 'mum tree' (Figure 4.3) this picture reveals the fused state of merger with the mother. However, whereas in Figure 4.3, the bubble was within the centre of the tree, here the figure is half-born and surrounded by a thorny and dangerous potential separation.

Figure 4.13 Birth

Here, the madonna mother of Figure 4.9 is pictured with a spider's web veil covering her face. The web is shaped like a shield, which offers protection and distance as well as part invisibility. The face of this mother is remarkably similar to the face of the male in Figure 4.5 (the candle), where he pictured himself with a spider's web/veil covering his own face. Here, the other head, which Carlos describes as himself, is part of the mother figure not yet born. This head appears to be cut off from the mother and, significantly, from his own body by a huge decorated sword. The top half of the picture shows the mother surrounded by thorny twigs and a small jewelled knife. The cross on the handle is reminiscent of the crusades. There seems to be a fairy tale or archetypal element in this image. The figure in the lower half of the picture appears like the sleeping beauty who can only be woken by a prince who fights through thorns and knives and drives the cobwebs away.

To the right of the picture is a huge jewelled sword and to the left is a hypodermic needle. Behind this is a mouth with jagged teeth. This combination of threatening and potentially penetrating elements seem to indicate the 'phallic mother' of Freudian theory. This, as we saw in Chapter 2, is the image of a mother who is simultaneously seductive and persecutory. It is considered to be an 'omnipotent and absolutely powerful, sexually neutral figure' (Grosz 1992: 315). It is thought that the boy may attribute the male genital organ to the mother and so she is experienced as intrusive, persecutory and potentially penetrating. This is an unconscious process and one which I would not see in any literal way. None the less, in this picture, the hypodermic and the swords, which all appear to belong to the mother's side, seem to indicate that this is the power which Carlos attributed to his mother. She was not merely the all-powerful female maternal presence but she also possessed, in his mind, the masculine attributes. This fits with Figure 4.4 (the bubble), where the skeletal figure was devoid of genitals.

It is likely that this image was evoked by the pain of the separation from his actual mother. The male figure's head, recognisably Carlos, is apparently asleep. Perhaps it is he who awaits rescue by the handsome prince of the fairy tales. This accords with his sexual fantasies and also perhaps relates to the desire for a dominant father to enable him to separate. His own reflected image is, it seems, held in this picture and it is important to recognise that, at a certain level, both faces represent aspects of himself. While he was identified with and dominated by his love for his idealised mother, his masculinity could not be born. In order to separate he needed to take up the sword and do battle himself. As we shall see, this is what happened.

FIGURE 4.14 (18) REACHING OUT 1. UNDATED. BLACK INK AND YELLOW PAINT ON WHITE PAPER. 12 × 8½ INCHES

From Carlos's study:
This picture is closer to me than I can ever explain in words. My true inner-self is trying to reach through the barriers which my physical self has created, I'm trying to find my true self. If you turn the picture upside down you are made to share something of my feeling of disorder. You will also

Figure 4.14 Reaching out 1

perceive my unhappiness in the tree. This picture makes me feel so good because it tells me what I cannot express, even to myself, in any other way.

The tree seems to grow from the jagged hole at the centre of the cliff precipice, which is similar to the one which featured in Plate 4 (The precipice). If we regard the two pictures the place seems to be similar but the terrain has changed. In Plate 4 the viewpoint of the spectator was high up and distant. If the artist was the spectator, one could assume he was looking at his body as if from far away. In the present picture (Figure 4.14) the spectator is on a level with the figure and the tree. The dark figure from Plate 4 seems to have risen and to be reaching out from within the larger yellow figure. The sun is higher in the sky and seems to be able to reach the standing figure who has its colour. Where there was barren or icy terrain, now there is grass and earth. The path seems to lead somewhere apart from directly into the sun; it disappears behind what appears to be a rock. The sun is ringed with black and from it black bats fly. One is above the path, perhaps it is threatening but it is also distant. The tree leans to the right like the tree in Figure 4.10, but the branches, although without leaves, are not drooping downward. If, as Carlos suggests, the picture is turned upside down then five faces become visible within the branches of the tree and a hand seems to point at them. Again the number five reminds one of Carlos's five siblings perhaps held within the mother tree which he is compelled to leave.

The hero takes on the solar attributes (Jung 1956) and here we see this beginning. It seems that Carlos has reached a point, which Jung likens to a stage in the alchemical process, indicated by the black ring around the sun. Jung suggests in *The Psychology of the Transference* (1946) that there is a stage where 'Sol is turned black' (Jung 1946: 96). At this stage:

> the pair who together represented body and spirit are now dead, and that the soul departs from them in great distress. [He continues] Although various other meanings play a part here, one cannot rid oneself of the impression that the death is a sort of tacit punishment for the sin of incest. . . . That would explain the soul's 'great distress'.
>
> (Jung 1946: 96)

However, there is a hopeful aspect to this; it is a death which comes about before a return of the soul and rebirth. This seems to fit with the stage of Carlos's process. However it is viewed, this picture, along with Carlos's strong feelings about it, would indicate that it is about integration. The unconscious or soul aspect is becoming integrated with the conscious solar light.

In this picture (Figure 4.14), his desire is revealed in the movement of the figure at the centre. The sun-drenched erect figure seems to herald a move to the symbolic, the masculine element, and to health, but he still yearns for a return to the family tree. Carlos acknowledges his desire in his comment of how much this picture means to him. His desire for separation and difference is struggling with the part of him that still wishes for a return to the maternal shelter.

If we regard the sun as symbolising the therapeutic relationship it would

Figure 4.15 Tree and pyramids

seem that the warmth, previously projected into the sun/therapist, is now reaching him. The art therapist and a certain female nurse were central in his treatment. We were both drawn into caring for him in different ways. The nurse dealt with the practical issues with regard to his body weight, food intake and day-to-day physical care. She became very important to him and involved in his world. At the same time the art therapist accepted his inner-world turmoil and was a witness as it emerged in his pictures. There was something of a split transference here which we attempted to hold together with the rest of the team involved in his care. It is likely that the transference represented the move away from the family. The therapist was drawn into the erotic, incestuous family atmosphere. This is a hopeful sign, as we have seen, because the desire constellated in the transference has a purpose. It is a channel which offers potential movement out of the fused state, towards the future and transformation. In response, the countertransference was very engaging and Carlos and his concerns were never very much out of mind. The erotic element in the countertransference was not overtly sexual but nor was it merely maternal.

FIGURE 4.15 (19) TREE AND PYRAMIDS. DATED 7 MAY. PENCIL DRAWING ON WHITE A4 PAPER

From the back of the picture:
A later picture.
The tree (me) is half grown . . . and longs to go away, very, very far away (pyramids).

The tree in Figure 4.15 which Carlos describes as half-grown symbolises himself, half-alive and half-dormant. If we look back at the 'mum tree' (Figure 4.3), it is possible to see that the creeper which, in that picture, clung closely to the trunk, is now loosening its hold. It would seem that if the creeper clinging to the tree in Figure 4.3 was himself clinging to his mother, a separation is beginning to take place. A path from the tree leads directly to a pyramid. This is rather like the mountains which were at the end of the flower-strewn path in Figure 4.3, but this path is more sparse but more direct. The pyramid sometimes has masculine or else spiritual associations (Cooper 1978). Throughout Carlos's pictures there is a strong sense of a spiritual quest which accompanies the physical journey to recovery.

FIGURE 4.16 (20) TRAPPED. DATED 10 MAY. PENCIL DRAWING ON A4 WHITE PAPER

From the back of the picture:
This is me inside the tiny room trapped amid bubbles.
Bubbles are important to me because they represent void.

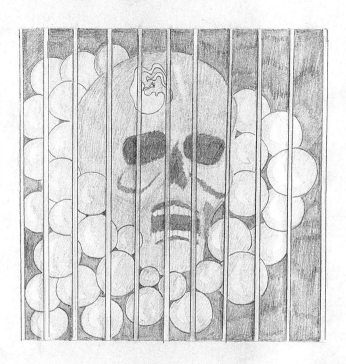

Figure 4.16 Trapped

From Carlos's study:
Trapped.
When I saw graphically how I felt I became more determined to change;
'there must be something better than this'.

After four months in the room he was getting very frustrated by the confinement. This image seems to depict this frustration. The skeletal head appears to be crying out, trapped behind the bars. In the forehead is a tiny embryo. Again this figure seems to reveal both death and potential life in the one desperate figure. Carlos describes this as the room, but it is also, I suggest, a picture of his inner conflict. The head is reminiscent of that of the skeletal figure in Figure 4.4. This is a regression to the earlier state but from a different viewpoint. This is part of the process, a movement

Figure 4.17 Body images

forward and a return to the earlier state, but from a different position. It reveals the negative feelings – his frustration at the undifferentiated state.

FIGURE 4.17 (21) BODY IMAGES. UNDATED. COLOURED CRAYON ON WHITE A4 PAPER

From the back of the picture: body images:
From Carlos's study:
There is an abundance of sunshine now compared with the picture, Plate 4.
The more aware I became of the process taking place, that is, the change within me, the more I found I could choose what I wanted to happen.
There are still many problems to face up to, as symbolised by the winding path, but at least I am able to face my true self now.
I realised that, a mirror, and the physical world, tells very little about what you really are.

This picture is drawn in different shades of yellow. Carlos stands flooded with the sun, which could be viewed as libido, life force, energy or his desire. He seems to be freer and to be looking back at the way that he has come. If we look back at Plate 4 (The precipice), where he was desperate, we see that this appears to be the same precipice. However, the viewpoint has changed and the figure seems to stand at the opposite end; he is now at the same end as the sun. He is naked and stands almost in full back view, looking at his reflection in a series of mirrors. In the first of these reflections his head and shoulders are seen and, in the second which is further distant, the top half of the body is visible. The path made by the yellow rays of the sun seems to be a different path from that suggested by the winding path of the previous precipice.

We could see this as an entry into the outer world and a beginning of differentiation. His own comment about the mirror is significant because it seems to indicate a separation from the state of identification. He is beginning to see the difference between his inner experience and his outer image. He is seeing himself and beginning to organise his perception of himself as a whole being. In Chapter 8 I will discuss the 'mirror stage' (Lacan 1977b). I suggest that this could be viewed as an example of the view of the self first seen in the mirror. Lacan discusses the infant's perceiving its own image in the mirror. The fragmented self-image begins to cohere in the reflection but this introduces the view of the Other and so alienation and difference. Once again the floods of yellow light could indicate that the transference feelings are metaphorically warming him.

Figure 4.18 Three figures

FIGURE 4.18 (22) THREE FIGURES. UNDATED. BLUE CRAYON AND BLACK INK ON WHITE A4 PAPER

From the back of the picture:
All three figures are me.

Carlos was now thinking about the future and described the picture in the following way. The cloaked figure is his mother and he is in the background with a male partner. It seemed that, if he were to have a close relationship with someone else, he would be dead to his mother. There are two crosses in this picture; the one in the foreground is dark blue, the same colour as the two male figures. The one at the back is turquoise and high above the couple.

He himself writes that all the figures are aspects of himself and the lovers appear to be very alike, almost mirror images. A way of understanding this would be that, if Carlos is to unite with him-'self', he has to separate from his attachment to the mother image. Until he has done so, there is little hope of a fulfilling relationship with another person – male or female.

FIGURE 4.19 (24) REACHING OUT 2. DATED 4 JUNE. PENCIL DRAWING ON WHITE A4 PAPER

From the back of the picture:
Reaching out and finding life.
From Carlos's study:
Reaching out. The bridge symbolises my crossing into a new life. The two trees at the top of the picture symbolise my reaching out and finding, touching people and life – communicating.

The rather obviously vaginal shape of the opening in the earth seems to suggest birth. There is a way out from the underground (possibly the unconscious), to the world outside (possibly consciousness), symbolised by the sun over a snow-capped mountain. The spectator's eye is led straight from the dark underworld viewpoint into the light of the centre by a short and direct path; this joins a more winding one which continues into the distance.

In view of Carlos's own comments on this picture it could be seen as a bringing together elements in the psyche. The two trees, one dark and one light, lean towards each other and unite at the top of the picture. This seems to indicate some form of resolution and to mark a stage in a process of integration.

It is again possible to make a transference link here in that the meeting, which is primarily an internal one, is also at this stage a meeting with the therapist. So that one way of understanding the comment that he is reaching out and touching people is to understand that, having left home, he now

Figure 4.19 Reaching out 2

Figure 4.20 Tree and cross

leans towards the therapist. He is met there and touches life. The unconscious element here is the erotic transference and countertransference
meeting between Carlos and the female therapist which was now beginning to intensify.

FIGURE 4.20 (25) TREE AND CROSS. DATED 11 JUNE. PENCIL DRAWING ON WHITE A4 PAPER

From the back of the picture:
The world shall finish with a hell.
I (the tree) cling to the cross because it's more real than life here.

Here the viewpoint is again from the sun's end of the precipice and, as in
Figure 4.17, the viewer is behind the sun. From the hole at the centre of the
path from Plate 4 (The precipice), grows a thorny leafless tree, its roots
limply attached to a cross. Behind the tree the path leads on to the clouds so
the viewer is high up in the sky almost like a view from an aeroplane. At
the end of the path there is a huge mushroom cloud like a nuclear explosion
which rises into the sky. This picture (Figure 4.20), made only a few days
after the previous one, demonstrates how fragile any advance was for
Carlos at this time. Here he seems again to be in the grip of fearsome
imagery. He says he clings to the cross for safety. He was now being visited
by the hospital chaplain with whom he had formed a relationship.

There is an additional way of viewing this – if the tree is seen to be being
uprooted by the cross. If so, it is possible to imagine that as before, the tree
is symbolic of the mother and perhaps, due to the physical separation, he is
becoming detached from the mother image. Jung writes: 'since the tree is
primarily significant of the mother, its felling has the significance of the
mother sacrifice' (Jung 1956: 421). This would accord with the three
pictures, shown as colour plates, which follow the next one (Figure 4.21).

FIGURE 4.21 (26) CANDLES AND COW PARSLEY. DATED 14 JUNE. PENCIL DRAWING ON WHITE A4 PAPER

From the back of the picture:
Candles and cow parsley
In my life now, there is –
light and brightness.
The flowers really struck
me as symbols of
My reaching out
The flowers break out, then
break out again, and again.

Figure 4.21 Candles and cow parsley

He included a close-up drawing of the parsley to demonstrate this and then wrote: 'keep reaching out'. A pattern is beginning to emerge whereby one negative or painfully difficult image is followed, a few days later, with a positive one. This seems to echo his mood swings at this time and reflects the process of integrating his conflicting feelings.

PLATE 5 (27) THE ROOM. UNDATED. PAINT ON WHITE CARTRIDGE PAPER. 19 × 16½ INCHES

From Carlos's study:
The blue shape is the bed in the room where I had to remain for ten months.
I felt I was trapped in the room. The blood is symbolic of myself draining
away – becoming part of the room.
I see it in a different way now; the blood represents my inner self. In that
room I 'opened-up' completely – I found my 'inner' self. The blood also
represents my pent-up frustrations and anger – something I was never able
to physically release. Painting the blood was a way of transmitting such
emotions from myself.

This last comment on Plate 5 confirms my view that the pictures were very often embodiments of the scapegoat transference. This 'transmitting' them from himself is just that; by painting he puts the emotions outside of himself. The picture is then a scapegoat in that it holds and contains the negative feelings. He has an outlet for them which damages no one and he is able to see the degree of his fury. Thus, he can own his aggression.

It was now June and the weather was very good. Carlos became frustrated and angry and demanded to leave the room. His weight was progressing slowly but he had still not attained his target weight. He no longer vomited nor devised tricks for disposing of his food and he seemed genuinely motivated to live and to gain weight. He had, since April, been studying with a volunteer tutor for O level English and had decided that he would aim for a career in either nursing or occupational therapy. Anorexic patients frequently express such a wish. However, Carlos seemed genuinely motivated and the self-awareness that he was gaining was very much part of it. He wanted to share this with others. This was an interest which persisted.

In this picture the sun is enormous and shining tantalisingly within his view. He is barred from it by barbed wire which seems to stretch across the entrance to his room. The room, which had at first been a safe place, was beginning to feel like a prison. When I discussed this picture with him he stated that this splat of blood was all that was left of him and that it was oozing away down the air vent (which did exist in the room).

This picture reveals the anger which Carlos was beginning to contact fully for the first time. It shows how painful it was for him to express anger. It is also evidence of the extent of the battle that was raging inside him. He wanted to escape from the room but also from the painful forces of the unconscious. These forces, as the next pictures show, were coming dangerously near to consciousness and his desperate need to leave the room was also a need to escape from the power of his inner turmoil. The air vent could be viewed as the way down into the underworld where these difficult aspects of himself were unconsciously experienced as residing.

It was seven months since his admission and, such was the power of his picture, that he convinced me that he should be allowed out of his room. I took the picture to the ward round and argued his case. There was lengthy discussion about this but eventually it was agreed that he had made a contract with the staff team and that we must hold to it. In the treatment of anorexia this is extremely important, so it was affirmed that Carlos must attain his target weight before he left the room. This may seem punitive but it is essential that the staff do not give in to pressure which the patient's family would probably be unable to resist.

THEORETICAL CONSIDERATIONS

This image seems to mark a turning point and so, before continuing with the rest of the pictures, I will analyse some of the transference and countertransference implications of my intervention. By now I felt intensely connected to Carlos and I was certainly affected by his desperation and the urgency of his appeal. I could sense his pressing need to leave the room. He and his picture combined to communicate the power of his anger, but also his fear, and I was concerned for him. This is the conscious layer. However, it is possible that I was unconsciously avoiding his fury and, not wishing to be associated with his imprisonment, sided with the part of him which wished to escape. In this way I would be permitting myself to be split off from the rest of the team.

This becomes significant if we think back to his earlier state where the asexual skeletal figure was trapped in the bubble room/womb. This I linked, through Lacanian theory, to the lack which, in this case, I saw as a total absence of desire. This fused state left no room for difference; there was only an 'us', not a 'me and you'. I suggest that it was this which was evoked in the almost immediate transference identification which generated the gift of his picture, Plate 2 (The name picture), in the early stages of our work together. The therapist became in-'corporated', almost literally into his inner-world state. Although on the one hand, this total fusion is what he desired, it was also what he most dreaded. We saw in Chapter 2, through the writings of Horney (1932) and Chasseguet-Smirgel (1984b) in particular, that this form of incorporation and engulfment is one of the major fears of male patients working with female therapists. The desire for fusion and the fear of being sucked back into the womb and so annihilated are the basis of the fear of death associated with the mother/female therapist.

In Lacanian terms this undifferentiated state is 'the Real'. The Real is a 'brute, pre-Symbolic reality which returns in the form of a need such as hunger' (Ragland-Sullivan, quoted in Wright 1992: 375). This would make sense in considering the manifestation of Carlos's problems which were expressed through a refusal to eat. A denial of hunger was also a denial of his desire. Moreover, this lack of differentiation is a form of psychic incest; it is a oneness which, because it is impossible, leads away from life. 'Sexual incest is possible, but psychic incest – where two identify as one – produces the structure of psychosis' (Lacan quoted in Ragland-Sullivan 1992: 375). Although they are very different forms of illness, the manifestation of both psychosis and anorexia is a concretising of experience. There is a lack of the symbolic in both.

This dangerous psychological state was expressed in anorexia for Carlos. It was this same, undifferentiated state which began to find expression in his pictures and, in the next chapter, I will suggest that they played the role of transactional objects. Art allows for an element of concretisation; the images which offer the bridge between the fused state and the differentiated one may take a physical form. They offer the possibility for the beginning of separation. Through the distancing from his state provided by his pictures, Carlos began to be able to differentiate. In his pictures he could see and so experience himself at a distance from the feared imagery which haunted him. By externalising this, he was able to begin to distance from the genuine dread which was revealed in the bubble picture (Figure 4.4).

My intervention with the staff team was significant. Carlos was a young man who was identified with his mother and so unable to enter the Symbolic order. His real father was absent and his stepfather did not seem to feature in his material. In Freudian/Lacanian views, we have seen, there is a need for the father to intervene between mother and the child. We saw in Chapter 2 that there are more positive ways of viewing the father's role and it is not limited to this rupture of the maternal bond (Samuels 1985b; Benjamin 1988). However, whether or not this role is attributed to the 'father', some form of boundary setting is a psychological necessity. In this case this was the function of the staff team. A contract had been agreed and was held to, thus the boundaries were maintained. The law of the 'father' held.

The countertransference could be understood to be significant in relation to this. I may have been seduced into playing the part of a seductive protective mother. Carlos's desire bound me to him and evoked a reciprocation. It was pleasurable to be his confidante. I felt an attachment to him, which, I suggest, was generated by an infantile incestuous bond. This is a combination of the maternal and the sexual. In Chapter 2, I quoted Searles (1959) who argues for the importance, at the oedipal stage, of the sexual attraction between a parent and the child of the opposite sex. This was part of the dynamic between myself and Carlos at this time. In the countertransference, there was a pre-oedipal protective element, combined with an oedipal sexual desire. It seems to me, in retrospect, that by siding with his vulnerability I would have kept him in the child role. Thus, the rest of the staff team were crucial in holding to the boundaries. As when a parental couple joins together to offer a clear boundaried message to a child, so we together gave him the structure to kick against and so the possibility to separate. Thus, the team as a whole, including the art therapist, held the dual aspects of the transference and so he was able to enter the Symbolic order. This came about by facing his fury with the womb/room/mother and breaking free of this internalised aspect of this image. His anger developed after this intervention and, terrifying as it was for him, it had a liberating effect, as we shall see, in the pictures which follow.

PLATE 6 (28) THE BATTLE. UNDATED. CRAYON AND PAINT ON BUFF SUGAR PAPER. 15 × 20 INCHES

From the study:
After six months of hospitalisation I was told that I must continue with the treatment for a further three months. This picture was the only way I had of releasing my anger. The ghostly figures represent everyone. Everyone has finally forced me to stop being over-dependent on others, especially on my mother. My childlike state has been/is being destroyed. This picture made me see how determined everyone was to help me find my independence and accept adulthood. The psychiatrists had constantly told me this; the drawing shouted it at me!
I discovered some very important things about my life when I came to understand this picture – some very deep personal truths.
Using art experience to reach behind our walls and images of the feelings we have disowned is a way of alleviating the alienation from ourselves. Visualising our fears can reduce their hold on us. This picture is an example of this.

Later I will discuss the picture as its own interpretation. Here Carlos makes this point very graphically. He writes that the picture shouted the interpretation that had been made by the psychiatrists. The picture here is seen as Other. This idea will be elaborated on in Chapter 8. The idea is that the picture, despite the fact that it is made by the artist, sometimes has the effect of giving an external perspective on an internal state. In this way the image feeds back to its maker in a way which offers a real potential for transformation.

This picture shows a marked change in style, medium and approach. This seems to accord with the state of mind he was in at the time. His anger, demonstrated in Plate 5 (The room), is now becoming overtly manifest. This picture, which is freer than most of his drawings, is drawn in crayon on a large sheet of paper and confronts the unconscious in very dramatic terms. To recap the recent pictures: in Figure 4.15 (Tree and pyramids) we saw that the vine is being freed from the 'mother tree', its hold loosening. In Plate 5 (The room) the blood seemed to seep down the air vent, perhaps into the deeper realms underground – the unconscious. Now Carlos confronts what the separation brings to the surface. This is maybe what he had unconsciously been attempting to avoid by leaving the room.

If all the parts in this picture are viewed as parts of Carlos, it would seem that the struggle is between those forces which battled to free him and those which were still fighting to bind him. The faceless figures in blue cloaks encircle an egg which they appear to have broken open. Within the egg a yellow foetus, in an embryonic state, is attacked and penetrated by vicious weapons, brandished by these anonymous figures. The fact that the foetus is coloured yellow may reflect that it is barely more than the yolk and unready to be born. It may also be significant that this is the sun colour, perhaps indicating some masculine element, which is not developed enough to survive the attack.

The figures are similarly clothed to others we have already seen. In Plate 1 (The family picture), the family are cloaked and, in Figure 4.10 (Tree and ghosts), the faceless figures standing near the tree are also clothed in cloaks. The implements which are used to attack the egg are also familiar – in Figure 4.5 (The candle) a pin, similar to the two which penetrate the head of the embryo, is stuck in the pin cushion and in Figure 4.13 (Birth) the sword and dagger surround the head of the mother. These, too, attack the egg, the sword penetrating its centre. To the right of the picture a figure stands, arms outstretched, holding a net reminiscent of the spiders' webs from other pictures. One figure uses what appears to be a piece of ice to penetrate the figure. Blood from the embryo drips downwards and to the foreground of the picture.

Carlos was angry, which was rare for him. He said that the figures were probably the staff in the hospital. By separating him from his mother, generally poking and prodding at him, breaking open the egg before it was ready, we were experienced as persecuting him. Regarding the son's internal battle for deliverance from the mother, Jung writes:

> The forward striving libido which rules the conscious mind of the son demands separation from the mother, but his childish longing for her prevents this by setting up a psychic resistance that manifests itself in all kinds of neurotic fears – that is to say in a general fear of life.
>
> (Jung 1956, CW 5: 297)

I think this encapsulates the problem which, for Carlos, was expressed through his anorexia. With this picture a point had been reached where the nature of the resistance could be seen. The anorexia was masking or expressing this conflict – the need to grow and leave the maternal shelter – and the desire to return to it. The seriousness of this conflict is addressed by Jung:

This fear of life is not just an imaginary bogy, but a very real panic which seems disproportionate, only because its real source is unconscious and therefore projected. The young growing part of the personality, if prevented from living or kept in check, generates fear and changes into fear. The fear seems to come from the mother but actually it is the deadly fear of the instinctive unconscious inner man who is cut off from life by the continual shrinking back from reality. If the mother is felt as the obstacle, she then becomes the vengeful pursuer.

(Jung 1956, CW 5: 298)

The art therapist, with the other members of the staff team, were all experienced as persecuting him. Although there was a basis in reality for this, its force was greater than this would merit. His fury was loaded with previously unconscious emotion probably repressed from the past.

This featured in the transference and he was rejecting and even hostile when I went to visit him. He showed me his pictures but he was beginning to be able to express his angry feelings, personally as well as through the medium of his pictures. He was no longer the acquiescent person he had been. He would accept no interpretations and he was clearly furious. We might understand his rejection of interpretations as a confronting of the anorexia in the following way. If the interpretations are understood to be something that is taken in, like food, the rejecting of them could be seen to be a form of spitting out. It is possible that one aspect of the anorexia is a distorted expression of his anger, anger turned inward. Now, instead of rejecting food whilst giving the appearance of being a victim of an 'illness', he was externalising his fury. These feelings were much nearer the surface than they had been previously and, although this was uncomfortable for all concerned, it was possible to accept his anger. For the art therapist the relationship was sustained by the affection for him which had gradually developed.

PLATE 7 (29) DEATH OF THE CHILD. UNDATED. CRAYON AND FELT-TIP PENS ON BUFF SUGAR PAPER. $16\frac{1}{2} \times 20$ INCHES

From Carlos's study:
I tried to remain childlike so that I could stay dependent on my mother. With one hand my mother 'forces' me to accept my own independance, with the other she remains passive and continues to be my protector, provider and guardian. I see from this picture that my over-dependance on my mother is as much her fault as it is mine.

Again here he tells us that he begins to realise from the picture about his over-dependence on his mother. We see from this that an inner-world separation was beginning, linked to the outer-world enforced separation.

Carlos's mother came to visit but she was not allowed to see him as the agreed separation time was not up. She asked for him to wave to her from the window of his room, but Carlos refused to do so. He felt great anger towards her and he described this picture as the hospital holding her at bay. However, the picture is far more complex than this, as his own comment indicates. Here, he confronts the internalised and archetypal image of mother/witch:

> we always forget that it is the unconscious creative force which wraps itself in images. Where therefore we read 'His mother was a wicked witch' we translate it as the son is unable to detach his libido from the mother image, he suffers from resistances because he is tied to the mother.
>
> (Jung 1956, CW 5: 222)

The battleground depicted here is predominantly an internal or unconscious one. However, it is precipitated by the absence of the physical being of his actual mother. Her enforced absence permits Carlos to begin to face what she has come to symbolise for him and to own it. The ban on his mother's visiting was enabling him to confront the internalised mother image.

In the picture the mother figure appears to be bleeding from a wound in her neck inflicted by a cloaked figure. She also bleeds from under her cloak. A sword in one hand and a spear in the other, she seems to keep one cloaked figure at bay by the touch of her sword on its hand. There are four figures on the left of the picture all dressed in blue cloaks. If we look again at Plate 1 (The family picture) we see a resemblance between these cloaked figures and the sisters in that picture; there is similarity of stance and dress. One figure appears to kneel shedding yellow tears which form a pool. In the foreground is a mass of blue which could be water, from which a hand reaches upwards, as if someone is drowning. This is reminiscent of the hand on the log in Figure 4.8. At the centre of the picture is a broken egg from which spills blood and a tiny yellow embryo. Carlos's own description of the picture indicates that this embryo is his child–self.

The cobweb or spider's web features prominently again in this picture. The cobweb or veil over the face of the female figure is rather like a display from a ruffled fighting cock. There is another net or cobweb, across the top of the picture, which encloses another embryo. This one is positioned similarly to that in the heads of the figures, in Figures 4.4 and 4.16. It is within a five-sided star and in a circle. This is reminiscent of a pentagram, which is often considered to be a symbol of wholeness. Usually the figure within it is a grown man whose limbs form the five points of the star, but here we have merely the very beginnings of a person. I suggest that the two embryos in this picture represent two aspects of Carlos's potential. The top one is perhaps his spiritual life and the lower his physical being. Both of these are in a fragile, exposed and embryonic state.

So far I have been assuming that the bleeding figure is the mother. However, in reading Carlos's own description, it is possible to see the cloaked and veiled figure as Carlos himself. In which case the hooded figures would represent the mother. It is possible for both views of the picture to coexist. To alter the viewpoint merely adds a dimension; bearing in mind that the picture is made by Carlos, we may consider all the elements to be aspects of himself.

In the discussion of the pictures I have been drawing attention to the repetition of images and trends of imagery which recur throughout the series. I would here make the point that this is an important part of the process because it reveals to the artist/patient the meaningful links between the pictures. These links are usually unconscious at the time the pictures are made and, in viewing them, their import begins to become conscious. As the words of Carlos make abundantly clear, such pictures tell the artist loud and clear what is going on. This is a form of interpretation and one that is sometimes more effective than all the words the therapist may utter. With the anorexic patient it has the additional benefit of permitting him to feel that he remains in control of his insights.

Furthermore, these pictures, which are embodiments of the transference, reveal the multiple projections such a transference may contain. Seeing the images laid out in this way illuminates the diverse layers of the transference, which is experienced but not normally seen, in other forms of psychotherapy. Here the transference was embodied in the pictures; the intensity was expressed within the imagery but it was also significantly played out between the people.

In Chapter 2, in connection with the case example of Mr B, I quoted Kristeva, who writes that: 'Matricide is our vital necessity, the sine-qua-non condition of our individuation, provided that it takes place under optimal circumstances and can be eroticized' (Kristeva 1989: 27–8). She continues on this theme:

> The lesser or greater violence of matricidal drive . . . entails, when it is hindered, its inversion on the self; the maternal object having been introjected, the depressive or melancholic putting to death of the self is what follows, instead of matricide. In order to protect mother I kill myself.
>
> (Kristeva 1989: 28)

Her discussion relates to depression but it is very relevant here as we can see from this picture (Plate 7). The tremendous resistance that Carlos had to staying in his room was, I suggest, associated with this. His terror that this destructive matricidal impulse would break through to consciousness was likely to have been part of the reason for his urgent plea to be permitted to leave the room. He was attempting to escape from becoming conscious of the terrible power of the implications of the imagery that was surfacing. This seems to be confirmed in the statement he makes in relation to the next picture (Plate 8).

PLATE 8 (30) CONFUSION. UNDATED. CRAYON, FELT-TIP PENS, AND INK ON WHITE A4 PAPER

From Carlos's study:
The ghostlike figure represents my mind. My mind vented its anger at my physical body – forcing me to waste away. In turn my starved body and brain became totally confused. Only now can I consciously and logically make sense of this picture. I drew then what I can only begin to understand and explain now.

This comment demonstrates how important it is not to attempt to ask questions regarding the meaning of an image when it is first made. Very often the artist cannot say what the image is about at the time. For the same reason it can also be intrusive for the therapist to attempt to make premature interpretations. We have to trust that it has its effect and, in time, its meaning will become conscious.

Carlos was now very near his target weight and this caused him tremendous anxiety. He insisted that he was now faced with the problem which had started him dieting in the first place. This had to do with the distribution of fatty tissue on his body and he requested surgery to remedy it and refused to hear any other interpretation of what this might symbolise for him. He insisted on wearing heavy loose sweaters in spite of the hot weather.

In this brightly coloured picture he shows more of his body than in previous pictures and he is seen from the front with facial features. However, it is a very violent image, the breast area of his body being violently attacked with an ornate axe. The cloaked figure which he attributes to his mind he told me, at the time, was his mother. Again a quote from Kristeva, regarding the son's bid to separate from his early identification with his mother, elucidates the significance of this image:

> I make of Her an image of Death so as not to be shattered through the hatred I bear against myself when I identify with Her. . . . Thus the feminine as image of death is not only a screen for my fear of castration, but also an imaginary safety catch for the matricidal drive that, without such representation, would pulverise me into melancholia if it did not drive me to crime. No, it is She who is death-bearing, therefore I do not kill her but I attack her, harass her, represent her. . . .
>
> (Kristeva 1989: 28)

The point is that the mother is experienced as castrating if the son is unable to make the move to differentiate himself from 'Her'. Like other writers Kristeva distinguishes the girl's difficulty in making this move from that of the boy. However, here it is the boy who is our concern and her words are borne out by this image where it seems that the hooded figure is cutting him off from his sexuality. This might be understood to be represented by the positioning of the jewelled sword and dagger in the foreground. This view of the sword may be affirmed by the three yellow rays of sun which seem to emanate from the sword. There are five orange crosses behind the figure and to the left of the picture. Behind these a huge eye is partly obscured by one of the crosses, two apparently seductive but disembodied female mouths are to the right. One of these has fangs and is clearly threatening, reminiscent of images of vampires or a vagina with teeth. These three elements seem to represent the threat of female sexuality. The eye could also be seen as a vagina. The sun is melting, tears drop from it and above bubbles seem to float away. In the lower left of the picture a chain is linked to three cobwebs which here seem to have less significance than in previous images.

Despite the apparent violence of this image, there is a sense that he has grown. Although he is no longer so directly in the power of the mother image it seems that it is still violently assaulting him. He is not yet free of it.

PLATE 9 (31) THE DRAGON. UNDATED. PENCIL, CRAYON, AND FELT-TIP PEN ON WHITE A4 PAPER

From the back of the picture:
I've killed anorexia/the dragon with the help of god/the cross.

This is another archetypal image and, like the tree from which the creeper or vine is being freed, conquering the dragon can be seen as a metaphor for the hero's freeing himself. Here a fiery dragon is being consumed by flames and killed with the cross. Fire is a traditional symbol of both rebirth and transformation. Jung writes: 'Fire making is pre-eminently a conscious act and therefore kills the dark state of union with the mother' (Jung 1956, CW 5: 211) [and] 'the hero who clings to the mother is the dragon and when he is reborn from the mother he becomes the conquerer of the dragon' (Ibid.: 374).

Carlos's own comments on the back of the picture seem to affirm this interpretation. In addition, the spiritual search which has been evident throughout this series of pictures, starting with Plate 2 and continuing with the many references to Christ throughout, is also present in this picture. Jung writes:

> The hero has much in common with the dragon he fights, or rather he takes over some of its qualities, invulnerability, snakes' eyes etc. Man and dragon might be a pair of brothers even as Christ identified himself with the serpent which conquered the plague of fiery serpents in the wilderness.

> (Jung 1956, CW 5: 367)

This seems to imply that to be free of the dragon it is necessary to accept what is in common with the dragon. This could be the flaming aspect, the fury and ability to destroy. The split-off and so unconscious negative aspect is as much a part of us as is that which we find easier to own, often the more positive. Through the last few images we have seen that Carlos seems to be beginning to accept the dragon as an aspect of himself.

FIGURE 4.22 (32) THE EGG. UNDATED. PENCIL DRAWING ON WHITE A4 PAPER

From the back of the picture:
You go through one stage/phase in life and what do you find . . . The next stage and the next.

Figure 4.22 The egg

From Carlos's study:
When I did this picture I wanted to show how every barrier we break
through in life only leads to the next barrier. Towards the end of therapy I
realised that the drawing shows the stripping away of all the barriers I'd
created around myself since being a child.
'I've removed all of the facades and discovered my real self.'

There is little for me to add to Carlos's own comments in relation to
Figure 4.22. The egg is often seen to represent the world and wholeness.

PLATE 10 (36) THE HERO. UNDATED. PAINT ON BUFF
SUGAR PAPER. 20 × 25 INCHES

Carlos was at last permitted to leave his little room. He had finally attained
the target weight and it was September – nine months since his admission.
He was now able to come to the art room to paint. There is a change in the
style and medium of the pictures which is affected by the physical freedom.
The room was large and light and he was free to mix with other people as
he chose. When he came to the art room he allowed himself to be more
spontaneous and he no longer pre-planned his pictures. It is notable that the
pictures from this stage are all on larger sheets of paper and much freer in
mode of execution. Two of these are shown as Plates 10 and 11.

In Plate 10 a figure, recognisable as Carlos, is shown full length and
painted in orange. He faces the sun without obstruction. This is very much
an archetypal hero picture. The figure, holding a sword, is coloured with
the solar orange. If we remember where he has come from, the slayed
dragon, the battle with the witch figure, then the hero is here seen emerging
from the underworld and entering the light or the sun. It seems like a birth
image as he stands atop a grassy mound. The sun is enormous and
dominates the whole picture. If we look back at earlier pictures in which
he was cut off from the sun we see that he is now free to face its power.

It could be argued that he has faced the unconscious and now faces the
light of consciousness. Alternatively, we could say that he has battled with,
and freed himself from, the feminine, and now he is able to claim his
masculinity in the form of the sword. The male figure, who stands with his
back to the viewer, appears to own his sexuality, anger and his power. The
fact that he holds the sword in his hands generates this impression. In
Figure 4.13 (Birth) the swords seemed to belong to the mother figure. In
Plate 8 (Confusion) he appeared to be cut off from the jewelled sword in
front of him. Here he owns the sword. It is bloody with droplets falling all
around – evidence, maybe, of having survived bloody battles. He commented that previously the sword would have been turned inwards.

The grey bubbles which have represented his problems and his feelings
of emptiness are still in evidence but at a distance. It is significant that,

although they have not disappeared, the figure is separate from them. Similarly there is a black bird flying towards the sun and it seems that these elements maintain a balance in what might otherwise seem a rather too positive image.

Carlos was delighted with the feelings he was experiencing now. He was enjoying talking with patients and helping them and he said that he got back ten times what he gave to them. He enrolled at an adult education college with the intention of getting qualifications – a first step on his intended path of a career.

THEORETICAL CONSIDERATIONS

It would be worth regarding Plate 10 in relation to the bubble/womb picture (Figure 4.4). We saw in that picture that the skeletal figure appeared atrophied, shrivelled, near to death and without any sexual characteristics. I have suggested that that image revealed the lack; it was an image of absence and devoid of desire. In this picture the triumphal figure seems transformed, appearing to burst forth from the earth/mother into the blaze of light from a huge sun. I have discussed how this might be viewed through the light of Jungian theory. A Lacanian frame would, in a different language, seem to offer a similar clinical understanding of the situation.

This triumphal image would suggest an entry into the Symbolic order. Finally differentiated, the figure stands holding his masculinity in his hand; he has survived the separation and emerged into the world of the adults. He is now sexually viable and also articulate, as is shown by the ways in which he is behaving in relation to the people around him. It seems that the total regression provided by his confinement in the little room, as well as the care and attention he received whilst in it, have liberated him and permitted a genuine differentiation to take place. He is now initiated into the Symbolic and so the social order. This is revealed in his identification with the staff and his keen desire to help others.

When discussing his sexuality, his homosexuality needs to be acknowledged. I am aware that the identification with the mother and absent father described throughout this case history could be understood through some forms of psychoanalytic theory to explain his homosexual orientation. However, I consider this to be neither necessary nor useful. If his sexual orientation is not a problem for the patient then it does not need to be resolved. The point is that Carlos has reached a position where he has a choice; he is now in a position to channel his sexual desire as he is inclined and to live a more fulfilled life. His sexual orientation is something that he will work out in his own way; it is neither attributable to any particular problem, nor does it need to be altered or cured.

PLATE 11 (40) THE SUN. UNDATED. PAINT ON BUFF SUGAR PAPER. 20 × 25 INCHES

As in Plate 10 the sun in Plate 11 is at the centre. Its rays seem to spread to all the areas of the picture. This seems to be in the celestial sphere, indicated by the clouds and the viewpoint level with the sun. Yellow light floods everywhere and illuminates a castle which is in the centre of the picture and slightly to the left. This position might indicate its relation to the unconscious, particularly as it is similar to the castle of Figure 4.7 and it is interesting to compare these two pictures. In Figure 4.7 some of the windows in the towers were in the forms of crosses. In this picture all the windows form crosses. There is also one large cross in the centre of the castle. This may indicate that the spiritual, conscious or sun element has become integrated with the unconscious which was revealed in the earlier castle. There are two lighted entrances whereas in Figure 4.7 there was one heavily barred entrance. Carlos writes that he had opened himself up in that little room and it seems that metaphorically he has let in the light.

There is a path leading to the castle apparently in the sky and made of seven yellow stepping stones. On the first of these is a brown seed, or apple, with a leaf growing from it. The next one has a sapling and each one after that has a slightly more mature version of a tree. The last one, which is next to the castle and in direct view of the sun, is a full-grown tree.

On the right of Plate 11, apparently suspended in the sky, is a white-cloaked winged figure who appears to have emerged from a broken egg. This could be seen as a positive male image or an aspect of his spiritual self. It is possible that the religious quest may have become mixed with a search for a positive father image. On the left in the foreground a figure in a white cloak with a grey face stands with arms outstretched. This figure, which might be seen as Carlos, is in a pose which we have seen before. In Plate 1, the family picture, the sister at the right-hand side of the picture stands in such a pose and a blue-cloaked figure stands in a similar position in Plate 7. It is not clear to me what the significance of this pose might be. It has been different each time it has appeared but I would suggest that here it has an aura of freedom about it.

This, too, might be a family picture, the white-cloaked figures being members of the family. The figures recede into the distance. The first is single, Carlos himself perhaps, then there are two and then three and finally, the last pair in the far distance are two figures, one much smaller than the other – a parent and child it seems. These could all be viewed as family members and then the last pair might be seen as his mother and little brother. However, it may be his child–self from which he is at last able to separate. It is possible that both interpretations have validity.

This is the fortieth picture in the series. There has been considerable urgency about the making of the pictures and they have sustained him through a very difficult phase. These last pictures indicate a resolution. Many aspects of the imagery that we have seen in the series appear to be reassembled in a different and more positive order. This is a stage where there seems to be an integration of certain elements within the psyche. This is not the end of treatment and, in psychotherapy, there would be the working-through process. Such a powerful outpouring of affect and imagery is a common first stage in psychotherapy or in analytical forms of art psychotherapy. This is followed by a necessary, and often lengthy, phase of assimilation. This is essential if the integration is to be consolidated, maintained and channelled into the day-to-day life of work and relationships.

Regarding the transference it is relevant to look back at Plate 2, the picture of my name, which was given to me in the very early stages of our work together. The castle, flooded with light, is rather similar in quality to this picture but in the picture of my name there is little shadow. The sunlight is relatively uncomplicated and there is little dark or earth colour. In retrospect we might understand this picture as being substantially without shadow. This fits with anorexia, the very nature of which is about keeping appearance good. However, the negative is split off and denied. This led to idealisation of the mother/therapist. The picture incorporates my name and reveals an idealised transference image.

If we now look at Plate 11, we see a much more integrated image. It contains many of the same colours but it has more substance. The castle could be seen to hold the shadow element which would indicate acceptance of the difficult negative feelings. This picture also suggests something of a resolution of the transference. Anorexia is an attempt to do away with the shadow; we have seen how Carlos confronted this in himself. These two pictures indicate that he is taking back into himself the positive elements which he projected and so gave to me with that picture.

SUMMARY

We have seen that, as the pictures began to reveal the unconscious processes, the initial idealisation broke down and aggression began to be experienced by Carlos. This was first, in relation to his pictures and secondly, in his behavior towards the therapeutic team and the art therapist. Thus, he began to separate from the fused state of identification with the mother and to enter the Symbolic realm. If we consider this in Lacanian terms we might regard Carlos as moving from the fused state of the Real through the Symbolic to the Imaginary and eventually to a place in the Symbolic order. This means that eventually he entered the adult world and was able to negotiate through language. The first pictures in this series demonstrate his turning away from life in a dangerous and life-threatening manner. The later ones revealed his beginning to engage with it in a more optimistic manner.

This chapter has been about the desire of the male anorexic patient working with a female therapist. However, in the context of this book, which is about desire, the female therapist's countertransference merits discussion. There was a real affection which sustained the therapeutic engagement throughout. At first the transference was infantile and pre-oedipal but later it was followed by an oedipal engagement where the erotic intensity increased and his aggression was admitted. I visited him in his little room in a physical situation which was more intimate than the average consulting room. Often, for example, he was in his pyjamas. However, this is a situation with its own boundaries, established by the nature of the clinical setting. I was drawn to him and certainly liked Carlos and found working with him rewarding. Many of the nurses also responded to him. Like most anorexics there was a need for him to feel in control and so often, despite the evident shared engagement, there was an emotional distance which had to be maintained.

CONCLUSION

When Carlos left the hospital, he took his pictures with him. That is all except those he made in the art room. He returned for these a year later and we discussed his experience of art therapy. He told me that he still kept his pictures safe and that he could now look at most of them. However, there were a few which he still found difficult to look at and these he kept under his bed at home. He said 'If I had not made these pictures what would have happened to these images?' He wondered how he would have coped with them because, although they were in an unformed shape, they were in his head. This is significant and shows the intense need that some people have to make pictures as part of their therapy. This has implications for therapists who are not art therapists. What happens to the images if the therapist discourages the bringing of pictures by interpreting it as acting out? What happens if the therapist feels disturbed by the visual material that their patient brings?

There is an argument here for psychotherapists, as well as art therapists, to familiarise themselves with the type of pictorial imagery that may emerge in the therapy of their patients. The imagery Carlos produced elicits strong reactions in the viewer. People are either attracted or repelled by these images. I suggest that this is because there is a conscious or unconscious recognition of these archetypal images from within the viewer's own psyche and this produces either a rejection of, or identification with, them. There are countertransference implications in these responses which I shall address in later chapters.

After leaving hospital in November, eleven months after his admission,

Carlos had many inter-personal difficulties to contend with. However, he maintained his weight and continued with his studies. Although he was offered alternatives, he decided to return to his family home, feeling that he was not ready to live on his own. A link with the hospital was maintained by means of a weekly appointment with a nurse who had been centrally involved in his treatment throughout. His study was written two years later.

Through Carlos's pictures, it has been possible to witness a process of growth and transformation. This evolved as part of a clearly defined treatment regime. For a while the pictures were a necessary link between Carlos's isolated inner world and the external world. However, this could not have taken place without the clear and boundaried situation offered by the inpatient treatment. Such a regime may seem to be rigid and harsh but it offered a space in which Carlos could take the risk of opening up and facing the terrifying power of his inner images.

In this chapter I have deliberately attempted to tell the story of Carlos's treatment through his words and pictures and so I will end this chapter, as it began, with Carlos's own words, which are an affirmation of the power and the importance of the art therapy process:

From Carlos's study:
Psychiatrists, doctors and nurses were all responsible for my eventual cure and recovery from anorexia nervosa. But looking back I realise that it was the art therapist who taught me to trust people again, and taught me how to like my 'self'.
It was through the medium of art therapy that I discovered the root of my illness, the change required in order to overcome anorexia, and a means of contacting my true self.

(Carlos 1983)

Chapter 5

The transactional object: art psychotherapy in the treatment of anorexia

In the previous chapter I discussed a case of anorexia in a male patient. In this chapter I will extract some theoretical implications from this study. The premise is that in the treatment of anorexia, art psychotherapy has a specific contribution to make. In the case of severe eating disorders the client's relationship to food may be understood to be a means of negotiating and mediating between the internal world and the external environment. It is a way of controlling desire in relation to food.

We saw with Carlos that pictures also mediate between the inner and outer worlds of the client and so between the client and the therapist. They offer an alternative means of understanding and coming to terms with the unconscious aspects of this desire. I suggest that through the intensity of engagement with the art process the pictures Carlos made first became objects of the scapegoat transference. As their importance for him developed, his libido, his desire for life and so the erotic drive became invested in this creative process. Gradually and unconsciously his engagement in them became a substitute for his interest in food. The picture then came to serve a positive function as a transactional object within the therapeutic relationship. In their subsequent disposal they were invested as talismans, empowered objects, within the therapeutic relationship (Schaverien 1991: 137–53).

In the last chapter the *content* of the imagery was the subject matter, in this chapter my investigation is into the *artwork as object*. We have seen that anorexia could be regarded as a borderline disturbance so the anorexic client is considered to be functioning at a pre-symbolic level. He or she is concretising experience, and unconsciously acting out, through the use of food. If this need for concrete expression can be converted from an obsession with food to a use of art materials, as in the case of Carlos, there is the beginning of a movement towards symbolisation.

This chapter is based on my experience of working as an art therapist with anorexic inpatients in two different NHS settings. The first of these was an adolescent unit and the second the psychiatric hospital, with a specialist approach to eating disorders, described in Chapter 3. The setting is significant because the problems encountered when working within a psychiatric hospital, as a member of a multi-disciplinary team, are very different from those encountered in outpatient psychotherapy.[1] None the less, the implications of the work I am describing are wider than psychiatry. The understanding gained from this inpatient experience has been the basis for my work with people with various eating problems in the more boundaried setting accorded by my present private analytical psychotherapy practice. It is intended that this understanding may also be of help to those psychotherapists, without art therapy training, whose anorexic patients bring pictures to their sessions.

Although the focus of the chapter is anorexia, my hypothesis also applies in a modified form to bulimia and compulsive eating problems. There is not the space here to review the literature on art therapy in the treatment of eating problems; instead I refer the interested reader to the following authors: Murphy (1984), Rust (1987, 1992), Levens (1987), Schaverien (1989). Similarly, I do not have space to comment on all the theories regarding the transference in art therapy but, in view of the topic of this chapter, it is necessary to offer a brief summary of the main debates. Psychotherapists may not be aware of the debates regarding the role of pictures in art psychotherapy. Because this overview is abbreviated I have to risk omission and over-simplifying quite complex ideas.

THE SCAPEGOAT AND THE TALISMAN: TRANSFERENCE IN ART PSYCHOTHERAPY

Until relatively recently there was little discussion of the transference and countertransference relationship in art therapy. In the USA some art therapists had discussed the topic, notably Naumberg (1953, 1966), a pioneer in the field. She worked with the transference and viewed art as a way of understanding psychoanalytic processes. Kramer (1971) on the other hand considered that the artwork was a 'container of emotions' and she, primarily, 'related to the patient through their art' (Waller 1991). Champernowne, a Jungian analyst and early champion of art therapy in Britain, published two papers (1969, 1971) in which she expressed the view that it was the role of the art therapist to elicit material through the art process. However, she considered it was for the psychotherapist to analyse the transference. Adamson (1986) worked in this way within psychiatry. He quietly and sensitively encouraged his patients to paint in the studio at the Netherne. They then took their pictures to the psychiatrist for discussion (see Cunningham Dax 1953).

In 1982 I published a paper 'Transference as an aspect of art therapy'. As far as I am aware this was the first paper in this country to address the topic directly. In 1984 Dalley produced the first edited collection of British papers on art therapy. This was followed by a coedited collection (Dalley *et al.* 1987). Since then, a number of books and articles have been published on art therapy; see, for example, Case & Dalley (1990, 1992), Waller & Gilroy (1992), Waller (1993) and *Inscape*, the Journal of the British Association of Art Therapists. The training now links art and psychotherapy and personal therapy is now mandatory for trainees. Thus transference and countertransference are increasingly accepted as part of the dynamic of an art psychotherapy relationship.

The debate regarding the place of the art process in art psychotherapy continues. A simplified explanation of the divergent positions might be characterised thus: there are art therapists who consider that art is healing in itself (Maclagan 1982) and there are others who espouse psychoanalytic concepts. The difference is in the priority accorded these different elements which are present in all forms of art therapy. The first group consider that transference interpretations disrupt a natural creative process (Thomson 1989; Simon 1992). The second group, usually with additional psychotherapy training, work with the transference and interpret the art process within an object relations framework (Mann 1990, 1991). The criticism of the first of these approaches might be that, whilst facilitating a powerful relation to the artwork, the interpersonal aspects of the transference are disregarded. The second view may undervalue the power of the art process by viewing the pictures as evidence of psychoanalytic concepts or as symptoms.

In an attempt to accommodate the view that art is healing in itself, but also taking account of the effects of the transference and countertransference, I have argued that there are times when the picture, too, becomes an object of transference. However, this is viewed *within* the frame of the interpersonal transference. This form of art therapy I have designated 'analytical art psychotherapy' (Schaverien 1991). Influenced by the work of Cassirer on symbolic form (1955, 1957), I have shown how art objects, made in art therapy, may be regarded as subject to mythical thought processes. Such thinking regards 'attributes and states' as transferable substances. This view is the foundation of traditional scapegoat rites and rituals throughout the world (Frazer 1922).

At times pictures may be understood, like the scapegoat, to embody attributes and states; they come to be experienced as embodying aspects of the inner world of the patient/artist. This is the 'scapegoat transference' (Schaverien 1987b, 1991). Cassirer demonstrates how it is, in part, through the making of tools and eventually artefacts that the 'I comes to grips with the world' (Cassirer 1955: 200). Following Cassirer, I have argued that pictures as self-made material objects offer a means through which a conscious attitude may develop. It is this *formative* function of the art medium that offers a way of bringing unconscious material to consciousness and it is through this process that a symbolic attitude may begin to develop from an undifferentiated state. The case study in Chapter 4, combined with the words of the artist himself, confirm this.

The scapegoat transference recognises the concretisation, which in developmental stages, precedes symbolisation (Segal 1981). It reframes identification and magical thinking as positive elements in the psyche which can be mobilised through artwork. However, this is facilitated *within* the context of the inter-personal transference and countertransference. Following Greenson (1967), I have proposed that when pictures are involved in psychotherapy, we might add an additional category to the conventional division of the therapeutic relationship: the real relationship, the therapeutic alliance, the transference and, in addition, the scapegoat transference to the picture. The pictures, once embodied as scapegoats, may subsequently become empowered. Such objects may be regarded as talismans in the therapeutic relationship because they are experienced as carriers or containers of magical significance. This initial identification with the artworks may lead, through a series of pictures, to separation, symbolisation and the ability to talk about the experience. Thus, a conscious attitude develops to previously unconscious material.

I will explain how I understand this process by referring back to some of the pictures made by Carlos. Carlos's pictures became embodiments of the scapegoat transference at an early stage. For example, if we think about 'The crucifix' (Plate 3), and 'The bubble' (Figure 4.4), these were powerfully invested with affect from the very beginning. The power invested in them meant that at the time he was engaged with making them, they were live; he was identified with them. This was evidenced in the intensity of his involvement and the fact that he did not wish to be disturbed when he was making them. They were an embodiment of his desire, and the lack of it, and so they became carriers of the transference.

In the disposal of individual pictures, it was demonstrated that they continued to be empowered, sometimes with magical significance. For example, the picture he gave to his therapist as a gift was an embodiment of the early stages of an erotic transference. This picture was significantly empowered and so was live between us for the duration of the therapy. This was a talisman. Carlos kept some of his pictures under his bed during his hospitalisation. These were the ones which disturbed him most. These, too, were carriers of magical significance. One even had to be destroyed because it brought the feared remembered image into the present. This continued after termination and he kept those that still frightened him under his bed. These, too, we might understand as being magically invested. Then he left some of the pictures in the art room when he left the hospital and this meant that he had to return to collect them, which he did a year later. Thus, these pictures maintained a physical link with the therapist.

The point about all these forms of disposal is that the object nature of the picture, its concrete and continued existence, is an important aspect of the therapy. The concrete nature of the picture and its unconscious employment as a talisman are significant aspects of the therapeutic process. The talisman is a form of transactional object. Unconsciously it is experienced as a link between the people. Carlos's pictures were embodiments of the scapegoat transference and further empowered as talismans. I am proposing, in addition, that they were transactional objects which became carriers of his desire and enabled him to begin to relate. They transformed his interest in food into a conscious awareness of the underlying problems. Through his relationship to his pictures, as well as his therapists, separation from his inner-world images began to take place. Subsequently, symbolisation and an ability to speak of the experience permitted them to come through to consciousness. This we see from his study written two years later.

There are cases where the healing effect of making and viewing pictures within the bounds of a therapeutic relationship effects a change in state without recourse to words. Then the artist/patient may come to own and reintegrate the affect which was embodied in the picture without directly discussing its meaning. Killick (1991, 1993) has discussed how, with psychotic patients, art therapy may bring the patient to the point where they can engage in psychotherapy. I am suggesting that it is similar with many anorexic patients. It is the effects of the concrete existence of the picture which distinguishes art psychotherapy from other forms of non-verbal communication within psychotherapy. For those therapists who are not art therapists it is important to be able to accept the imagery that is brought to sessions and not to be experienced as rejecting it. This can be difficult if the imagery contained in the pictures is unfamiliar and disturbing.

When practising psychotherapists engage with the idea of the scapegoat transference the suggestion is, understandably, often made that what I am describing is merely a form of projective identification. The scapegoat transference, as I have discussed it, involves processes which include splitting and disposal, both fundamental aspects of projective identification. However, despite its similarity, this idea is based on a different type of understanding, drawn from anthropological researches on the one hand, and aesthetic theory on the other.

There are two elements in the therapeutic relationship in art psychotherapy. These are the artist's relation to the artwork and to the therapist. Elements of projective identification (Klein 1946; Rosenfeld 1965; Ogden 1982; Grotstein 1981) may be involved in the patient's relation to the therapist and even, at times, in relation to the picture, but this is insufficient to encompass the phenomenon notated as the scapegoat transference. An understanding of projective identification sheds some light on aspects of the client's psychological relationship to the therapist, and even sometimes to the picture, as has been shown by Case (1994), but it cannot, in itself, provide an adequate account of the multi-faceted effects of the interaction of therapist, client and picture.

Samuels (1993: 276–7) has pointed out that far from being a culturally neutral technical concept, projective identification is itself an image and, moreover, a highly culturally contingent one. The concept of projective identification rests on a whole set of given, cultural and political assumptions that propose a fundamental separateness as the basic state of affairs between people as far as communication is concerned. In projective identification something is thrown or hurled across an empty space, penetrating the other. Such an image or trend of imagery is inadequate when we come to consider the complicated psychological processes that affect the therapist and client as viewers of pictures. In circumstances where art exists, we need to recognise that there is a cultural realm to be considered.

Artworks, whether viewed in galleries or in therapy, offer a way of making visible some shared states; they convey already existing links between people and offer a means of recognising and bringing to consciousness something which cannot easily be expressed in any other way. Sometimes pictures come to be experienced as carriers of transference and countertransference. This has been discussed by writers other than myself (Kuhns 1983; Spitz 1985, both of whom write about aesthetics and psychoanalysis). However, the processes I discuss could also be understood in terms of the 'collective unconscious' (Jung 1959b). Schwartz-Salant (1989) has pointed out that there are 'archetypal foundations of projective identification' and he makes connections between Klein (1946) and Jung in this regard (Jung 1946).

This could generate a lively and lengthy argument but here I can merely point out that there are many different ways of describing the phenomenon that I have identified as the scapegoat transference. I turn now to another related theme and that is the picture as a 'transactional object'.

THE TRANSACTIONAL OBJECT

The transactional object which I propose is different from both the transitional object (Winnicott 1971) and the transformational object (Bollas 1987). The transitional object is the first 'not me' object to which the infant becomes attached. It is an object which mediates between the mother and the environment. The transitional object is an actual object with a physical existence, a teddy bear or a piece of blanket, to which the infant forms an early attachment. Sustained by the transitional object the infant begins to be able to retain a sense of the continued existence of the mother in her absence. Winnicott demonstrates how this attachment gradually disperses and becomes sustained by the whole environment. This leads eventually to cultural life and appreciation of art.

There is clearly a relation here between the transitional object and the picture, which has a mediating function in anorexia. The picture mediates in the transitional space and so it may sometimes become a transitional object; it may enable the patient to sustain the relationship to the therapist in her absence. This is the beginning of the ability to symbolise and relate as a separate person and it is one facet of the artist's relation to her pictures. But it is not this function that I am exploring here. I am suggesting a more direct and, in some ways, less complex role for the picture. I am proposing that the picture is an object through which unconscious transactions may be acted out and channelled. Initially an unconscious acting out, it may lead to a conscious attitude and enactment.

Bollas argues that the transitional object is 'heir' to the transformational object (Bollas 1987). The transformational object is a part–object relation, an internal process, which is a result of the earliest attachment to the mother as mediator. 'Not yet identified as other, the mother is experienced as a process of transformation' (Bollas 1987: 14). The mother transforms otherwise unbearable anxiety or intolerable feelings; she metabolises the infant's experience and returns it in a manageable form. Bollas considers that the transitional object belongs to a later stage and is dependent on the satisfactory negotiation of this earlier developmental phase. Clearly this, too, is relevant when working with disorders related to food. However, unlike the transitional object and the picture, the transformational object is not a tangible object and it does not actually exist between the mother and the child.

The transactional object that I am proposing offers an additonal category. It owes a debt to both of the above theories but it comes from a different root. The idea is based on anthropological explorations of the use of art in different cultures throughout the world.[2] The word transaction implies a category where the object is used in exchange for something else. It is an object through which negotiation takes place. This may be thought to imply a conscious transaction but the process to which I refer is primarily unconscious and may be magically invested.

Like food, art materials have a physical presence and, like the mother offering the child food, the art psychotherapist provides art materials for the patient to use. The concrete nature of this transaction, within the therapeutic boundary, sets up a resonance with the problem. This can be observed in the use made of the materials; often they are related to in a similar way to food. For example, it may be some time before the anorexic will dare to engage with the art materials. She may be suspicious of them and refuse to use them at first. Then she may tentatively try them out in private well out of the view of the therapist. When eating, the anorexic takes a small helping of food and then plays with it; likewise, when offered art materials, she may take a pencil in preference to any of the more sensual materials offered. She may then make a tiny mark and fiddle around, tentatively marking the paper, but never 'biting' into it. Alternatively, she may binge on the art materials, going wild and splashing paint around. This is more likely with the bulimic patient as has been shown by Levens (1987). So the relation to the art materials is significant even before a picture is made.

Once made, the picture becomes an object through which unconscious transactions may be negotiated. The pictures reveal the significance of the role played by food, but the pictures, as objects, may themselves be the medium through which the patient relates to the therapist. This may reproduce elements of the mother/child feeding relationship in the transference. The use of food as a transactional object might be understood to be an unconscious displacement of anxiety or fear. If this displacement can be channelled through art materials, it may be possible to bring the original impulse to consciousness. The pictures, as temporary transactional objects, may facilitate the beginning of movement from an unconscious fused state to separation and differentiation.

THE ANOREXIC

As we have seen the entire existence of the person suffering from anorexia is centred on food. All her energies are directed to controlling her own intake of food.[3] Her thoughts are constantly concerned with what she will eat, what she can eat and what she has eaten. She makes bargains with herself, and with others, about what she is permitted to eat and inflicts penance on herself for transgressions of her self-imposed regime (McCleod 1981; Chernin 1981, 1985). This is a very conscious interest. Food and its effects are her sole, and usually total, preoccupation. The refusal to take food into herself is a way of controlling her own body, destiny and ultimately her life. Consequently when she begins to achieve this control, which is a denial of her desires, she comes to feel omnipotently powerful.

The anorexic might be understood as suffering from a form of borderline disturbance characterised by a powerful defence system and distorted relationship to the body. In place of an imaginal world the anorexic has her own symbolic rituals, ideas and actions connected with food. These are a way of concretising her experience. She exerts control through the ingeniously designed patterns of monitoring intake and excretion of food. Thus, if she eats, she will take laxatives to ensure that the food does not remain too long inside her, or she will purge herself by induced vomiting. She will only eat certain foods and any transgression will be atoned for by excessive self-directed punishments, such as exhausting exercise. The whole effort is directed towards control of the uncontrollable: the body, sexuality, other people and ultimately, life and death. Her body is often reduced to a dangerously low weight level and menstruation ceases. She then feels a sense of power and omnipotent control.

The anorexic uses food to mediate between herself and the world. The attachment to, or interest in, food is obsessional. The borderline thought processes which underlie anorexia mean that food is often invested with magical powers. Its presence in the body is desired but also experienced as intrusive and disgusting. Terrified of loss of control and so fragmentation, the anorexic is frozen on the borderline between life and death or control and madness.

FAMILY RELATIONSHIPS

The infant's omnipotent power in relation to her mother is centred on the need to feed and the reciprocal need of the mother to gratify her, to feed her when she is hungry. As the infant grows and develops her needs change and gradually she begins to test her independence, to leave the mother and return on her own terms. The first evidence of this is when the infant is able to crawl away, then to walk and explore the world for herself (Eichenbaum & Orbach 1983). This can only be achieved if the mother can provide a base to which the child may safely return (Mahler *et al.* 1975). The mother, or parenting adult, is needed to provide a good-enough holding environment (Winnicott 1971), which allows the child to experience safety but also a tolerable amount of failure of the maternal environment. The child needs to be nurtured and fed but learns to sustain a certain degree of frustration which would have been intolerable in infancy.

As the child develops, vestiges of this early relationship remain, and are, at times, to be recognised in battles at the dinner table over food. In some cases these last into adolescence and beyond. The anorexic's control of the world, via food, could be understood as an extension of this ability to interest her immediate maternal environment through her refusal to eat. This evokes the mother's primitive anxiety, her need to respond and ensure the survival of her child. The mother's ambivalence regarding the adolescent daughter's impending sexuality and separation from her may be a contributary factor in this anxiety. In Chapter 3 we discussed the possible effects of gender difference when the anorexic patient is male.

We have also seen in Chapter 3 that theories regarding the aetiology of eating problems abound. There are sociological factors as well as developmental theories which contribute to my understanding. However, it is not my intention to review the literature nor to discuss the diverse theories regarding the origins of these problems. My aim is to draw out the central factors which lead to the efficacy of art psychotherapy as a method of treatment for this client group. The premise of this chapter is that for the anorexic food is significant. It is a symptom, a means of expressing something else.

I will compare two pictures made by another anorexic patient to two pictures made by Carlos. There is a similarity which may have wider implications for understanding the imagery produced by the anorexic patient.

CASE ILLUSTRATION: PART 1

The following is an example of the very early stages of engagement in art therapy with an anorexic patient. Although this did not develop into long-term art psychotherapy due to certain external factors, I offer this here because it shows how the pictures begin to reveal and embody the inner-world state of the patient. With May, as with most anorexic patients, there was a mild resistance to making artworks. There was little understanding of the reason she was being asked to draw or paint. I suspect she complied initially because the therapist requested it. Only gradually does the process become meaningful for the patient.

May had made a few decorative pictures in the two weeks since her admission. Like Carlos she was an inpatient on bed rest and I would leave a selection of art materials with such patients in their rooms. At first the pictures she made were all similar to Figure 5.1. This is a very common type of picture for anorexic patients. Although it could be understood to be revealing in several ways, the controlled nature of its execution is typical. Such a picture echoes the transference to the therapist in that it affirms, as does the patient herself, no matter how emaciated, that all is well and she does not know what all the fuss is about. Both pictures, Figures 5.1 and 5.2, are carefully drawn, the use of the material is sparing and they are drawn on very small pieces of paper. This is typical of the relationship of the anorexic to the art materials in the early stages.

May's slim fairy figure which floats above temptation, high in the sky, could be understood as in flight from reality. She is not earthed but rather an 'earthereal' creature with the ability to fly. Associated with the crescent moon, this could be understood as the unconscious element in the psyche. Thus, the picture states the problem. The female figure is suspended, neither child nor woman she is poised between earth and sky. However, the patient was in no way ready for such an interpretation at this point. Her attitude to it was defensive and protective. For her the picture was no more than it appeared, an attractive image drawn in coloured felt-tip pens. This image was apparently unconnected from her feeling self. It was of little significance to her and, in this way, it echoed the transference to the therapist. This picture was not a transactional object in any embodied sense. In contrast the tiny pencil drawing on the back of this 'pretty picture' was the start of engagement in art psychotherapy for May. It

Figure 5.1 May's first picture

took a great deal of courage for her to make the drawing – Figure 5.2 – which will be discussed below.

Despite the apparent decorative quality of Figure 5.1, there are several indications of the problem. There are also considerable similarities to Figure 4.2 (The badger) made by Carlos at a comparable time in his treatment. It is in the childlike quality of these two early images that the correspondence resides and also in certain elements in the imagery. May's figure floats between earth and sky and appears to be poised or in transition. Similarly, Carlos's badger is poised outside the doorway but about to enter, also in transition. The mushroom seems to be a common image from anorexic patients and might indicate poisonous food. May's is a giant mushroom which appears to be an edible variety. Carlos's mushrooms on the other hand appear to be some form of poisonous toadstool, as indicated by their spots. In both pictures these are positioned at the bottom of the picture and both also have the moon in the top right-hand corner. In May's picture it is the crescent moon and in Carlos's a full moon, partly obscured by clouds.

The significance of these images is clearly different for each person. However, a traditional view of the moon might be that it indicates the unconscious and, as it is on the right-hand side, it might be obscuring the conscious element. This type of thinking can never be fixed and such generalisations only offer a suggestion for further consideration. This is most useful if it takes place within therapy and with the patient.

The point for the present discussion is that neither picture was a transactional object in the sense that I intend it. Both were beginnings of embodiment but the relationship of the artist to these pictures meant that in no way did these pictures substitute for the use of food.

FOOD AS A TRANSACTIONAL OBJECT

For the anorexic, food is empowered. As we have seen, the power attributed to it affects the relationships between the anorexic and those people who care most about her. For her, food is a focus on which many bargains are struck, bargains with herself and bargains with others. In this sense food becomes for her a transactional object. It is here that the anorexic is fixed.

The interest of the anorexic in her food consumption frequently extends to other members of her family. In addition to controlling her own food intake, the anorexic may have a compelling interest in the food consumption of other family members. Often, while starving herself, the anorexic will take an abnormal interest in the diet of her family. Sometimes this becomes manifest in her insistence on cooking food for the family which she will not eat; sometimes it is evident in her obsessional concern that they should eat healthy foods. She may attempt to strike bargains with them over food, insisting that they eat what she will not. She may sit at the dinner table eating only lettuce, pushing the rest of her food into piles or hiding it under a lettuce leaf. Meanwhile the rest of the family becomes increasingly exasperated, angry and worried in turn.

Battles for control of the life of the child/woman/man rage in the family around such behaviour. The symbolic nature of such life and death struggles is vividly expressed by Spignesi (1983). Both intra-personally and inter-personally these are highly emotive and complex methods of relating, with food as the currency and endless focus of attention and concern. For the anorexic food becomes a medium by which deals with others are negotiated and a distorted independence is accomplished. The anorexic structures her social existence and her private world through food; she controls her own body and exerts some control over others through it. Food, which is essential for life and health, becomes an unconscious way of symbolising conflict. Anorexia could be seen as an unconscious acting out of the splits and stresses of the divided inner world of the sufferer. It is her own unique and self-invented solution, which is a symbolisation of an internal battle for control of her life (Shorter 1985).

THE PICTURE AS TRANSACTIONAL OBJECT

It is here that we can begin to isolate one reason why it is that art psychotherapy is potentially effective in treating such patients. Art offers an alternative, a way of enacting and symbolising the inner conflict and it also provides another potential transactional object. Anorexia could be understood to be a form of acting out. *Acting out* is behaviour which is motivated by unconscious pain, a form of splitting. The relation to food could be understood to be such acting out. Conversely, *enactment* implies that there is consciousness and so the act has meaning. The artwork, as a transactional object, might at first be the channel for unconscious acting out; later it may develop into an enactment.

The transactional object is very different from the other transactions which involve discussion of body weight. Whether the therapist is working as a member of an inpatient team, or with the client as an outpatient, she needs to know about the rest of the treatment programme. It is essential that she is in contact with other workers so that she does not become split off and manipulated by the patient. However, she must not negotiate any contract with the client over weight gain or loss or regarding food intake. Art should never become a bargaining counter itself; this can be very destructive. For example, I have known a situation where the patient was only permitted to be engaged in art therapy when a certain weight was attained. Furthermore, weight loss meant forgoing art therapy. In this behavioural approach art becomes a privilege which is gained or with-drawn according to external factors. Art psychotherapy cannot be effective if it becomes part of a bargaining process itself.

The transaction to which I refer is less conscious and less obvious than this. When a picture is made it is private; it belongs to its maker. The content of the imagery may not be conscious, but the artist has the option, at any time during its creation, to obliterate or destroy any part or the whole picture. In practice it is relatively rare that a picture is destroyed, but it is this option which is, for the anorexic patient in particular, so essential. The picture can be viewed in private and then shown. This makes a space between the 'utterance and the performance'. We saw this in the case of

Carlos. He kept some of his pictures under his bed and did not show them to anyone. He then showed them to the art therapist when he chose to do so. Ultimately he chose to destroy one of them. The freedom to do this is very important because he is in control of his own material. This is an important aspect of the mediating function of art and it is a transaction which is controlled entirely by the patient. Throughout the process, access of other people to the picture is controlled by the artist. The picture thus becomes, like food, a private matter. It is an object through which mediation for control may be negotiated without the necessity for verbal intervention.

The picture is less important than food and so it is not as emotive in terms of family dynamics. Parents may be curious to see the picture, but it is not a matter of life and death as is eating. Thus, the patient may find this is one area where she can express herself and yet find a refuge. Here she may explore how she feels without invasive questioning of her motives. The picture offers a forum where unconscious conflicts and conscious concerns may be externalised and the internal theatre of the patient may be revealed. It can then be viewed by the artist herself, and subsequently by others – but only if she chooses. The picture, and the inner constellation which it exhibits, may become accessible for discussion but at a remove from the patient. The picture is 'out there', a third object, a potential transactional object which is not food.

The anorexic is preoccupied with ways of controlling her desires and keeping the people around her under control and at a distance. Her inner-world patterns reflect this, so for her the picture may offer a real solution to the problem of maintaining her own space in relationship. A picture creates space and it offers a way of potentially sharing that space by permitting the imaginal world to be viewed. The anorexic does not usually permit herself imaginal space; she does not dare to dream or risk chaos; nor can she permit her vigilance to lapse for a moment. She fears mess and intrusion and by either she may be overwhelmed. A picture, even the first tentative attempts of the anorexic, permits the possibility of contained mess, within the framed space of the picture. Here chaos may be held safely within the boundaries of the paper, separated from its creator, and it may exhibit the imaginal world.

This picture may become a scapegoat in that it may embody the chaos, the feared aspects of the inner world; on the paper these may become 'live' within the therapeutic relationship. Here the client may engage in a way she cannot dare to venture to engage with the therapist. The framed and separated nature of the picture serves two functions for the anorexic. It separates the pictured image from her and, in doing so, distances her from her own fears. Paradoxically it brings the pictured fears and fantasies nearer to consciousness because they are to be seen. Simultaneously, the picture protects the transitional area (Winnicott 1971), it keeps the space between patient and therapist. The imaginal world may be revealed in the picture but there is no automatic right of access to it. No one else has a right to see or even question it.

FOOD AS SUBJECT MATTER

The initial pictures made by anorexic patients are often about food. A skeleton sitting on a huge pile of food which reached to the edges of the paper was the way that one young woman pictured her predicament. The pictures which refer to food are often the first ones, the ones which state the problem. I submit that they also test the therapist. By assessing the therapist's reaction to the *content* of the imagery, the patient measures the therapist's reaction to her attitude to food. The reception of these early pictures is then crucial. If the therapist is able to convey that she accepts these pictures, without getting drawn into negotiations about the consumption of food, she may gain the trust of the patient. Despite her defences the anorexic is likely to be desperate for her plight to be understood.

It is possible for the therapist, by not showing any particular interest in food, to encourage the patient to relinquish her obsession, at first only in her pictures. This is not an overt ploy, merely that the therapist is genuinely more interested in the person than her food intake. The interest in the person, without the interest in food, is unusual for the patient who is used to defining herself in relation to her food intake. As soon as she enters hospital negotiations regarding weight gain and food consumption are formalised. Art permits her to be an ordinary person with ordinary worries. Through the making of pictures she may redefine her existence. In finding another means of expression for her conflicted and divided inner world the focus may shift, the patient may begin to permit herself to eat more normally. The problems, fears and fantasies which have been displaced into food are released. The fears which have been frozen with the imaginal aspects of the self may come to the fore at this stage in frightening and powerful images. A freedom and self-understanding develops through assimilation of the pictured image. An understanding of the unconscious meanings of anorexia becomes clearer and the need to enact the drama of life through food is gradually relinquished.

When the patient is courageous enough to risk picturing food and her relation to it, the therapist merely accepts this as any other statement or image of feeling made by the patient. Overt interpretations of the content of the patient's pictures or behaviour tend to be experienced as invasive. Transference interpretations are rarely useful with the anorexic; the very nature of her transference means that they meet with denial and rejection. However, the picture could be understood to be a kind of visual interpretation; it is seen by both people and even when nothing is said the picture has, as it were, 'had its say'. The patient who fears invasion will not find it easy to show the therapist her pictures. She is likely to feel extremely exposed when she has made an image which has any real meaning for her. When the picture gives access to her imaginal world, in however tentative a manner, there may be an overwhelming feeling of risk.

This we saw clearly in the case of Carlos. His early pictures – Plate 3 (The crucifix), and Figures 4.5 and 4.6 (The candle and The squirrel) – made reference to food but, as he became more engaged with the image-making process, Carlos's pictures began to be about his life in a much more direct way. The obsession with his eating gave way and the conflicting desires which were underlying this broke through to consciousness. I submit that this came about in part through the medium of his pictures. He was able to express his intense emotions in a contained form and now the pictures began to become transactional objects. He was able to relate to the art therapist through the medium of the pictures. This meant that there was a third object which could be the focus of the gaze of both people.

TRANSFERENCE

The transference with this client group presents a rather different set of problems from other client groups. In the transference the therapist is likely to be experienced as 'a parent' and to be expected to relate in similar ways. Thus, there is an immediate problem for the development of a working alliance within which a transference may develop. The client will treat the therapist as she does all adults, as a figure of authority, so she may anticipate loss of control. She will need to keep the therapist at a safe distance, in order to maintain her control of the situation. The transference in psychotherapy effects the unfreezing of old patterns. The anorexic has learned to live without trusting imagination for fear that she will be overwhelmed by chaos. Similarly she will not trust another person for fear that she will be overwhelmed in the relationship. The imaginal world will thus remain frozen (Spignesi 1983).

The transference to the therapist is likely to be a repetition of the powerful cycle of resistance. Attempts on the part of the therapist to mobilise unconscious forces are likely to be frustrated. The anorexic is the expert at this relational game and she is terrified of letting go. We have seen that there is often a similar resistance to engaging in the art process. However, in my experience, it has become noticeable that, like May, she just may permit herself to start to imagine on paper, usually in private, or out of sight of the therapist. She may have been good at drawing at school. Alternatively, she may never have had any previous abilities in this area but she may have a little confidence in making controlled pictures. These are usually pale pencil or felt-tip-pen drawings – both mediums which allow for maximum control of the end result – paint is rarely used. This may be the start. Eventually a transference may be mobilised in relation to the paper. The pictures which were initially decorative, tight and diagrammatic may begin to embody feeling.

By altering the currency and also the nature of the obsession by the gradual substitution of art for food, the therapist is offering the client a different method of negotiating with the external world. This is a delicate task. The therapist initiates the creative process; in this sense she teaches the client that it is possible for her to use this medium. At the same time she must maintain a distance from the final picture and from the picture in progress. She accepts but must not be experienced as curious, interested or enthusiastic. The therapist must be prepared to wait without expectation while the patient is given space to be private and even secretive. The patient needs to have the option to destroy her pictures or to hide them. It doesn't matter if the therapist does not see everything that is made. It is far more important that the patient can find refuge in her artwork, that she can begin to explore for herself the constellations of the images of her inner world. If she can begin to do this, then later there may be the opportunity for discussion of content with the therapist. Links and connections may then be made which further the progress of differentiation. This will all follow the initial involvement of the client with the art materials which she can control. The triangular pattern of child–food–parent may be replaced by one in which the picture becomes the apex of the triangle. We then have patient–picture–therapist. The concrete element which was food now becomes picture. The potential for a symbolic dimension enters the therapy.

CASE ILLUSTRATION: PART 2

For May the unfreezing began tentatively and I propose initially through the image Figure 5.2. I spent a good deal of time with May listening to her story, hearing about her life, her relationships with her family and looking at the pictures she had made. Before leaving her on one occasion I suggested that she might think about what she had told me and perhaps she could find a way of picturing it. The direction was not specific, but it was designed to give her permission to picture her distressed feelings on paper. It was also intended to affirm the seriousness of what she had told me. This session was the beginning of a real engagement in the process I was permitted to see, and side with, the real, distressed part of herself.

When I returned to see May in her little room, a few days after the session described above, she showed me first her pretty picture, Figure 5.1, and then, tentatively, she showed me her secret image drawn faintly on the back of the paper. It was a very small pencil drawing of a girl curled up in an

Figure 5.2 May's second picture

oval shape, reminiscent of an egg. We will see in a later chapter (Chapter 7) that the beginning of movement is frequently first evident in the manifestation of the image of a child. This is such an image. In its own way this vividly portrayed her situation. It did not need immediate interpretation. The image revealed her regressed state; at this stage words would have intruded in her relationship to the image. The image was hidden on the reverse of the picture, Figure 5.1, which she considered to be more acceptable. It showed her something of which she may have been only partly conscious prior to making the drawing. The therapist saw the image without needing to ask for explanations. It is an eloquent image, an exemplification of a feeling rather than an explanation (Henzell 1984). May knew that I understood that she was showing me how withdrawn, small and regressed she felt. In this way she was starting to let me into her world, to show it to me. She could not find words to tell how she felt but she did not need to because it was evident from her picture.

This tiny doodle on the back of what she considered, at the time, to be her more important picture was an 'embodied image' (Schaverien 1987b, 1991). It was the first tentative step in admitting to herself, and to the therapist, how she felt. This very small picture engaged her feelings on a real level in contrast to a performance level. She was permitting a public expression of her private experience. In so doing she was admitting, only partly consciously, that her pretty picture world was an act, a false self-construction. I submit that this change occurred because trust and a positive transference was beginning to become live in the therapeutic relationship. After our previous meeting she was prepared to allow herself to experience, in a tightly controlled and safely small pencilled image, how she felt. This was an embodied image and so a potential scapegoat picture. The tiny picture, which risked admitting feelings of vulnerability, was a tiny picture but a very large potential step.

The picture was the medium through which a transaction could begin to take place between us. The patient could experiment with relating to the therapist but without actually facing her. Both could regard the picture while talking about the feelings. This enabled May to test the triangular space. Perhaps she was, unconsciously, testing whether the space between us would remain once her inner world was exposed. To use a feeding analogy – she was nibbling, testing whether if she took a small bite, interpretations would be stuffed into her. By showing the picture she was using an object to mediate between herself and the therapist. Thus, this picture was a transactional object that was not food.

In Figure 4.4 made by Carlos shortly after his admission to hospital we see a figure enclosed in a circle which is a bubble/womb. There is a similarity with May's picture as she, too, has drawn herself enclosed within a circle. Her figure, too, is without sexual characteristics except for her hair, which is used to hide her body. Both of these people were being treated in the same way. Each was held in a small room as part of the treatment. None the less I have noticed this regressed type of image, where the person is enclosed within a circle, as a common picture made by anorexic patients. On the one hand this is not very remarkable if we accept that regression is part of the problem in this condition. However, I consider that this type of image marks the beginning of embodiment of the transference to the picture. Often it echoes the interpersonal transference. It is a real as opposed to a false self-image. For this reason it may offer the beginning of engagement, which may lead to the picture becoming a transactional object in the place of food. Thereby the picture may offer the possibility of movement from a frozen or atrophied state.

CONCLUSION

The aim in this chapter has been to develop the theme of the last two chapters and to illustrate one way in which pictures offer a medium for relating, first to the self and then to another person. The pictures may begin to embody some of the power which was previously invested in food and so they become transactional objects in place of food. The therapist is present to witness and receive the picture and so it is likely that the relation to the therapist may repeat some of the power which was invested in the parents. Thus, there are two ways in which the transference may begin to come live into the present of the therapeutic relationship – first, through the transference to the picture in place of the relationship to food and second, through the transference to the therapist in place of the parent. These case examples were from art therapy within a psychiatric setting. However, as suggested in the beginning of the chapter, my intention has been to demonstrate the potential significance of the transference which is embodied in the artwork and this may apply in other analytical psychotherapy settings. I have argued that for this particular client group art in psychotherapy may offer an important means of beginning to relate to the self and the other.

In discussing the role of the picture as a transactional object the focus has been the object nature of the artwork. However, as we have seen, the images which emerge in a series of pictures in long-term work are highly significant. The pictures may reveal powerful unconscious forces which are at play in the inner world. The visual nature of art means that the images are seen. This viewing, in itself, effects a change in the state of the artist. The externalisation leads to a conscious attitude because the images are seen out in the world. Eventually it may be possible for the artist/patient to discuss the pictures with the therapist. The additional understanding gained from some verbal discussion may be helpful in fixing meaning and bringing a further consciousness to bear. However, with an anorexic client group this may not always be possible or beneficial. Art can offer a means of bringing the anorexic to a stage where she can relate directly to another person. The art process, mediated within the transference, may facilitate a journey from a relatively unconscious or undifferentiated state, through stages of concrete thinking, to the beginnings of separation and eventually to symbolisation.

Chapter 6

The aesthetic countertransference: desire in art and psychoanalysis

Desire: Unsatisfied appetite; longing; wish; craving; request; thing desired.

(Concise Oxford English Dictionary)

We can apprehend this privilege of the gaze in the function of desire, by pouring ourselves, as it were along the veins through which the domain of vision has been integrated into the field of desire.

(Lacan 1977a: 85)

In the second chapter of this book I discussed the erotic transference and countertransference in the female therapist/male patient dyad. The last three chapters have centred on a male patient and anorexia, which, as we have seen, could be understood to be a manifestation of desire, and denial of desire. We have followed this through his pictures. This chapter and the one that follows are also linked. They offer an exploration of theoretical considerations regarding art in psychotherapy and, in particular, the aesthetic countertransference.

It is sometimes stated as a negative of the therapeutic encounter that pictures in psychotherapy can seduce the therapist. It is my premise that pictures *can*, and sometimes *do*, seduce both the therapist and the patient and, far from this being a negative indication, this is one of the essential elements of an analytical encounter with art in psychotherapy. I propose that, unless a picture does have the power to seduce the therapist, it is unlikely to be an affective element in the treatment. Such seduction is rarely overt, it may be subtle or unconscious. It is also likely that the pictures concerned will in some way seduce the artist/patient. I need, however, to make it clear that the type of seduction to which I refer is not the simple seduction which is sometimes described by analysts when the very act of bringing a picture to therapy is interpreted as seductive. On occasions this may be the case but what I am discussing are the more complex affects of the whole interaction – including the imagery – on the viewers.

Not all pictures have the power to seduce the therapist. The pretty chocolate-box image, to which some patients initially aspire, does not have the power to seduce the viewer. Conversely, the raw, untamed and sometimes unnameable image, which at first glance may not look pretty, may well have the power to do so. This is an aesthetic consideration which we might recognise if we recall that which is pleasing in 'public' art.

The initial appeal of a work of art is an attraction which invites the viewer to make a closer inspection. Subsequently a successful work evokes feelings in the viewer and provokes a response. This attraction is complex and may be understood in its broadest sense to be a seduction. This seduction is not necessarily sexual, although sometimes it may have an erotic charge. Nevertheless it is characterised by desire. To have such effect a picture will have substance and convey a tension, it will be an 'embodied image'. Subsequently such an image may become empowered and be valued as a 'talisman' (Schaverien 1987b, 1991). A picture of this type may disturb the viewer because of the feelings it evokes. The response may be a rejection, dislike of certain marks perhaps, or a distaste for the figurations or shapes. On the other hand it may be an identification with the image, enjoyment of the sensuality of the colour, the way it is painted or the combinations of the figures. Whatever the response, a work which is aesthetically integrated will not leave the spectator unmoved.

The picture which is aesthetically pleasing may be said to evoke desire and yet can only be appreciated with a suspension of desire as well as of judgement (Kant 1928). Bion (1970: 41), discussing the psychoanalytic encounter, indicates that the therapist can only meet the patient in his present reality if there is an absence of memory and desire. The aesthetics of art and psychoanalysis are similar in this respect. In terms of understanding what is meant by this suspension of judgement, this absence of memory and desire, closer examination is required. At first glance such a statement appears paradoxical. It might be said that desire and memory are the very substance of the appreciation of art and also of the transference and countertransference in psychoanalysis.

DESIRE IN PSYCHOANALYSIS

Freud began by recognising the desire of the patient when he came to understand 'transference love' (Freud 1915). It is when the patient's desire enters the therapeutic encounter that analysis begins to come alive. It is then that the therapist's desire becomes engaged and, inevitably, both people are affected and changed. Thus, desire is intrinsic to the transference. Freud wrote that the pattern for conducting erotic life, laid down in the early years, will influence the aims and objects of love in later life. 'If someone's need for love is not entirely satisfied by reality, he is bound to approach every new person he meets with libidinal anticipatory ideas' (Freud 1912: 100). Thus, in the transference, the analyst very often becomes the desired object. This is only gradually relinquished as con-sciousness takes over from the unconscious drive. Desire is a characteristic of both analysis and art.

The suspension of judgement and the absence of memory and desire, in a situation where desire is evidently a central element, appears to be a paradox (as already stated) – but perhaps it is not so very paradoxical. To be able to work with the desire of the patient, in the present, the therapist must first relinquish her need for the patient. This might be a wish for the patient to get better, or it might be a longing for the patient as an 'ideal' partner or for any combination of conscious or unconscious desires which the patient may evoke in the therapist. The patient's desire will inevitably evoke a reciprocal desire in the therapist. This, if tempered with eros, places the therapist immediately in the area of a taboo. As we have seen, in Chapter 2, it evokes images of incest and of illicit love affairs. Moreover, it often engages the same feelings in the therapist as a person, as does any other intimate relationship.

The topic of desire in psychoanalysis has been approached by many analysts since Freud. Most agree that it is the re-experiencing of desire in the transference and the abstinence from acting on it which brings the origins of the drive to consciousness. It is this which transforms the inner world. Manifestations of desire in the transference make powerful counter-transference demands. Bion claims that it is only through the relinquishing of memory and desire that the analyst can be totally available to the patient in the present. Thinking about this may help in considering the aesthetic countertransference. He writes:

> A bad memory is not enough: what is ordinarily called forgetting is as bad as remembering. It is necessary to inhibit dwelling on memories and desires . . . the more the psychoanalyst occupies himself with memory and desire the more his facility for harbouring them increases and the more he comes to undermining his capacity.
>
> (Bion 1970: 41)

Bion distinguishes between memory and desire. Memories are often treated as possessions whilst desires, although often spoken of as if they too were possessions, in fact tend to possess us (Bion 1970: 42). The past is contained within memory; in this sense the past is fixed and 'memories can be regarded as possessions' (ibid.). When we hold on to memories, even the memory of the last session, we become rigid or inflexible because something is fixed in mind. We tend to behave as if we own memories. Desires are different: 'Desires while just as much "in" the mind as are memories, and therefore just as much "possessions" are spoken of as if they possessed the mind' (ibid.) and, when desires possess the mind, we are on the edge of psychotic experience.

It is this possessive nature of memory and of desire, the yearning for the object, which becomes manifest in the transference. If desire is evoked in the countertransference it obscures the analyst's vision. Bion elaborates the need for the analyst to regress, in the analytic session, to a state where he is almost unconscious: 'The nearer the analyst comes to achieving suppression of desire, memory, and understanding, the more likely he is to slip into a near sleep, akin to stupor. Though different, the difference is hard to define' (Bion 1970: 47). I understand this as a state where, in order to be more directly available in the present, the analyst attempts to relinquish all that is consciously known about the analysand. He/she is then more open to receive communications from the unconscious in the present. This availability of the analyst is a temporary surrender of the external world, a relinquishing of consciousness. Bion warns that the danger of this state is that it may take the analyst to the edge of his own psychosis.

Although their theoretical approaches are very different there appears to be some similarity between Bion and Lacan in this regard. I understand them both to be attempting to articulate the gap – the space between conscious and unconscious – and between patient and therapist. This seems to lead to the borderline area – the very edge of psychotic experience. Bion writes that patient and analyst are separated by a gap – the gap between container and contained. He questions whether the distance between analyst and analysand, the difference between their different perspectives, can be measured. The gap is between their perception of the analytic situation as well, perhaps, as the analytic space (Bion 1970: 93). It seems he feels that in this gap is the focus of the work.

In this, and the next chapter, I will be discussing this gap and linking it to the role of art objects in therapy. Art objects illuminate the space in between patient and therapist, for which there is no other symbolic articulation. The figure–ground relationship in pictures themselves sometimes reveals the area between the conscious figurations and the artist's own unconscious. In addition the picture illuminates the unconscious aspects of the relationship between patient and therapist. It is the complexities of the figure–ground relationship in psychoanalysis that I understand both Bion and Lacan, in their very different ways, to articulate. They are both rather like abstract painters attempting to convey their insights through unusual juxtapositions of diverse, and often apparently unconnected, elements or images. Both confront the limits of written language in their attempts to write of the ineffable.

At times working in this area – the spaces in-between – challenges the analyst's sanity and therefore the analyst must be familiar with the terrain. The analyst, as patient, must learn through her/his own exposure something of what the patient experiences. 'The training analysis has no other purpose than to bring the analyst to this point I designate in my algebra as the analyst's desire' (Lacan 1977a: 10). We have seen that when the desire of the patient enters the therapeutic encounter, analysis begins to come alive and change is possible; this is when affect is mobilised. This makes considerable demands on the therapist and we need to learn to use desires which arise in the consulting room rather than acting upon them. Similarly we learn to understand the affects of desires embodied in pictures.

Lacan writes that it is the analyst's desire that interested Freud and it is the analyst's desire which comes first. According to Lacan desire is the link between the unconscious and sexuality in the work of Freud (Rose 1982: 29–30). It is the gap between the need and the demand that constitutes the desire. Desire 'is a perpetual effect of symbolic articulation. It is not an appetite' (Sheridan 1977: viii). Evidently this is rather different from the more common understanding of desire. The movement towards an Other is, as I understand this, desire. So that to speak is desire and, if we follow this argument, so too, is to paint.

For Freud desire is motivated by a need to reinstate the lost object but Lacan avers this as impossible. It is the impossibility of ever retrieving the lost object which is at the heart of desire. The impossibility of 'oneness' is linked to 'need' and 'demand' but in a complex way. It is this search for the 'Other' that leads to symbolisation and language. It is therefore significant for understanding the role of the pictures in psychotherapy. When the patient in psychotherapy makes a picture, it is made for an audience – usually the therapist. Here the therapist is the Other and the movement – the desire – is embodied in the picture.

Like language art, too, 'presupposes the Other to whom it is addressed' (Sheridan 1977: viii). At times the picture itself may be experienced as that 'Other' and the therapist is then, less centrally, involved as witness. 'That which comes from the Other is treated . . . as a response to an appeal, a gift a token of love' (Sheridan 1977: viii). A picture 'feeds back' so that, although a picture cannot actually give anything, it may be experienced as doing so – something comes back from the picture. When we view our own picture it may be experienced as a response, but this response has, at some point, to be acknowledged as originating in the self. This is then a narcissistic form of experience but very often in a positive sense.

We have seen that Bion considers that the absence of memory and desire is a surrender of consciousness. The purpose of this is to be available and alert in the present but the effect is that it brings both patient and analyst close to their own psychosis. In Lacan the fragmented and undifferentiated state of psychosis is 'the Real'. The object we seek does not exist and yet we continue to seek it and so the Real is not the real object which is re-found, i.e. the breast, but rather the drive, the seeking. The real object of desire is rather confusingly 'not the Real but rather the Imaginary, in the Lacanian lexicon' (Ragland-Sullivan 1992: 375). The Real – characterised by the desire – is embodied in the gap between the creation of the object and the wish. The reason for this discussion here is that the Real brings us to the centre of the debate, to the role of desire in the analytic encounter. It brings us back to incest and its taboo.

In Chapter 4, in relation to the pictures where Carlos appeared to be totally absorbed by his mother (Figures 4.3 and 4.4), we saw that one reason for the incest taboo is because incest leads to psychosis. I quoted Ragland-Sullivan, who explains that the structure of the taboo of the 'Oedipal myth is a taboo against Oneness' (Ragland-Sullivan 1992). This is because:

> Sexual incest is possible, but psychic incest – where two identify as one – produces the structure of psychosis where the Real appears in the undifferentiation of an unborn subject. . . . The incest taboo against identificatory fusion with the mother is a structural taboo of the Real, a forbidding of what fails to create a proper name, a Symbolic identity, a social link.
>
> (Ragland-Sullivan 1992)

The act in itself is not impossible; what is impossible is the return to the fused state. Psychologically the desire for this state and the yearning for a return is symbolic. If it is misunderstood as real, then it may lead to madness. In practice this is often the case and, in part, may account for the fear of incest. We saw that a fear of engulfment was often the foundation of the resistance to their therapy in men working with a female therapist. This engulfment could be understood to be the loss of the self through the loss of the Symbolic. An undifferentiated state is just that. There is no name for it, no symbolic representation and so no separation. For Lacan it is the name of the 'father' which admits the Symbolic and enables separation. For Lacan, without language, there is the desire – the gap – but no separation.

The point of this discussion here is to develop an understanding of the seduction by the image to which I referred in the beginning of this chapter. When we succumb to the surface attraction of a picture we are lured initially into a relationship. Later this relationship may connect in a deeper sense with the gaze. Lacan writes of laying down the gaze in relation to looking at pictures (Lacan 1977a: 103) (this will be discussed in Chapter 9). I think about this as a similar process to that elaborated by Bion in relation to the absence of memory and desire. To surrender to the experience of viewing a picture is to temporarily abandon consciousness. To be available to pictures, as to persons, in analysis requires a similar attitude. To be uncontaminated by memories of the past, or desires which lead to anticipation of the future, means relinquishing the hope of gratification or reparation. When viewing pictures within the context of psychotherapy, we view person and picture together. We 'lay down the gaze' (Lacan 1977a: 101), make ourselves available and attempt to be alert in the present.

In analytical art psychotherapy the pictures are the central focus of the treatment. In other forms of psychotherapy and analysis there may be times when the picture takes a central role. The aesthetic countertransference is not merely the appreciation of pictures it is the appreciation of the artist, in part through the pictures. Thus, in therapy, where pictures are the medium, the analyst's desire is influenced by the gaze which is engendered through the picture.

THE AESTHETIC COUNTERTRANSFERENCE

Desire in art and desire in psychoanalysis converge when, in the context of therapy, the patient engages in the art process. There are similar affects whether pictures are made in the session, with the therapist present, or at home and brought to the session. In both of these instances it is likely that the artist will have, at the least, a pre-conscious awareness of the therapist as a future viewer of the work.

It could be argued that it is in the nature of art that the desire of the artist is, consciously or unconsciously, embodied in the pictures she or he creates. Wollheim (1987), who has written widely about art and psycho-analysis, discusses the embodiment of desire in art when writing about the artist Ingres. He proposes that repetition of themes in the work of this artist is conditioned by an unconscious need to reorder his world, 'as a way of bringing about something in the world; of getting something done, or altered; of rearranging the environment somewhat' (Wollheim 1987: 271). This secondary meaning of the picture is unconsciously evoked by something desired by the artist. It is a form of search; a need to reinstate something lost. This is the 'centrifugal retracing' (Lacan 1977a: 62) which I will discuss in the next chapter in relation to clinical examples. Wollheim writes that such a

> painting acquires the status of a wish: the wish being best thought of as a thought, a thought which is about a desired object . . . under the shadow of the wish, massive condensation, massive displacement, massive associative thinking, obscure, indeed destabilize the object of desire.

> (Wollheim 1987: 271)

A picture, which is a product of such a process, comes to embody the artist's desire and thus it could be understood to be an object of transfer-ence. I will argue that the viewer's response to such a picture is a form of countertransference. Furthermore, the spectator/therapist and the artist/patient are both viewers and so both subject to a countertransference to the picture. This is the aesthetic transference and countertransference.

Countertransference was originally understood to be a problem in ana-lysis caused by under-analysed elements of the analyst which impeded the work. The solution to this was further analysis of the analyst. It was subsequently understood to be helpful in understanding the communications from the patient's unconscious to that of the analyst (Heimann 1950). Currently it is understood to be a response, evoked in the analyst by the patient, and furthermore it may extend to include the analyst's response to the whole of the therapeutic environment (Little 1950; Racker 1968; Fordham 1978).

Additional complexity is introduced when pictures are produced in therapy; the countertransference, which includes the therapist's response to the whole of the therapeutic environment, involves the affects of the artworks. In the analytic encounter, the therapist engages in the feeling tone of the session but also observes her own responses. In this way she uses the countertransference to better understand the patient. The pictures add to this; they, too, contribute to an understanding of the unconscious aspects of the relationship.

When we view pictures, whatever the setting, our impressions could be understood to involve a countertransference to the image. This has been discussed by Kuhns (1983) and Spitz (1985) in relation to pictures viewed in art galleries and, elsewhere, I have developed this to include pictures viewed in the therapeutic context (Schaverien 1991). In viewing art in galleries the spectator engages with what is offered by the artist but, at the same time, stands apart from it in order to permit the affects of the picture to permeate consciousness. In viewing pictures in therapy the therapist/spectator goes one step beyond this. She engages with the picture, stands apart from it, but she does so in order to understand it as a conscious or unconscious communication from the patient. There is an awareness of the patient and the history of the therapeutic relationship to consider at the same time as the picture. For the therapist the countertransference is the aesthetic appreciation of the picture within the frame of the therapeutic relationship and moreover, in the presence of the artist.

In addition to the foregoing I am proposing that the artist/patient responds to her or his own picture and this, too, might be understood as a countertransference. If we regard the complexity of the relationship of the artist to her or his work, we see that there are different stages in the creative process. For there to be a countertransference there has first to be a transference. I have argued that, in the making, some pictures come to embody a transference. This is the scapegoat transference. Subsequently the artist stands back and views the completed work. Now the image feeds back and the response to this feedback may include a countertransference. There is some new understanding gained from the artist's viewing of the picture. The aesthetic countertransference of the patient, then, is an appreciation of the completed picture which, in the case of therapy, takes place within the frame of the therapeutic relationship.

There are two strands to the aesthetic countertransference – that of the therapist as spectator and that of the artist/patient. It is my aim to attempt to distinguish the various elements which contribute to the response to pictures in therapy. Aesthetic appreciation is inevitably an aspect of regarding a picture. The aesthetic countertransference, both that of the therapist and that of the patient, follows the initial embodiment of transference in the artwork.

THE AESTHETIC COUNTERTRANSFERENCE – THE FRAME

In discussing the aesthetic affects of pictures in analytical art psychotherapy I am not only addressing art therapists who work in institutions nor am I exclusively addressing art therapists. Many psychotherapists of my acquaintance find themselves in a position where they are looking at pictures made by their patients. Pictures brought to sessions, whatever the form of psychotherapy, have similar effects. Thus the psychotherapist whose patient arrives one day with a picture or even, as sometimes happens, a bag full of pictures, is faced with similar issues. Often pictures are made at home during the course of therapy. Psychotherapists also have patients who wish to paint or draw during their sessions and, if the therapist does not provide art materials, then the patient may sometimes bring her or his own. We need to be able to understand our countertransference responses to all aspects of the therapeutic relationship. Therefore I hope that these considerations may be of interest to psychotherapists as well as to art therapists.

The therapeutic relationship in analytical art psychotherapy has often been described as triangular. The three points of the triangle in the clinical setting are made up of patient–picture–therapist. Although this is often stated by art therapists, as far as I know the meaning of it has never been the subject of a detailed investigation. This will be the subject of this chapter and Chapters 8 and 9. I will argue that the points of such a triangle are linked by the gaze and furthermore, there are a number of inextricably linked gazes within this triangle. Figure 6.1 may help visualise this. These

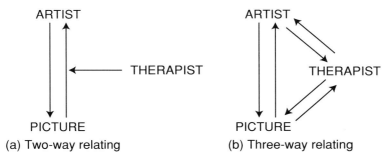

Figure 6.1 The therapeutic relationship in analytical art psychotherapy

indicate different forms of relating and are connected to the state of the patient and her or his ability to meet the therapist as person. In the early stages the relationship can be understood as two-way: artist to picture and the return of picture to artist. Here the therapist is witness. Later it is triangular: artist to picture to therapist and back again from picture to artist to therapist. Here the therapist is centrally involved in the transference.

I am addressing both art therapists and psychotherapists and so some attention to the way that I work and the place in which I practise is relevant. In Chapters 3 and 4, I discussed a case of analytical art psychotherapy within a psychiatric hospital. In Chapter 2, I discussed three cases from my current analytical psychotherapy practice. Thus, I am discussing issues related to both art therapy in its traditional settings – analytical art psychotherapy in private practice, as well as analytical psychotherapy. This might seem complex and, in order to avoid confusion, I will describe my current working situation. The approach depends on the referral and the wishes of the patient. The art materials are in the room but are not used by all patients.

My consulting room/studio is arranged with two chairs which face each other but at a slight angle. I sit in one of these. Against one wall is the couch and against another is a table with art materials. This means that the patient has a choice of how to use the room. The two chairs enable patient and therapist to look at each other and to look away. They may focus on the other person or the inner world. A different experience is evoked by the couch. When the patient lies on the couch the therapist sits to one side, slightly behind, and so out of the line of vision. Here the patient's gaze may turn inwards, untrammelled by the visual reminder of the presence of the therapist.

There is a table with paints and drawing materials which are arranged so that patients may draw or paint with their back to the therapist or else sitting in the chair. The patient may sit alone, and paint or draw. The therapist may watch the process of the creation of the image or she may look away; in either case her presence is a factor but this phase is, initially, a meeting between the artist and the picture. This is a form of two-way relating. When the picture is finished, the patient may return to the chair facing the therapist and show her picture. At this stage a three-way interaction becomes activated. Thus the triangle patient–picture–therapist may become animated.

Through its imagery and/or its aesthetic quality a picture may embody or evoke desire in patient or therapist or both. Alternatively it may repulse or disturb in some way; it may be attractive, repulsive, fascinating or merely mildly interesting. It may reveal the unconscious or unstated aspect of the therapeutic relationship. Thus, it may deepen the patient's relationship to herself and it may also deepen the transference and countertransference.

This – the aesthetic affects of the picture – within the bounds of this privileged relationship is the 'aesthetic countertransference'.

AESTHETIC JUDGEMENTS

The life *of* the picture (Schaverien 1991: 117) is the stage following the creative act. It is when the picture is complete or else when the artist has finished making it. At this stage it is viewed by artist/patient and spectator/therapist.

Art mediates in the area between subjective and objective experience. It mediates between the artist and him/herself; 'the "I" comes to grips with the world' through the objects it makes (Cassirer 1955b: 204). Thus, individual consciousness is mediated. Subsequently art mediates between artist and spectator. In psychotherapy the pictures mediate in the area between the private experience of the artist/patient and the semi-public world of the shared viewing with the observer/therapist. There is an interplay between inner and outer experience. However, I shall argue in the following chapters, that art is neither merely a means of self-expression, nor is it merely a mirror of the inner world, although both of these could be regarded as facets of it. The need for art is fundamental and, like other symbolic forms such as myth and language, art perfoms a formative function for the individual and for society. Through the artefacts that we make we come to know ourselves and consciousness develops (Cassirer 1955a, b: 93). Thus art offers an empowered form of relating with self and other through the mediation of a substantial object.

With art in psychotherapy, there is a constant interplay between subjective experience and objective appraisal. As in any analytic setting the therapist is available to identify with, and experience whatever occurs within the setting, but needs to be able to draw back from too close an identification with the client. The therapist views pictures and person together. In the subjective viewing of pictures there is reference to private experience. Whereas, in the case of objective judgements it is social criteria which must be acknowledged, in therapy there is constant interplay between these two. There is movement between subjective and objective, and private and public, experience.

Kant (1928) develops a distinction between subjective and objective judgements and between the agreeable and the beautiful. Such a distinction may contribute to our discussion of desire. The agreeable is a subjective judgement but the beautiful is universally acclaimed:

It would be . . . ridiculous if anyone . . . were to think of justifying himself by saying: This object . . . is beautiful for me. For it merely pleases him, he must not call it beautiful. [This is merely a subjective judgement] Many things for him may possess charm and agreeableness

– no one cares about that; but when he puts a thing on a pedestal and calls it beautiful, he demands the same delight from others. He judges not merely for himself, but for all men, and then speaks of beauty as if it were a property of things. [an objective judgement]

(Kant 1928: 52) [my brackets]

This difference is exemplified by two picture postcards which are on the wall of my room as I write. The first is a picture which I like; it touches me but it is not 'art' in the public sense. It is a picture of a cottage drawn on silver paper with a rainbow overhead and flowers in a garden surrounding it. It is not a painting but an illustration made as a postcard. It is an idealised image of a dream cottage. If I show it to my friends, it does not touch them in the same way. I cannot explain my delight in this image but it is certainly agreeable to me and constitutes a subjective judgement – it gives me pleasure. It resonates with some aspect of my inner world. Despite the lack of aesthetic depth, it has allure for me.

The second picture is a painting by Auguste Macke. It is called *Red House in the Park* and it is a reproduction of an oil painting. It is, for me, similar to the other picture in that it touches a similar part of myself. However, this is a painting, one of an artist with accepted status in the world of art, but this is not all that separates it from the other picture. The first picture, the illustration, is unambiguous. The Macke painting shows a red house deep in a wood but here there is something that is unclear, implied, not stated. It appeals to the imagination and evokes a sense of mystery. The sky is dark, and the trees have light and shade, which suggest to me that there is more here than might at first appear. This picture is universally known to be a 'good' painting whereas the other is merely an image that I like. But this is not the factor which distinguishes art from illustration. The difference is in the depth of the image and the struggle that is evident in the latter picture. This is not a glossy picture-book image of an ideal cottage, it is a house which is hidden, a centre which has secrets. The first picture I like, and admit it is purely a subjective judgement. The second has a wider appeal. The common element for me is that both resonate with some unspecified and, probably unrealisable, desire. Both have allure but the second picture engages the gaze and rewards a deeper investment in it. (This distinction between the al'Lure' of the picture and the gaze will be elaborated in Chapters 8 and 9.)

A difference between these two is in their ability to affect the viewer. I began this chapter referring to pictures of 'chocolate-box' normality. The first picture I describe, the rainbow cottage, is like the chocolate-box image; it does not disturb, it changes nothing, it causes no ripples. Conversely, the second picture is raw and mysterious, some unanswered question remains in mind for the viewer. Everything is not spelled out and something could happen or change as a result of viewing or making this picture. Its effects have a continued resonance even after viewing it.

Very often the art objects made by the client in therapy do not please in any general sense. They are rarely acceptable in the wider context of art. However, within the shared context of the therapeutic relationship, they may be pleasing in one way or another. They are not beautiful in Kant's terms (Kant 1928: 60), but they are affecting and perhaps also gratifying. They may please one or both of the viewers involved and may resonate with the inter-personal relationship. Moreover, this response to the object may affect the therapeutic relationship and influence the transference and the countertransference. If such a picture is taken out of the therapeutic context, it loses its power. This is because it does not have general appeal. It belongs in the context in which it was created.

It is likely that certain pictures, viewed within the context of a psychotherapy session, might touch me in similar ways to the two pictures described above. I might recognise my own transference to the image and, as with other predilections when they are evoked in therapy, we question our response. Like other countertransferences, we must own our personal preferences and even transferences to certain images. In addition we might ask ourselves – why this image at this time? In this way we use the countertransference to analyse the transference effects of images within the context of the therapeutic relationship. The aesthetic countertransference will engage the analytical art psychotherapist just as fundamentally and intensely as any other form of countertransference. The fact that such a transference or countertransference is affected by the gaze of the viewer does not lessen its impact. As we saw with Carlos's pictures in Chapter 4, there are times when viewing the inner-world image in a picture, rather than merely experiencing its affects, increases its impact.

Pictures made and viewed within the limited culture of the therapy setting may be valued as a poignant depiction of the state of the patient. They may reflect the transference. Thus, they may touch the viewer(s) in a profound manner. This is not a criterion which has any definite status as art outside of the therapeutic context. However, within the limits of the therapy, such pictures may be considered agreeable, disagreeable or even occasionally beautiful. It is the case that therapeutic pair or group elevate the pictures to a status beyond any objective judgement of their aesthetic value. This viewpoint is sometimes coloured by desire. If the picture is an embodiment of desire, it will influence the viewer and, I am proposing, that this is one of the elements of the seduction of the therapist through the picture.

If charm or emotion share in judgement, if it is coloured by desire, then judgement is tainted, i.e. it is not pure, not objective. This is where the art in psychotherapy is different from art created for the public arena. Art which is produced and viewed within a therapeutic relationship is presented within an affect-laden context. Thus, it is likely that emotion and even, perhaps, charm may colour the viewer's experience. That is the intention. In therapy, attention to the affect of any interaction is of prime significance. There is often an emotional response whether it is delight or horror or something in between. Thus, emotion is likely to influence any consideration of the artwork. The question arises then of how to separate these different elements of the appreciation of picture and of person. This is the purpose of this investigation.

IMAGINATION AND DESIRE

Aesthetic pleasure is not merely evoked through art. It may be a response to nature. It is, in part, an effect of imagination:

> The astonishment amounting almost to terror, the awe and thrill of devout feeling, that takes hold of one when gazing upon the prospect of mountains ascending to heaven, deep ravines and torrents raging there, deep-shadowed solitudes that invite to brooding melancholy, and the like – all this, when we are assured of our own safety, *is not actual fear*. Rather it is an attempt to gain access to it through imagination . . . . For the imagination, in accordance with laws of association, makes our state of contentment dependent upon physical conditions.
>
> (Kant 1928: 120–1)

Although this is an evocation of the power of nature it could also be a description of the power of the inner world. These words simultaneously evoke the real world, the world of nature, and also the imaginal realm. Furthermore, this passage resonates with the type of imagery which at times emerges in dreams, fantasies and pictures in therapy. There are occasions in all these when we are confronted by such immensity. Viewing the feared areas of the psyche could, at times, be described in similar words. In it too, we may confront awesome images, as we have seen in Chapter 4. When viewing pictures which reveal disturbed states associated with, for example, psychotic areas of the personality, the fragmented elements sometimes depicted can induce terror or awe. At times this may be unambiguously terrifying for patient and therapist. At others it might be similar to the paradoxical pleasure sometimes gained from being indoors during a storm. When the imaginal world is unveiled in a picture, we may view an awe-inspiring state, maybe of loneliness, violence or horror, and yet maintain a base in the more solid material world. If we are drawn too much into the imaginal, however, we may be in danger of being overwhelmed by its magnitude.

Using the countertransference the therapist enters into the inner-world experience of the client, and yet observes it and, in doing so, she uses her imagination. She travels with the client into her story, or picture, using her own subjective state and ability to empathise. Yet she maintains an ability to move to a more objective stance. Gradually this enables the client to do the same, to view the state depicted and simultaneously maintain a foothold in the world (as we saw with Carlos).

Desire is a form of yearning and, when it is unconscious, there is merely an identification but no gap for the imaginal. The aim in therapy is to open up this area to reveal the gap, the loss. This enables the experience of grieving to take place so that a separation may begin. If there is some psychological movement, some form of symbolisation, then the object of desire may be linked to imagination. When an art object evokes desire, or seduces the viewer, this may be an effect of imagination. 'The delight which we connect with the representation of an object is called interest. Such a delight always involves a reference to the faculty of desire' (Kant 1928: 42). There is a movement towards the object which appears to offer realisation of some unspecified desired state. The object may be a person, a painting or it may be a disembodied longing. The viewer is motivated by some imagined pleasure. If someone wants to arouse our emotions 'he must get us to concentrate upon a single image, and must try to prevent us from passing rapidly from one image to another' (Warnock 1980: 38).

We saw at the beginning of this chapter that desire is linked to such a concentration upon one image, whether that relates to a person, a picture or something else. We saw that desires as well as memories may be regarded as possessions although very often they possess us (Bion 1970). The point is that imagination is a bridge between self and other. This has been discussed in varying ways by Warnock (1980), Plaut (1966) and Wetherell (1988). Imagination bridges the gaps in therapy. These gaps are interpersonal and also intrapersonal. They are the gaps in understanding, between container and contained (Bion 1970) and between conscious and unconscious (Lacan 1977a). It is in these gaps that pictures play their part. They reveal that which was previously unconscious and present it in a visible form. This will be developed in the next chapter through discussion of the 'gap' in relation to the spaces in-between in pictures, and the appearance of the image of a child.

Chapter 7

Desire, the spaces in-between and the image of a child[1]

> What does seeing the figure now this way now that consist in? – Do I actually see something different each time; or do I only interpret what I see in a different way?
>
> (Wittgenstein 1980: 2)

In the last chapter I discussed seduction through the pictorial image and the ways in which desire could be understood to emerge in the gap. This gap we saw was that between container and contained for Bion (1970), for Lacan (1977a) the gap between desire and its object and, for both of them, that between conscious and unconscious. In this chapter this will be further explored in relation to pictures. When painting a picture the object which is painted, say, for example, a vase of flowers, will be set against the shapes surrounding it. This is the space in-between the object – in the foreground – and its setting – the background.

Figure/ground relationships have a resonance with the therapeutic relationship in several ways. In a psychotherapeutic relationship we might consider the figure to be the conscious level. For example, the conscious reality of the therapist and patient sitting together in a room might be considered the figure; here the ground would be the gap. The spaces in-between would be the silence of the unconscious communications. Sometimes this reverses when the unconscious dominates and becomes the figure. The real relationship then recedes into the background and thus the priority has temporarily changed. In psychotherapy there is a constant interplay between these two, conscious and unconscious, communications.

When art is central in a psychotherapeutic relationship there is an additional factor. Here the figure/ground will also resonate between therapist and patient, between conscious and unconscious, but the unconscious may be revealed and so become conscious through the mediation of the art object. That which fills the silence may be revealed in the imagery. Thus the artist's unconscious becomes visible and so potentially conscious. The artist's two-way relationship to the picture, described in the last chapter, means that first this is an interaction between the artist and him/herself. It is likely that this will extend to three-way relating where the interplay between conscious and unconscious includes the effects of the picture. The picture reveals what remains unsaid or even unsayable in the therapeutic interaction.

The psychoanalytic transference is based on repetition. It is when regression takes place that feelings from the past become live in the present and change is possible. Traditionally the mobilisation of the transference is understood to occur through the reproduction of affect often, though not exclusively, from infantile stages of development. In this chapter I plan to demonstrate how this transference element may be echoed by, and resonate in, the pictorial images made by patients in analytical art psychotherapy.

THE IMAGE OF THE CHILD

Very often one of the first pictures made spontaneously in analytical art psychotherapy is of a foetus or a child. This often corresponds with some element of desire becoming embodied in the art object and it echoes the transference to the therapist as person. Regression may evoke the image of a child but this is not necessarily, nor exclusively, a return to infancy. The image may be understood less literally to reveal some underdeveloped aspect of the self rather than an actual child. I propose that such pictures reveal the desire of the patient and sometimes, as with Carlos, the lack-in-being. Moreover, the age, or developmental stage of the child image, seems to correspond to a significant moment in the development of the personality. MacGregor (1989) has pointed out that the child, in a sequence of pictures, appears to develop and grow in correspondence to the progress of the therapy.

Jung (1946, CW 16, paras 376–81: 182–5) suggests that the appearance of the child in therapy may mark the onset of the transference. He discusses the dreams of a patient. In the first dream there is a baby of about six months; the dreamer realises that a character in her dream has known this baby even before it was born. This child Jung considers to be a symbol of the self and he describes it as the 'child hero or the divine child'. He requests that the dreamer look back at her notebook to see what happened six months previously. She discovers that, six months earlier whilst she had been writing up a dream, she had a clear vision of a golden child lying at the foot of a tree. This Jung equates with the birth of the divine child. Through further reviewing her notes the dreamer finds out that nine months prior to this, she had painted a picture which Jung suggests is the likely moment of symbolic conception. He suggests that this image marks the onset of the transference.

The fact that it was painting which marked this 'onset of the transference' leads me to wonder if it was the act that made the difference. The act of painting could be seen as the move towards the Other, equated, in this case, with the sex act as the moment of symbolic conception. Art could then be understood in a similar way to Lacan's application of language, as a form of symbolic articulation. I will further discuss this link below.

Hillman (1975: 5) suggests that 'the abandoned child' which, frequently, first appears in dreams is one who has been known already at some level. He writes that although it is abandoned, we can 'still hear it, feel its call' (Hillman 1975: 13). It is clear that what I am suggesting is not new; it is a known factor that, in therapy, the child image returns bringing with it repressed or forgotten emotions, images and memories. My intention is, then, not merely to show that this happens, but rather to offer some thoughts on the ways in which pictures contribute to an understanding of this facet of the therapy.

This discussion brings together two apparently incompatible analytic views – those of Jung and Hillman, on the one hand, and Freud and Lacan on the other. The apparent incompatibility is that for Jung the central element to which we regress in therapy is the self. For Lacan, following Freud, it is the lack which is central. For both it is desire which leads out of the undifferentiated state but they discuss it in very different ways. Despite this apparent incompatibility, I find both useful in thinking about the clinical aspects of working with pictures in therapy.

I propose that it is at the nodal point between the conscious and unconscious, in the gap between the object and the desire, that the image of the child appears. Sheridan (1977) explains that, for Lacan, desire is not 'an appetite: it is essentially excentric and insatiable. That is why Lacan co-ordinates it not with the object that would seem to satisfy it, but with the object that causes it' (Sheridan 1977: viii). Very often the child image relates to the lost object; the desire is for the object which originally evoked the desire and is experienced as its cause – perhaps the mother. Conversely, it is the object which seems, in the transference, to offer satisfaction of the desire which re-awakens the image – possibly the therapist. Thus, the infantile, erotic and incestuous strivings, which 're-present' themselves in the transference, do so in the picture but they are evoked by the desire, demand and need for the therapist as person.

It is an abandoned element in the psyche which is unconsciously carried by the child image. Hillman considers that to view this merely as a transference regression is to do violence to the imaginal:

> The cue to the future is given by the repressed, the child and what he brings with him, and the way forward is indeed the way back. But it is difficult to discriminate among the emotions that come with the child mainly because he does not return alone.
> It is as if the little girl abandoned returns with a protector, a new found father, a strong male figure of muscular will, of arguments and cunning,

and his outrage, his blind striking out mingles with her pained tantrums, his sullen melancholy becomes indistinguishable from her withdrawn pouting. Though they coalesce child and guardian also struggle for separation.

(Hillman 1975: 22)

This graphic description of that which is often, so problematically in Jung, called the animus makes its potential clear. Further, Hillman distinguishes the boy child from the girl in equally vivid terms:

In the little boy a similar pattern occurs for it is equally difficult to distinguish him from the milkmaids and nymphs and sisters who have succoured him during the repression. The softness and vanity and demands which he brings with him, passivity and vulnerability, the reclusive nursing of himself, hardly differ from what psychology has called anima states.

(Hillman 1975: 22)

The female therapist may find herself idealised in the transference with a male patient, and so drawn into identification as one of these milkmaids or nymphs. If she can detach herself from this identification and, by her stance and/or interpretations separate from it, then the male patient may be able to begin to separate from the image and so find his male power.

This was rather the way that Carlos presented himself initially: gentle, passive and amenable. It was when he became conscious of his negative feelings that he was able to contact his 'true self'. Hillman writes that the return of the child brings with it access to memory and the imaginal. It is when the child returns that there is access to the unconscious. The child image needs to be freed from its identification with actual childhood: 'our cult of childhood is a sentimental disguise for the homage to the imaginal' (Hillman 1975: 22). This is potentially liberating. His poetic evocation of the multiple possibilities, of the child image, frees us from the application of fixed frames of reference, from continually seeing communications from the adult client exclusively in terms of infantile impulses. Following this, maternal and erotic responses in the countertransference may potentially be viewed in a less rigid manner.

The emergence of the child image could be understood to be one form of the embodiment of desire in the transference. But this is not all. The play between conscious and unconscious, between the imaginal and the real, or between the child and the adult may take place in the creation of the picture. 'Desire is a perpetual effect of symbolic articulation' (Sheridan 1977: viii). For Lacan this symbolic articulation is language. I am suggesting that art, too, is a form of symbolic articulation and therefore pictures may well be embodiments of the desire of the artist. The picture reveals otherwise unseen imagery which emerges in the space in-between the two in therapy; it may characterise the only possible movement towards the Other at the time. This may subsequently lead to the valuing of the picture as a talisman as a carrier of desire.

It is within the context of a 'good enough' therapeutic alliance that the child is revealed. This is when movement begins and a transference to the therapist emerges. It may be that such an embryonic transference first appears in the picture and only later is echoed within the therapeutic relationship. However, it may be the other way round. The transference to the therapist may evoke the regression which is revealed in the picture. The readiness of the client for transformation may not be a conscious decision; it may merely be that a level of resistance is relinquished through the picture. The child will appear spontaneously if the process is not interfered with by artificially imposed interventions such as inviting the client to make a picture of a child. When the time is right, when the feeling tone of the relationship permits, this occurs spontaneously and there is no need for invasive therapeutic techniques.

The regression, and so the child image, introduces the incest motif with all the conflicted feelings of attraction and repulsion that accompany it. This includes the incest desire and the dread that the desire will be realised. This holds a fascination because it is archetypal, it is an experience where the collective psyche meets with the personal. We have seen in Chapter 2 that these evoke the original parental imagos and that there may be an added intensity when this emerges in the opposite gender pairing.

PICTORIAL AND MENTAL IMAGES

The image in analytical art psychotherapy can be produced without recourse to words and before the artist is conscious of what she or he is revealing. If the appearance of the child is an unconscious regression, it may be a result of the medium. The pictorial image offers a means of by-passing language and so conceptualisation. Thus, the visual medium may sometimes depict the source of the problem and reveal it much more quickly than other forms of psychotherapy.

The meaning of a picture is embodied in it. Pictorial images are often likened to mental images, but they differ from them in practice and effect. A mental image is occasionally a pictorial image. More often it is an unspecific feeling or a formless intuition. Dreams, memories and, in psychotherapy, the constellation of the transference, evoke visual meta-phors which might be considered mental images. A pictorial image is different from these. It is visible and tangible; it can be seen and experi-enced as an object. In the process of picture making, the mental image is transformed into a visible pictorial one. This echoes, but does not repro-duce, the original intuition. The unspecific mental image is pictured and so given form.

Thus, in the cases where the image reveals the child in its state of abandonment, or frozen in the present by its past, the picture is not merely a portrait. It is not a replica of a mental image; it is a picture previously unseen. The picture reveals to the artist aspects of the inner world of which she/he was previously unconscious. This primary function of the image is followed by its secondary function, the making of links. These include observing the connections within an individual picture. Within a series of pictures links are made between this picture and others, and within the therapeutic relationship, these links may lead to interpretation of the transference to the therapist.

The pictures which reveal the child, in the way I intend here, occur spontaneously. They are embodied images. These are different from the diagrammatic images which may also show a child. The difference is that the latter are usually consciously conceived and very often made as an illustration or to tell something to the therapist. Embodied images are different; they are spontaneous and, if a child image appears, it is because for some reason it needs to be there. For a more detailed discussion of the difference see Schaverien (1987b, 1991: 85–93).

This embodied image of a child has an immediate correspondence with unconscious desire. It may be added as an afterthought or suggested as the result of the picture-making process. It appears to grow out of the marks that are made and to suggest itself to the artist. In this way, although the thought to put the child in the picture may have been conscious, its full implications are unconscious. This is more likely to occur when there is minimal intervention from the therapist. If the therapist intervenes, by asking for pictures on specific themes, the client will make pictures as an aid to talking. It is common for a directive approach to evoke diagrammatic images. A non-directive approach is more likely to lead to images which embody unconscious desire and it is these which mobilise the psyche and affect some change in state.

Both Carlos and May, described earlier in the book, made pictures of a child. I have described how, when she felt that it was acceptable to express her real feelings, May made the tiny picture (Figure 5.2). This reveals a girl with her legs crossed and head bowed, enclosed within an egg. This we might see as a picture of her regressed child–self. I have described how, at this early stage in the work, it seemed to reveal the beginning of a therapeutic alliance, trust was only just emerging in the therapeutic relationship.

In Chapter 4 I showed the picture Figure 4.4, The bubble picture, which Carlos made spontaneously, within a few days of being admitted to hospital. As a self-image it is very disturbing and we saw how it dramatically revealed his state. We could see this atrophied foetus, skeleton as a very stuck form of regression. This was a dangerous state, depicting his wasted body and revealing its correspondence to the wasted inner world.

The second picture of Carlos's child is a little more hopeful; made nine months later, it is Plate 6, in Chapter 4. Here an embryo, in very early stages, is being attacked, penetrated and broken from the egg in which it is still contained and held. It is as if the embryonic child–self was here being rescued from its imprisoned state in Figure 4.4 by the external forces which attack the outer shell. This has already been discussed but here my point is a general one – it is to note that the child or foetus image is common early in therapy. Further, it is very often an unconscious progress report during the course of the therapy.

My third example refers back to an earlier work. I discussed the case of Harry in detail in *The Revealing Image* (Schaverien 1991). In colour plates I showed a picture which seemed to be about conception – Plate 1 in that book – and then another made a few days later which was Plate 2 (shown here as Figure 7.1). In Figure 7.1 an embryonic foetus was suspended in a tear-drop womb/heart. This was made spontaneously and within days of Harry engaging in analytical art psychotherapy. The point for discussion here is that this picture seemed to embody the desire of the artist. It

Figure 7.1 Harry – Foetus 1

Figure 7.2 Harry – Foetus 2

revealed his regressed state in a way that no words could substitute. Here already we see the incest constellating in the, as yet unconscious, desire for a return to the place where the problem is located. The picture which was Plate 12 in *The Revealing Image* was made two months and forty-six pictures later and is shown here as Figure 7.2. It again showed a foetus, but this time more developed and in rather more welcoming surroundings. It had developed facial features and hands and, although it was not ready to be born, there was a sense that the world may have become a more friendly place. This foetus also has the glow of the divine child about it; it was suspended in light above a chalice or communion cup.

By now there was an erotic element in the transference and the counter-transference between the male patient and female therapist. This probably reproduced the mother/son dyad. The point for discussion here is that the pictures influenced that transference and were also evoked by it. For the therapist the attraction to the need of the patient was compounded and intensified through his ability to express his desire in visual terms. Thus the imaginal world of the patient becomes the shared environment of the therapeutic relationship. The therapist is drawn into this and attracted to the person through his picture.

The common point in the pictures of May's child and Carlos's and Harry's foetuses is that they first appeared early in treatment. The artists were not asked to draw a child and each emerged spontaneously. Each seems to reveal a child–self image and to indicate the starting place of the therapy. In Carlos's and Harry's series there is a reappearance of the child or foetus image which seems to act as a progress report in the therapy. In each of these cases the image stated the problem and the stage of the child graphically. The picture revealed the patient's distress in a way which had no correspondence in words; none of these people could have stated the depth of feeling so eloquently in any other way. It could not be formulated because there was no conceptual equivalent to the image. At the time they were made, there was no more than an intuition of what they might mean for the artist. There was a clear recognition that they were important but neither patient nor therapist could formulate the nature of their import.

I suggest that these pictures invited deep interpretation but this would have been inappropriate at so early a stage. Pictures 'bare the phenomenon' (Schaverien 1991; Cassirer 1955b), they reveal deep levels of the psyche far more quickly than the client is prepared for; thus the client needs to catch up before she is amenable to interpretation of such material. The phase of familiarisation with the image is essential prior to verbal acknowledgement. Thus, I am suggesting that in psychotherapy, when art is a medium of expression, the spontaneous depiction of the inner child may indicate the client's readiness to engage in therapy. It is when the client can permit dependence, and so regression, that the deeper layers of disturbance can be revealed and worked with in the transference. A form of erotic transference may begin to emerge when the picture embodies the desire of the artist in this way.

I would like to make it clear that I am not suggesting that it is *necessary* for a *picture* of a child to occur in all cases; there are many successful therapies where no such thing happens. Moreover, if it does appear, it is not *always* in the early stages of therapy. My point is that this is one way in which the transference deepens and so the client's relation to her or his inner world also deepens. The apparent developmental stage of the pictured foetus or child may indicate that it was at this stage that the world first impinged in some way.

THE GAP OR THE SPACES IN-BETWEEN

The depiction of the child image may be a manifestation of desire. Such desire embodied in the picture may be an expression of the unconscious. Lacan puts it thus: 'it is in the very movement of speaking that the [patient] constitutes her desire' (Lacan 1977a: 12). We could perhaps extend this to include the movement of painting as also constituting desire. Lacan continues: 'It was through this door that Freud entered . . . what was . . . the relation of desire to language and discovered the unconscious' (Lacan 1977a: 12). Lacan suggests that the relation of desire to language was not fully elucidated by the notion of transference. Transference is based on the idea of repetition but he questions what it is that is repeated and proposes that it is 'the absence'. This absence is the gap between desire and its object. It is this which constitutes the unconscious. It is the source of the desire, the original movement towards the desired object.

As I understand it this could be the perceived – or actual – loss of the mother. The moment of separation, which may have been the negotiation of a normal phase of development, has a profound effect. Lacan indicates that the effect of this original absence is that the child does not immediately watch the door through which the mother has disappeared. This would indicate anticipation of her return – rather:

His vigilance was aroused earlier; at the very point she left him, at the point she moved away from him. The ever open gap introduced by the absence . . . remains the cause of a centrifugal retracing . . . the activity of the whole symbolises repetition.

(Lacan 1977a: 62)

This 'centrifugal retracing' is the unconscious desire and thus the origins of the transference. Lacan distinguishes this 'centrifugal retracing' from the demand for the mother to return, which would be manifest in a cry. Instead, this is the repetition of the moment of the mother's departure, the moment of separation. This absence, the gap, the foundation of the original desire, is truly unconscious. Perhaps because it is preverbal it has no voice, no name. Lacan nominates it negatively, defines it by its 'not' quality. For Lacan the repetition, which is the transference, is the repetition of this absence. The desire and the yearning are sustained in this gap which is unconscious.

I suggest that this is also the place to which the artist/patient may unconsciously be returning when the child image is depicted. The gap – the absence – might be understood in terms of a common phenomenon in art. When I was an art student painting the human figure or still life, the tutors used to emphasise the importance of observing the 'spaces in-between' the objects. In the depiction of an object, they would point out the relationship of the figure to ground, drawing attention to the 'spaces in-between'. They would emphasise that these are as much a part of the whole picture as the main area of interest. The spaces surrounding an object define its shape. One exercise for fine art students recognises this. The task is to paint the figure by painting only the shapes surrounding it, the shapes it makes in space. This sensitises the student to seeing the pattern of the whole and the interconnectedness of objects. Milner (1977) has described her personal discovery of this phenomenon. The awareness of the relationship between the object of focus and the gaps which surround it, is an essential element in creating a painting. It is the figure–ground relationship which informs the viewer and gives meaning to the whole. This is an acknowledged element in visual perception (Gombrich 1963).

Wittgenstein distinguishes between what he calls '"continuous seeing" of an aspect and the "dawning of an aspect"' (Wittgenstein 1958: 194). He shows a diagram which can first of all be seen as a duck's head and subsequently as that of a rabbit. The picture remains the same but something changes which permits us to see both at once – the difference is a perceptual one. First, we have 'continuous seeing', we see the picture as a duck only. When it has also been seen as a rabbit, the other aspect has dawned and then it is no longer possible to merely view the picture as a single thing – it constantly flips between the two.

Here I am using this is an illustration of the impact of the effects of interpretations in therapy. Something said may seem quite simple and straightforward until its unconscious significance is pointed out. At this point something is transformed and we see the other aspect as well. We could liken this to the visual dawning of an aspect. When pictures are involved in therapy there is a more obvious similarity to Wittgenstein's example. Here a picture which we have made consciously intending to show one thing is transformed by our perception into something else as well. This has the effect of an interpretation. I will give an example of this in the case illustration with which I will conclude this chapter.

The distinction between the diagrammatic and the embodied image is also relevant here because without awareness of the figure–ground relationship we have only a diagram. In such a picture there is a lack of relationship whereas in an embodied image figure and ground resonate. Put another way, and linking this argument to Lacan, we might see that the diagram takes no account of the 'gap', the negative aspect. It shows that which is already consciously known. It illustrates, it tells, but it reveals little. The embodied image, on the other hand, is one in which the figure and ground resonate and, through it, something additional comes to light. There is then the potential for change.

The gap, the negative of what is said in therapy, is of similar significance. The psychotherapist may hear what is being said but she also listens to the silence, to what is not said. She is tuned in to listen for that which is negatively present. Thus, we might understand that the psychotherapist listens to the spaces in-between in therapy. When Lacan (1977a) nominates the unconscious negatively I think he is discussing something similar to this. He evokes the area of the gap, the unconscious, that for which there are no words. In his discourse, which is often indirect or even obscure, we might understand him to be attempting to paint the shapes around the object. He refers to the unconscious by discussing the actions which surround it, the spaces in-between. Thus he nominates it by its 'not' quality. If it could be spoken of directly it would, by definition, not be unconscious.

Pictures in analytical art psychotherapy may reveal the content of that space in-between. They may reveal what is hidden in the silence. Pictures and art objects made in therapy may be seen as an embodiment of the negative. In this way they open up the spaces in-between. They reveal the content of the gap. They open up the reverse side of that which can be spoken. In this way they are a window on the unspoken and the unspeakable and reveal previously unconscious material. This area which Lacan calls the 'Real' is the area of the centrifugal retracing. It is the central element in the desire, the yearning for that which can never be named. In psychotherapy that which exists in the gap remains unnamed; in analytical art psychotherapy such an unnameable element is knowable because it can be seen, it appeals to the gaze. Sometimes in that space the image of a child appears.

CENTRIFUGAL RETRACING REVEALED IN THE PICTURE

I will now return to the 'centrifugal retracing' which Lacan indicates is a result of the moment at which the mother moved away. I will give an example of the way this may come to light, and be worked through, in a series of visual images. Once again I make the point that the implications of this analytical art psychotherapy case illustration are twofold. First, it reveals the way in which art in psychotherapy may work. Art offers a medium for bringing the unconscious to consciousness and so for transformation. However, it also illustrates the material that is regularly worked with in other forms of psychotherapy. The pictures are like illustrations. Thus, in addition to their transforming potential, they also reveal material which is commonly active in the psyche and present it in pictorial form.

The resistance in analysis produces a tension which both holds the key to, and opposes consciousness. This is a necessary dynamic force in therapy as in life itself. There is the paradox of the wish to become conscious and a fear of it. There is an attraction to the revelation of self-knowledge and, at the same time, a resistance to it. The avoidance of unpleasure in anticipation of the revival of previously experienced pain underlies the resistance. The fear of madness may also underlie such resistance. The centrifugal retracing is an enactment of this conflict – it embodies both the wish and the repression simultaneously. The centrifugal retracing is an enactment of this unconscious conflict.

For the patient it is the therapist who holds the tension of these feelings. She or he may be experienced as the polar opposite of the feeling which is admitted to consciousness. When pictures play a role in therapy they may be experienced as holding the tension of the opposition. As the 'Other' they may be the complement to the patient's conscious attitude. Thus a patient who is never violent may express violent fantasies in the pictures. Alternatively, the opposing forces may be held together in one picture. The tensions which are pictured may be raw and uncomfortable and they may correspond to feelings which are aroused in the transference. In embodied images resistance may be bypassed. Then painful, unconscious and feared areas, which are usually defended against, may be revealed quite unexpectedly. The desire may find pictorial form, and the centrifugal retracing may be seen in its raw and painful reality.

ELISABETH

The case illustration which follows is different from most of the others in the book in that it is of the female therapist–female client dyad. This is acknowledged but not discussed in any detail. The implications of the erotic transference and countertransference of the same gender pair requires a deeper analysis. It remains for a planned future work and is not the topic of this book nor this chapter.

The emergence of the child image early in therapy may be understood to indicate the source of the centrifugal retracing: the moment of the origin of the desire. The repetition for Elisabeth was vividly embodied in her pictures. The abandoned child appeared very early in our work together and, although we did not at the time realise it, stated the problem.

Elisabeth, in her early thirties, came into the art room in a state of anxiety and desperate to talk. She had been admitted to the psychiatric hospital as a result of anxiety and depression which had been precipitated by recent life events. The major crisis which had now passed was her husband's serious illness. It was only now, when he had recovered, that she was able to experience the desperation that this illness had evoked in her. She talked as if a dam was breaking, as if she had been holding inside the sorrows of the world which now flowed out in a torrent. This could be understood, with hindsight, as the attempt to resolve something; to find something lost. The repetition of the story, which is so common in therapy, may be just this attempt to nominate the unspecified desire, the initial trauma, the moment at which the mother moved away. 'In the very movement of speaking the [patient] constitutes her desire' (Lacan 1977a: 12).

The therapist listened to her, then moved away while she made a picture. The first picture (Figure 7.3), was a landscape, and when the therapist returned to Elisabeth, she showed the picture and talked some more. Then, just before the end of the session, she painted a tiny, black figure huddled under the trees on the left of the landscape. Then she reversed the picture

Figure 7.3 Elisabeth – Landscape

Figure 7.4 Elisabeth – Child

and, on the back of the paper, she painted the small figure (Figure 7.4). This one she described as being in a fog. In terms of the use of art as a medium, Elisabeth first made a landscape. This is formally an acceptable art form. It was only after talking to the therapist that she put the figure in the picture. Having done that, something suggested that she put the other figure on the back of the picture. This was the beginning of engaging with the art process. It reveals her developing understanding of the possibilities of the medium.

The next picture (Figure 7.5) she made in the following session, one week later. This was also a landscape but with two distinct groups of trees – three on one side of the picture and five on the other. A small black figure (she was actually a white woman) is crouched on the ground between the two groups of trees. The therapist asked her if the numbers three and five had any meaning for her. She paused, thought, and then realised that they did. The group of three, she realised, could be her current family consisting of herself, her husband and her child. The five could be her family of origin with her parents, herself and two siblings. The black figure crouched on the ground equi-distant between these two groups she realised depicted her current predicament. Her back was turned to the family of origin but she was not free. Unconsciously she had made a picture which revealed her

Figure 7.5 Elisabeth – Between the trees

situation. It uncovered something of which she had previously been unconscious and showed it to her.

Earlier in the chapter I discussed the duck–rabbit picture which was shown by Wittgenstein (1958: 194) to illustrate the 'dawning of an aspect'. I suggest that this is the operation which took place here. Once Elisabeth had realised that her tree picture was also a picture of her family, neither she nor the therapist could any more see only the trees. It was now a graphic embodiment and a manifestation of the previously unconscious root of her current problem. The picture was both a picture of trees and a picture of the family. In this way the dawning of an aspect operates as a visual interpretation, but one which can never again be denied because it has an actual, real, presence in the external world.

Elisabeth's fourth picture, Figure 7.6, was made the subsequent week in response to a group theme – to make a picture of her earliest memory. Here she pictured herself as a small black child alone with her mother when her older sibling had gone to school. She said she remembered feeling that her sleeping mother had left her; there was silence and emptiness all around her. Here is a picture of silence. This is how she described it and we can also see it. It is revealed in the spaces in-between the objects in the room. Furthermore, her urgent and rapid speaking filled all the therapeutic space between us and so left no room for silence in the present. In the transference repetition, in-between patient and therapist, the original fear of the

Figure 7.6 Elisabeth – Memory

silent space becomes apparent. The source of the silence, the unconscious or the negative of consciousness, is thus revealed in the picture.

Moreover, we could see this is a classic picture of the depressive position and later we came to understand that it was likely that her mother had been depressed at this time and, therefore, the feeling was, possibly, originally her mother's. It became clear over the subsequent weeks and months that this feeling had always been with her. It had resulted in an inability to live for fear of loss. The original loss, the moment when the mother moved away, is graphically captured here. For Elisabeth the centrifugal retracing and the origin of her repetition, her transference, was here in this picture for us both to see. The child was depicted in the first four pictures, this time finding its way back to the original gap.

Elisabeth was not making pictures of chocolate-box normality. In her pictures her pain was embodied. These embodied images revealed the 'lack', the gap which was both the source of her desire and the origin of the 'centrifugal retracing'. The problem was stated in visual terms and the child was revealed. As we have already seen in psychoanalysis, the problem and the direction of future therapeutic work is often stated, unconsciously, in the material brought to the first session. This is some-times a dream. It is similar in analytical art psychotherapy. The first image frequently states the problem, and formulates it pictorially. Elisabeth's first picture was such a picture and it was an embodied image.

Viewed with the knowledge of hindsight we can see that (Figure 7.3) depicts a division between good and bad. This is indicated by the use of green and black. The hills in the front are painted green, whilst those in the background are painted black and grey and the figure under the trees is painted black. Throughout our work together Elisabeth used green to represent health and good things and black to represent the bad. This division, which was an echo of an inner-world split, was such that it affected her life and held her in a depression. In terms of Kleinian theory it is the division between the good and bad breast. The child embodies the depression which is still affective in the present. We might also view the landscape as the maternal body. The child is then seen held, depressed within not this time a womb, but a 'bodyscape'. This could be linked to a desire but also fear of being merged with the body of the therapist/mother. Thus again the transference is both revealed and embodied in the picture.

A further insight occurred much later in therapy. In Figure 7.4 the grey and black figure on the back of the picture meant very little to either Elisabeth or myself, at the time. It was clearly a child and not a baby, in this grey which she described as fog. Many months later, she made another picture of fog after being alone in her house one foggy day. It had made her feel lost and the next day she made this picture (Figure 7.7).

At the time this, too, meant little more than the conscious level which she described. However, some months later as we looked back at the pictures, it emerged that when she was 10 years old her beloved grandfather had died suddenly one foggy night. This had been a time of great trauma for her which had been forgotten, partly because she had been unable to grieve. The recovery of this memory was centrally important in understanding the intensity of the fear she had experienced associated with her husband's recent illness. It had reawakened the still repressed memory of that early tragic loss. This was linked to her earlier feeling of loss of her mother who left her through her own depression and fatigue. Again the picture is an early form of interpretation not always, at first, understood. It is only when the continuous seeing, which could be understood to be the conscious aspect, gives way and permits the alternative aspect to 'dawn' that consciousness is transformed. Thus the 'dawning of an aspect' is when previously unconscious material is admitted to consciousness.

These four pictures of Elisabeth's child are, I suggest, examples of the centrifugal retracing, the inevitable and constant returning to the point at which the mother moved away. This is the repetition, the gap, the absence. The black depressed child and the one in the fog were Elisabeth's transference repetition. They revealed the place to which she constantly returned in her unconscious search for that which was lost – the moment of the loss. As we worked together it became clear that her depression,

Figure 7.7 Elisabeth – Fog

although precipitated in the present by current life events, had always been with her. Her desire was exemplified and embodied in these first images. It was these images, rather than all the words that she spoke, that revealed the true nature of her distress to Elizabeth. The pictures stated the problem more eloquently than the artist could have done in any other way. This was because what was revealed was unconscious at the time the image was made. Unconsciously the gap was known, but it was the pictures which enabled it to become conscious. It was rather as if the pictures in-between Elisabeth and the therapist peeled back the layers of repression.

Elisabeth's first picture was an embodied image, the 'life in this picture' (Schaverien 1991) revealed her desire. In correspondence to this the therapist was interested and, as we saw in the last chapter, interest is a form of desire. The desire of the patient may have evoked a corresponding desire in the therapist as viewer of the picture and partner in the patient's quest. It may have aroused all kinds of desires in the therapist at an unconscious level – her need to be a therapist; her need to offer good mothering to the abandoned child of the patient. In Bion's terms these are all motivations which must be relinquished in the therapeutic work. However, before they can be relinquished they must become conscious.

The emergence of these images was probably an echo of the transference which was already beginning in this first session. The landscape was painted after Elisabeth had told her story to the therapist. Furthermore, it was after the landscape had been seen and accepted by the therapist that the abandoned child was added to the picture. These interactions might be understood as the beginning of the intensification of the therapeutic relationship

The essence of the transference in any form of analytical psychotherapy is desire. At times this may be characterised by hate or fear or other less acceptable emotions as well as by love need, etc. The patient, in her desire, is attached to the therapist. That 'Other', which is an aspect of her own psyche, is temporarily embodied in the therapist. I have suggested that it is sometimes also embodied in the picture. The effect of transference desire is to fix, and to temporarily hold the two in thrall, to fascinate. In the transference the therapist's ability to move in and out of this state eventually makes it less powerful. Whether such investment is made in the therapist or in the pictures, or as in this case both, it allows deeper layers of the psyche to find outer expression.

The appearance of the abandoned child is no solution. It is merely the beginning. The undernourished child we meet, pictured by adult clients, has remained frozen since its abandonment at one year, at two or at ten. Once pictured it can be recognised and its needs acknowledged, though not necessarily fulfilled. We have seen that sometimes this child image develops and grows within a series of pictures. This sequence is an unconscious process which is often surprisingly logical and corresponds to some development in the personality which is revealed in the images.

The aesthetic element in the pictures plays a part in the transference and countertransference manifestations and this is the topic of the last two chapters of the book. It will be discussed in relation to the lure of the image and the gaze.

Chapter 8

The lure and reflections

As some peoples believe a man's soul to be in his shadow so other peoples believe it to be in his reflection in water or a mirror.

(Frazer 1911: 92)

Pictures in analytical art psychotherapy are sometimes considered to be reflections of the inner world. Moreover it is suggested that they are mirrors. This is not strictly accurate. There are similarities between reflections in mirrors and pictures but they are also very different. Pictures are, in fact, neither mirror images of the outer world nor reflections of the inner world, rather they are themselves formative.

Cognition, language, myth and art none of them is a mere mirror simply reflecting images of inward or outward data; they are not indifferent media, but rather the true sources of light, the prerequisite of vision, and the well-springs of all formation.

(Cassirer 1955a: 93)

In this and the following chapter I will discuss two different ways in which pictures may embody desire in analytical forms of art psychotherapy. In this chapter the focus is a form of two-way engagement between the artist and picture, which is usually the first stage. However, the transforming potential of art takes place within a context and, in therapy, this context is the transference and countertransference relationship. It is the nature of the relationship, as well as the affects of the imagery, which leads us to consider two distinct ways in which pictures function in the analytic encounter. In Chapter 6 I discussed how the triangle of artist–picture–therapist may be an equally balanced three-way form of relating. The picture is central but so is the engagement with the therapist. This three-way engagement will be the topic of the next chapter. In Chapter 6 I differentiated this three-way engagement from the rather different balance in the triangle of the two-way form of relating. In this the triangle might be: artist–picture– – –therapist (see Figure 8.1a).

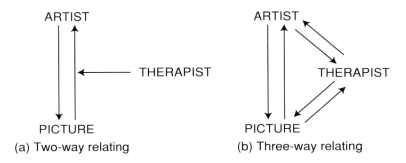

Figure 8.1 The therapeutic relationship in analytical art psychotherapy (also shown as Figure 6.1)

Here the therapist appears, and sometimes feels, peripheral. In fact her role is central but it is not acknowledged as such. This form of art psychotherapy usually occurs with the more disturbed patients. Very often borderline, psychotic or narcissistic patients engage in a two-way relationship with their picture. Only later do they begin to enter into a relationship that is three-way and so includes the therapist. It is this two-way relating which is the subject of this chapter.

I should make it clear that I am intentionally applying the terms two-way and three-way relating and not the more usual two- or three-person relating. This latter applies in psychoanalysis and refers to the mother/child dyad as two-person relating. When the father becomes a factor, usually in the oedipal phase, it is said that three-person relating begins. This is when the inner-world separation leads to the ability to symbolise. Clearly there is a connection here. I am discussing a related but rather different type of situation. The relation to the artwork is a self–Other relationship, and later an-'Other' person is introduced. This is a specific form of relating when pictures are central. However, Wright (1991) suggests something of this sort in his discussion of the development of an analysis. He suggests that to begin with the analyst is sometimes an observer, hearing about the significant people in the patient's life. It is only later, as symbolisation begins, that a three-person relationship is possible and it is at this point that the analyst is admitted. He then becomes a significant other himself and so is central in the material.

In the type of engagement I am proposing the erotic transference may be embodied in the artwork. This may act as a lure, seducing the therapist, and drawing her into a more intimate form of relating than is consciously admitted. The seduction of the therapist, through the image, may occur in a rather intense and also unconscious way. However, in this case the first seduction, the real lure, is that of the artist/patient and the picture. Like

Narcissus the patient may be lured into an erotic connection with her/his own image.

The aesthetic countertransference is often an unconscious mix which is evoked through the gaze. There is an attraction, an affinity, for the art object and it is this which lures both artist and viewer into a deeper engagement. This lure is at times like Narcissus looking into the pool, a relationship with the self. At other times it is an interpersonal lure where the attraction draws the pair into relating through a shared gaze. The implication is that when the desire of the male patient is embodied in the art object, the female therapist may be lured into an intimate engagement with the image. Her desire is thus evoked and this resonates with the interpersonal transference/countertransference. These gazes may be considered to be reflections but they are very different from those which we see in a mirror or in the eyes of another person.

MIRRORS AND MIRRORING

'The Mirror Stage' (Lacan 1949) is associated with the developmental stage prior to the acquisition of speech and independent mobility. It is the stage at which, despite the infant's lack of motor skills, there is a recognition of his own image in a mirror. The recognition is followed by mimicry by which the child explores the relation between his own gestures and those of the reflection. This can take place from the age of six months. This recognition, which precedes the use of language, reveals a primordial sense of self or sense of I. 'The mirror image would seem to be the threshold of the visible world' (Lacan 1949: 3). The mirror image is different from the 'imago of one's own body present in hallucinations or dreams' (ibid.). It establishes a relation between the organism and its reality (1949: 4). This offers the first cohesive view of the 'I' as an entity.

The internal thrust of the mirror stage is to move from a fragmented body image to a 'form of its totality'. This Lacan relates to clinical practice. He suggests that the fragmented body image usually manifests itself in dreams in analysis at a point at which the analysis encounters a certain level of aggressive disintegration. As with other psychoanalytic understandings this, too, becomes manifest in pictures. It is evident in Plates 6 and 7, which were pictures made by Carlos when he was in just such a state. His fear of his own aggression was mixed up with a fear of disintegration. In the pictures we can see this reflected in the persecutory figures which appear to resonate with his inner world. Lacan agrees with Freud's (1914) distinction between sexual and narcissistic libido and suggests (Lacan 1949: 5) that the mirror stage, which comes to an end about the age of eighteen months, heralds the onset of social relations characterised by 'the drama of primordial jealousy'. This is the point at which the desire for the Other enters the equation.

Winnicott (1967) acknowledges Lacan's paper but he proposes a rather different view of mirroring. In Winnicott's developmental model there is fusion between mother and infant which gradually separates. As the infant begins to experience the difference between me and not-me objects the mother is gradually perceived as separate. This is usually achieved through her survival of an aggressive attack by the baby. In the early stages the baby sees him/herself reflected in the mother's face:

> What does the baby see when he or she looks at the mother's face? I am suggesting that, ordinarily what the baby sees is himself or herself. In other words the mother is looking at the baby and what she looks like is related to what she sees there.
>
> (Winnicott 1967: 130)

This is a form of mirroring in which the baby learns to forecast, from the mother's face, her ability to tolerate his demands. He/she soon learns to adapt to the mother's moods and to know how safe it is to be spontaneous. If the mother accepts the moods and demands of her baby he/she is affirmed, and grows psychologically. However, if the mother's face is preoccupied, reveals depression or some other self-involved state, the baby learns to adapt to please the mother. If the mother's mood dominates, the baby learns not to make demands and this may affect emotional development. This interpersonal mirroring is not about actual mirrors.

This was exemplified by James who, it seemed, had suffered a lack of positive mirroring. From his account it became evident that, from the first months of his life, he had adapted his demands according to his vulnerable mother's needs. In the transference he quickly became regressed and found all analytic comments or interpretations offensive. If no words were spoken he would watch my face. If he could not read my expression he would ask what I was thinking. He could not bear me to have my own thoughts because it felt as if I was leaving him. Whether I interpreted or remained silent, it made little difference. He felt persecuted and became angry. After several months his fury drove him to a point at which there was a genuine danger that he would give up his therapy. Interpretations were not working and he told me vehemently how abusive he found them. I suggest that this was because interpretations introduced the gaze of the 'Other'. The effect of this was to make him feel separate from me and so fragmented and separated from himself. For this reason I suggested that using the art materials might help.

James responded to this with some enthusiasm and he would now paint in each session with me sitting next to him. He relaxed visibly and seemed to enjoy these sessions. He chatted happily while he drew, telling me what was going on in each picture. From my point of view it felt like being with a small child who was telling the story of his pictures as he drew. During this phase, although there were many references to the therapeutic relationship in the pictures, I refrained from interpretation. All went well unless I made a comment which linked the picture to the transference. If I did, James would become furious, again feeling intruded upon and abused.

I suggest that, in the first phase, when he was sitting looking at my face, James was adapting in the way that Winnicott suggests. He was watching his therapist/mother's face in order to adapt to what was required. 'If a mother's face is unresponsive, then a mirror is a thing to be looked at but not to be looked into' (Winnicott 1967: 132). He was identified with me but also alert, watching to see what I wanted him to be for me. This related to his experience of his mother's depression, of which he had been aware from very early in life. His early experience had been such that, when the mother looked at her baby, she looked with despair and fatigue. Thus, James had come to feel responsible for the despair and fatigue. He also felt invisible. When he searched my face, for clues of what I saw, he was looking for a mirror but all he saw was that he was a burden. He was adapting to a mood he had seen in his mother and which, by projective identification, I often came to embody. My words were experienced as fitting him into my preconceived framework. This could be understood as like the Lacanian mirror: the words introduced the view of the Other. This in his experience was alienating and thus terrifying. It seemed to threaten the disintegration of his body–self–image.

Painting offered an opportunity for a different sort of reflection. It permitted him to play in the therapist's company and to talk freely. The pictures resonated with the healthy, creative part of the self. Through them we moved from the stuck, interpersonal transference to a form of self-affirmation. At this stage he needed the mirroring provided by his own creativity. This was a form of two-way relating with his own pictures which were a series of narcissistic self-objects which provided an inner mirroring. Here he could find images corresponding to his own experience which remained within his control. Unlike interpretations these pictures enabled James to feel seen, to reveal his inner world but on his own terms.

Newton (1965), discusses this type of patient who has an ideal of 'oneness' which is ultimately unattainable. The patient she discusses made pictures and art objects. Newton describes the problems and despair experienced by her patient and the difficulty for the therapist in refraining from being drawn into conflict. The patient was ultimately 'held' by her analyst, whose understanding was based on Winnicott,'s idea of 'the mother's ego supporting the infant's incipient ego'. It is this being together and holding, without interpreting, which constitutes the therapist's role in the two-way relationship to the artist/patient's own image that I am proposing. This comes before a separate and interpersonal relationship can be established. This form of reflection of the inner-world state does not have the same effect as real mirrors.

Winnicott does mention real mirrors. He considers that the actual mirrors that exist in the house provide opportunities for the child to see the parents and others looking at themselves. 'It should be understood, however, that the actual mirror has significance mainly in its figurative sense' (Winnicott 1967: 138). Here he differs from Lacan who discusses real mirrors based on observation of the infant responding to his own mirror image.

An incident with a real mirror in art therapy is discussed by Case. She writes about a 9-year-old girl who had experienced a great deal of rejection (Case 1990: 141). During the course of an art therapy session a mirror, in which the child was looking at her reflection, was accidentally broken. Case discusses the complex impact of this event.

> It was possible to understand this in several ways . . . the mirror brought external reality into the room, in contrast to the acceptance and reflection that Ruth was receiving from the therapist's eyes; the mirror as critical eye, of conscience, of society, disapproving of mess, make up. Or, that the mirror showed an inward depth, the cracked self-image underlying the surface made up image.
>
> (Case 1990: 148)

Case links the acceptance and reflection that Ruth was receiving from the therapist's eyes to Winnicott's mirroring – it is interpersonal. She suggests that the mirror that broke could be thought of with reference to Lacan's 'mirror stage' (Lacan 1977b). Through seeing her own image, reflected in a real mirror, the child was beginning to organise her self-perception. Thus the breaking of the mirror could have a profound effect. It seems it was experienced as shattering the fragile self-image and revealing 'the cracked self-image underlying the surface made up image' (Case 1990: 148). My point, in quoting this example, is that it gives a vivid account of the theories of both Winnicott and Lacan in action. The child was receiving mirroring from the mother/therapist and this was an affirmation that she was accepted. Until the mirror broke and so became persecutory, she was beginning to perceive herself in the reflected image as an embodied person.

Thus we see that these theories may be compatible and applicable for art in psychotherapy. The maternal role of the therapist, combined with the reflection, offers two different, but linked, engagements. These simultaneously take place when art is made in therapy. In this example there was a real mirror involved whereas in the majority of art psychotherapy interactions, as in the case of James, it would be a picture. The connection I am proposing is that, at times, we might view the pictures in a similar way to Lacan's mirror. It is often through the picture that the fragmented elements of the personality first begin to cohere. This may introduce a view of the

Other: it is not a view of the body as a whole but it offers a distance, a perspective on the inner world. Although the picture is not literally a mirror it does bring fragmented elements together and sometimes presents them in a coherent frame. The two-way relating artist–picture may then enable the artist to begin to establish a sense of her/himself as an embodied person.

THE PICTURES AND MIRRORS

The reflection in a mirror tells us little about the person reflected in it; it reveals what the person looks like but it does not tell us how it feels to be that person. This was stated by Carlos when writing about his picture of his reflected image (see Figure 4.17). Zinkin (1983) points out that, as well as affirming the self-image, mirrors can be destructive. The reflection in a mirror is not a true reflection, it does not bare the soul, but only the features of the person. The reflection in the mirror is a flat two-dimensional version of a multi-dimensional being; it is cold. In regarding the reflection we may like or dislike what we see and our view may be distorted by projection. (For example, the anorexic may view an emaciated body as grossly over-weight.) Further, the image which regards us from the mirror is passive, it lacks the spark which lights the face, the life which others see when the face is animated. Without the 'Other' person the image is hollow.

There are some similarities between the pictorial image and the reflection in a mirror. Some of these have been explored in relation to art therapy by Seth-Smith (1987). Both the mirror image and the picture are framed visual images. The mirror image is always figurative while pictures may not be. They may be abstract. Yet they could be said to offer a more recognisable reflection than the mirror image. Pictures may offer a truer likeness because they reflect the animation the mirror lacks. A portrait, for example, may not show the correct lines and marks in the exact place where they are in reality. Rather, a picture reveals some essence of the person. Further, when we paint a face it is simultaneously our own face but also that of the Other. In the act of painting I become subject and object of my own gaze, sometimes also subject and object of my own desire. Thus, I am lured by my own picture.

Winnicott describes the reflection in the eyes of the mother as an empathic response to the infant. The mother's vision is not merely perception but apperception. This is a more subtle reflection than the mirror's gaze. The mother sees, not with the cold gaze of the mirror, but with the warm gaze of empathy. She sees, not merely the object of the gaze, but all around it. The embodied image is also warm and the reflection the artist sees in the picture usually gives some self-affirmation. Even negative images give feedback and so affirm a sense of self. In addition the pictures may offer an opportunity for the development of a new conscious attitude. The nascent self may develop in relation to the self-created art objects and thus the narcissistic and mirroring function of pictures offer an additional medium for transforming undifferentiated states. When the original disturbance has occurred at the stages of early mirroring, pictures may serve an important mediating function. Narcissistic injury may be mediated through the creative act of making and viewing pictures.

There are further distinctions to be made between the reflections in mirrors, or water, and those which look out at us from the pictures we create. Transference desire is a yearning often for something not clearly focused. This may manifest in both the need to make images and in the pictured images themselves. The reflection then may be of some opposite, some element which is felt to be missing – the lack – the gap – the unconscious.

MAGICAL THINKING, REFLECTIONS AND THE TALISMAN

Often there is an element of magical thinking associated with pictures and these may be similar to those which underlie traditional beliefs. Magical beliefs regarding reflected images could be considered cultural phenomena. In developing the idea of the scapegoat transference I discussed the magical thinking involved in various scapegoat rituals (Schaverien 1991). This was based, in part, on Frazer's (1913) researches which show that the scapegoat is a widely applied means of purging communities of ill-effect and pollution. Such magical beliefs also operate in relation to reflected images in mirrors, water and portraits (Frazer 1911).

Patients involved with art in psychotherapy may consciously, or unconsciously, imbue their pictures with magical powers. These pictures may come to be valued as talismans felt to hold the power for good or evil. Sometimes this means that the artist comes to fear their picture. The fear can be such that there is a need to cover or hide the image. There may be many reasons for such fears. They may be evoked by a belief that the image might attack the artist or perhaps someone else. The image may be thought to reveal some unacceptable aspect of the shadow or some unnameable fear. There are numerous other potential reasons for fearing one's own picture which can only be elaborated in the individual case. The point is that it is worth considering that such apparently incongruous thoughts may have roots in once accepted beliefs.

Fear of loss of soul related to mirrors and other forms of reflected or depicted image is common. In many cultures mirrors are covered, or turned to the wall, in the event of a death: 'It is feared that the soul, projected out of the person in the shape of his reflection in the mirror, may be carried off by the ghost of the departed which is commonly supposed to linger about the house till the burial' (Frazer 1911: 94). In some cultures pictures, like reflections, are thought to embody the soul. This is why portraits and photographs are feared. The associated dangers are similar to those attributed to reflections:

> As with shadows and reflections so with portraits; they are often believed to contain the soul of the person portrayed. People who hold this belief are naturally loth to have their likeness taken; for if the portrait is the soul, or at least a vital part of the person portrayed; whoever possesses the portrait will be able to exercise a fatal influence over the original of it.
>
> (Frazer 1911: 96)

Thus, images may be regarded as potentially endangering life. Similarly, it is believed that photographic images can take the shadow away and, as the shadow is equated with the soul, the person is believed to be in mortal danger. A related fear is that possession of the photographic image gives power over its subject to the person who acquires it (Frazer 1911: 92).

There are traditions which consider reflections in water to be the soul (Frazer 1911: 92). The associated fear is that the reflection–soul is believed to be subject to the same dangers as the shadow–soul. Homeopathic magic indicates that, for example, if the reflection is struck in the eye, the person reflected will suffer a similar injury. The person whose shadow or reflection is injured may be injured as a consequence:

> An Aztec mode of keeping sorcerers from the house was to leave a vessel of water with a knife in it behind the door. When the sorcerer entered he was so much alarmed at seeing his reflection in the water transfixed by a knife that he turned and fled.
>
> (Frazer 1911: 93)

The scapegoat picture is an image which embodies affect. If it is additionally empowered as a talisman, it may be similarly employed by the artist/patient who may believe that, if left in the art room, it will keep the unwanted attentions of other people at bay. This may be a conscious or unconscious enactment which is not necessarily psychotic. Magical thinking may be considered to be a healthy attitude to facing the shadow aspects of the personality. It is only when the magical thought processes dominate that there is danger of psychosis. Frazer reports peoples who will not look into a dark pool for fear that the beast who lives in it will take away their reflections and so they will die. This is not psychotic thinking because it is culturally appropriate; it is shared in common with the group. Such thinking is more likely to become, or be viewed as, psychotic if it emerges in a culture where the belief is not shared.

There are many such beliefs associated with water. For example: 'that crocodiles have the power to kill a man by dragging his reflection under water' (Frazer 1911: 93). In Melanesia: 'There is a pool "into which if anyone looks he dies; the malignant spirit takes hold upon his life by means of his reflection on the water" ' (Frazer 1911: 94). Beliefs that 'the water spirits would drag the person's reflection or soul under water, leaving him soul-less to perish', it seems are universal.

Frazer gives many such examples from European sources. These, he suggests, were precursors of the Narcissus myth and, in this regard, he mentions an English belief that 'whoever sees a water fairy must pine and die' (Frazer 1911: 94). In ancient Greece it was believed that it was an omen of death if a man dreamed of seeing himself reflected (ibid.). Frazer proposes that the idea that Narcissus languished and died of love through seeing his own image reflected in the water was probably derived from such tales but devised later when the old meaning of the story was forgotten (ibid.).

NARCISSUS

The story of Narcissus as told by Graves (1955: 286–7) is as follows: Narcissus was the son of the blue nymph Leiriope. She was told by a seer that 'Narcissus will live to a ripe old age, provided he never knows himself' (Graves 1955: 286). From childhood Narcissus was very beautiful and at sixteen he was desired by lovers of both sexes. Echo's voice had been taken from her as a punishment and so she could only repeat the utterances of others. She fell in love with Narcissus but he rejected her and she pined until all that was left of her was her voice repeating the words of others. Narcissus was responsible for the death of another lover to whom he gave a sword with which he killed himself. The gods avenged the death of this lover by condemning Narcissus to fall in love but 'denying him love's consummation' (Graves 1955: 287).

> He came upon a spring, clear as silver . . . and as he cast himself down, exhausted, on the grassy verge to slake his thirst, he fell in love with his reflection. At first he tried to embrace and kiss the beautiful boy who confronted him, but presently recognized himself, and lay gazing enraptured into the pool, hour after hour. How could he endure both to possess and yet not to possess?
>
> (Graves 1955: 287)

Echo, who had not forgiven Narcissus, grieved with him as he stabbed himself with a dagger. His blood soaked the earth and from this grew the white Narcissus flower. Mitchell (1974) relates this myth to child development and to psychoanalytic practice. She points out that Narcissus was unreachable and he dies in love with himself as if he were another person. 'Narcissus was forever grasping his shadow which was the object of his own desire, but what eluded him was himself' (Mitchell 1974: 38). She considers that Echo, who witnessed his fate, 'was the absolute Other to whom none could get attached because she would not listen', she could only repeat his words.

There is a parallel with the narcissistic patient whose gaze is invested in the picture. At times he or she may be like Narcissus, enraptured with his own image. The picture may be a trap, into which artist is lured, to find there only his own image reflected back at him. It may indicate that he/she is unable to leave this state and make relationships in the world. At other times this is a highly productive two-way engagement which is sometimes an important transforming element. Thus, the two-way relating, which I am proposing, is sometimes a negative self-absorption and, at others, a positive form of self-affirmation. It may be an expression of a necessary form of self-love which eventually leads the patient into a relationship and eventually love of an-'Other'.

When the patient is so totally engaged with her or his own picture, the therapist may feel outside, an observer, excluded from an important relationship between the artist and his picture. When the artist/patient is involved with his own picture, in a narcissistic phase, then the therapist may find that she is playing Echo's part. Naomi Segal (1989) points out that this relationship is a common one in literature where the woman in love with the male protagonist can only watch as he commits suicide. She gives examples from literature where the male is the central protagonist while the 'woman is required to serve him as his mirror', she is silent (Segal 1989: 171). Although she is discussing this through literature, there is a similarity here. The female therapist working with the male client may be perpetuating a social role. I would suggest that for a while she watches the display of narcissistic love without intervening. However, this stage usually fails to move beyond a certain point because what is needed is relationship. The need is for a real person with thoughts and a will of her own and the therapist needs to intervene – a mother who is not just a mirror but who interacts (Mitchell 1974; Chodorow 1978; Benjamin 1988). Mitchell writes that no one could have done any more than Echo, 'Narcissus is confined in intra-subjectivity'. She makes the point that, developmentally, 'the baby has to find out . . . who he is in the eyes of other people' (Mitchell 1974: 39). The narcissistic stage can only be negotiated through the medium of an 'Other'. Sometimes that Other is first a picture and second a person.

The Other is the desired object and at first this may be found in a picture and secondly in the therapist. As we have seen in Chapter 2, the analyst or psychotherapist may become this loved 'other' for a time. The erotic transference and countertransference are made up of many fantasy images and projections. Among these is the hope that this person will be that Other who will make the difference. This may be irrespective of the actual gender of the pair but, as we have seen, it may be intensified in certain combinations. Consequently, the falling in love which takes place within an analytic encounter is often a narcissistic form of self-love reflected in the eyes of the Other. When pictures are an embodiment of the desire of the patient they play an important role in this dynamic.

PSYCHOANALYTIC THEORIES OF NARCISSISM

The link between the myth of Narcissus and the psychoanalytic concept of mirroring is an important one for my theme. It was on the myth of Narcissus that Freud founded the concept of Narcissism. He distinguished between auto-eroticism, which he considered was present from the beginning, and narcissism, which was a result of an additional psychical action (Freud 1914: 77). This distinction rests on the difference between ego libido, a form of attachment to the self, and object libido, a subsequent attachment to another. The first auto-erotic sexual satisfactions are experienced by the infant in connection with vital functions which serve the purpose of self-preservation. The sexual instincts are at the outset attached to the satisfaction of the ego-instincts (Freud 1914: 87).

The additional distinction between primary and secondary narcissism is the difference between attachment to self and attachment to other. Primary narcissism derives from the fact that: 'The human being has originally two sexual objects – himself and the woman who nurses him' [Freud writes] 'we are postulating a primary narcissism in everyone, which may in some cases manifest itself in a dominating fashion in . . . object choice' (Freud 1914: 88). This first attachment is made to the person who provided the original experience of satisfaction; usually the mother or mother substitute. The second type of object choice is that where the love-object has become the self and this he termed narcissistic (ibid.). He links this to homosexuality but asserts that this does not mean that human beings are sharply divided between these two types of object choice, rather he affirms that 'both kinds of object choice are open to each individual, though there may be a preference for one or the other' (ibid.).

The difference between the effects of primary and secondary narcissism is eloquently stated by Winnicott (1971: 133): 'The man who falls in love with beauty is quite different from the man who loves a girl and feels she is beautiful and can see what is beautiful about her.' The first is an effect of primary narcissism, the second, secondary narcissism.

A number of Jungians have discussed narcissism. Following Fordham (1974), Gordon (1980) emphasises that narcissism is healthy unless it serves a defensive function. In Fordham's view the primary self, which is in existence from the very beginning, is not merely one self but it is made up of many deintegrates or self-elements. Narcissism cannot be understood separately from the concept of the self and yet it does not easily coexist with Fordham's concept of the primary self. This leads her to question which part of the self is loved in narcissism (Gordon 1980).

Ledermann has written a number of influential papers on narcissism. She quotes Kohut (1971), who sees the narcissistic patient as 'arrested at a very early but healthy state of infantile development' and Kernberg (1975), who considers that narcissistic patients are unable to love themselves. She is in accord with the latter view and considers patients whose 'feelings of aloofness and superiority . . . arise as an early complex defense structure against the terror of not being able to relate and of "non-existing" (Ledermann 1979: 108). This is a useful way of understanding the clinical manifestation of narcissism. I am proposing that these are the sort of patients who may be particularly helped by using art in their therapy, as indeed some of Ledermann's patients do. Ledermann (1982) writes of patients who need to barricade themselves against any form of intimacy with their analyst. They come up with images of fortresses. One described the couch as a castle with a moat surrounding it (Ledermann 1982: 106). As we have seen this is an image which Carlos depicted (see Figure 4.7). One way of viewing his picture would be similarly, as a picture of the gap between the intimacy expressed in the pictures and the relationship with the therapist. This changed over time but when this image was made, this is a likely interpretation. Moreover, anorexia is often considered to be a narcissistic disturbance.

THE LURE

The topic of this chapter is transference desire reflected in pictures and so the subject of narcissism is important. The erotic transference and counter-transference involves a state similar to falling in love. Carotenuto (1989: 18) discusses falling in love as double narcissism: 'It is exactly the violent rupture of basic narcissistic defenses that characterises the condition of love' (Carotenuto 1989: 20) and 'The beloved always symbolises the potential of the lover' (Carotenuto 1989: 37). Thus we might understand that, if the analyst is the temporary beloved, it is because she/he symbolises just that potential in the patient. Similarly, if the analyst temporarily falls in love with the patient, she/he is finding something for which she/he is searching in the patient as other.

> The greatest mistake we can make is to think the other has seduced us. The truth is rather that I have been seduced by my own image. When I fall into the arms of my lover . . . in reality I am preparing to risk all for the sake of realising my inner world. The lover offers the bait.
>
> (Carotenuto 1989: 39)

Thus, he is suggesting that each of the lovers sees his own reflection in the other. Each falls in love with her/his own potential in the other. This seems to have been the situation with Gary. He had recently been rejected by his girlfriend and this had aroused feelings associated with many past rejections and losses. He made numerous pictures of faces with tears falling from the eyes. The most powerful of these was painted in red paint on black paper. The face had a fearsome aspect. The eye was red, with tears falling from it. It was life size and he said it was his girlfriend. However, as he continued to look at it, he realised that it was also himself. It was simultaneously a picture of the girlfriend and himself. Here was the 'beloved' who 'symbolises the potential of the lover' (Carotenuto 1989: 37). The woman who had left was experienced as having taken his potential. It is likely that his love had been fuelled by a narcissistic projection which may have contributed to his inability to accept that it was quite hopeless.

This image could be understood to be a form of reflection but it was clearly not a mirror image – smooth and cold. The image showed him as frightened, tragic and bereft. In association it brought back memories and it became clear that this picture was about more than the current loss. It revealed a previously unconscious connection. The 'phenomenon was bared' in this image and we see the 'centrifugal retracing' of the transference beginning to peel back the layers. Like Elisabeth, discussed in Chapter 7, his fragmentation – the gap – was starkly apparent. Very quickly, through the picture, it became evident that past losses were loading the feelings associated with this most recent one. The image of the lover was also an image of the self.

Carotenuto, quoted above, uses the term 'bait' in connection with the lover. The bait is also a 'lure'. It is this lure of the other which attracts. The importance of this realisation for the therapist working with patients who play out their need for love in the analytic encounter is considerable. It is the deepening of the relation to the self which is the object of falling in love and analysis offers the opportunity for such a transformation. It is the privilege and also the demand of such work that, for a limited time, the analyst becomes the beloved. Eventually disillusion sets in or the projection is withdrawn.

Sometimes the pictures embody transference desire. The transference and countertransference effects of this mean that patient and therapist may be drawn into an erotic connection through the artwork. I am proposing that the artist and beholder of the picture are lured into engaging with the picture. The lure is the thread which connects us to the image. This idea is engendered by Lacan: 'Generally speaking, the relation between the gaze and what one wishes to see involves a lure' (Lacan 1977a: 104). The lure of the image could be understood to be a seduction, a response to the surface of the picture. This is an initial impression, a surface attraction, which may lead into a deeper relationship with the picture. This, in turn, may lead to a deeper interpersonal relationship. The gaze brings together the surface image and its depth equivalent; it may be the embodiment of the erotic. The lure may be understood to be the sign, and the gaze the symbol. 'The

French word translates variously "lure" (for hawks, fish), decoy (for birds), bait (for fish) and the notion of "allurement" and "enticement"' (Sheridan 1977: xi).

Thus, we see the 'lure' is a deception – it stands in for something else. If a picture acts as bait, what does it lead us towards? The surface attraction, its allure, is the first impression. If I walk into an art gallery where many pictures are displayed, one may catch my eye, perhaps I am attracted by the colours or a figure. Something makes this image stand out and I am drawn to it. At this point I am lured towards it – this is the enticement. The picture may be one of substance which holds my gaze beyond this. Alternatively, I may turn away, drawn to another image. In the gallery I am searching for an experience. I desire something from the pictures and my gaze searches for it.

Spitz refers to desire in this context in her chapter which is called 'looking and longing' (Spitz 1991). She writes of the 'pleasure of desire' which is located in the object (Spitz 1991: 4). This 'constitutes the special quality of the aesthetic experience' (ibid.: 5). In the same book, writing of the beholder's viewing of the painting 'Olympia' by Manet, she writes:

> The painted image serves a mirroring function, reflecting to the beholder his own gaze; compelled to behold himself beholding and struggling to avoid a confrontation with his own self-alienation, he is both *moved* and *held* – spellbound, bewitched by the painting.
>
> (Spitz 1991: 17)

This is about the viewing of pictures in the formal setting of the art gallery. Given that the quality of the imagery of the pictures viewed in therapy is rarely, if ever, comparable to an artist such as Manet, none the less we might make a comparison of the effects on the beholder. If the pictures in therapy challenge the viewer in this way, if they facilitate a confrontation with the self, then their influence will be considerable.

A picture, as an object of the gaze, is an affective carrier of the desire of the artist. It may exemplify desire, reveal it, or be the object of desire itself. The picture lures the artist into a relationship with the self through the attraction to the 'Other'. Subsequently the self-created image reveals that necessary other to be an aspect of the self. It also lures the therapist who may be attracted, first of all through the image, and this may lead her into seeing the potential of the artist/patient.

> The lure plays an essential function therefore. It is not something else that seizes us at the level of clinical experience, when, in relation to what one might imagine of the attraction to the other pole as conjoining masculine and feminine, we apprehend the prevalence of that which is presented as travesty.
>
> (Lacan 1977a: 107)

I understand this to mean that initial glances and sight of a person or a thing offers a performance. The allure may be viewed as a travesty but with profoundly serious consequences. We initially respond to a performance: 'It is no doubt through the mediation of masks that the masculine and the feminine meet in the most acute, most intense way' (Lacan 1977a: 107). The artist sees the image unfold and it may come to embody the desired 'Other'. This is a form of looking which goes beyond; which penetrates into deeper layers of the psyche. The therapist is then involved and, through the gaze, this may lead to a deepening of the relationship.

THE LURE: THE EMBODIMENT OF DESIRE IN ART

The embodiment of transference desire in an art object created within a therapeutic setting is illustrated by David. David's art object was the lure for him and potentially for the therapist. Once again I make the point that, although this took place in an art therapy studio setting, the enactment can be understood to have implications for other forms of psychotherapy. This type of enactment reveals some of the unconscious processes which are happening in most forms of psychotherapy. I suggest that the creation of this art object was an unconscious attempt to reinstate the 'lost object' and so it embodied the desire of the patient. This art object was the 'lure' for the artist.

David was in his twenties, a day patient in a therapeutic community, and he used the art room freely. He considered the work he did 'art', rather than art therapy. By this definition he resisted interpretation of his artwork and attempted to control the therapist. The therapist was thus outside the relationship between himself and the art object. This might be understood as a narcissistic engagement. It was a two-way relating as distinct from a two-person relating. If we think of the triangle of patient–picture–therapist,

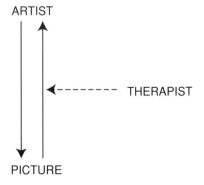

Figure 8.2 Two-way relating in analytical art psychotherapy

here the engagement is artist–picture– – –therapist. Dave was totally engaged in the process and the therapist is apparently irrelevant.

Patients were free to use the art room whether the art therapist was present or not. There were no structured appointments. David worked in the art room much of the week and showed his work to the therapist when she was in. (There is a similarity here to private practice when the patient brings artwork created during the intervening days, or week, to the session.) The art therapist worked mainly with individuals in a group but there were also opportunities for individual work. The constant analytic environment and interpretive milieu enabled a deep analytic engagement which is not always possible in open group settings. This environment has been described in more detail elsewhere (Schaverien 1991: 159).

On this occasion, when I arrived, David was alone in the art room. He was creating an object from papier-mâché made from newspaper soaked in flour and water. From the low ceiling hung an inflated balloon which was turning white as he stroked the thick pasty liquid over its surface. The object was suspended, slightly weighed down with its coating and, as he stroked it on, the milky liquid dripped to the floor.

When I came upon this enactment, it seemed as if the milky balloon was a breast. It was positioned just above David's head and, if his head had been that of a baby, the proportions of the object, its size and position, would have been just right. I do not know how conscious he was of this. I felt he intuitively knew what he was doing. There was a combination of consciousness and unconsciousness in the creation of this object. I suggest that this object, which was so tenderly caressed into being, was an object of transference desire. David was realising an inner image. The internal object was taking an external concrete form and, in that moment, he was regressed.

Let us now look more closely at what may have been taking place here. This was a form of regression through an artwork which is different from the examples given in Chapter 7. It is a manifestation of desire but not this time evoked through a picture of a child. It was rather as if David himself embodied the child and the balloon/breast the desired object. The enactment was fuelled by infantile needs which thus were revealed, live, in the present. We could understand this as an attempt to recreate the lost object in a very literal sense. The art object could be understood to be experienced simultaneously as the actual object of desire – the mother/therapist's breast – to which the 'centrifugal retracing' (Lacan 1977a), the repetition of the transference, had led him. We can also see that an aspect of the psyche was split off and held in the object and thus this was an embodiment of the 'scapegoat transference'.

This was a form of two-way and not two-person relating. David was in no way amenable to interpretation and, at this stage, I made none, intuitively knowing that any such intervention would have been experienced as intrusive. The therapist was none the less significant as a witness to the enactment and moreover, her presence was a form of affirmation. The experience of the creation of the object was, for now, all that was needed. David's object was no mere representation, it was not made to *tell* anything, but it did reveal a great deal. It evoked considerable affect. Live in the present and resonant with his current feelings, it was made primarily for himself. I submit that initially this was experienced by David as a real breast, it was no mere imitation. It was not a 'symbolic substitution' but a 'real physical transference' (Cassirer 1955b; Schaverien 1991). In the regressed state this was more than a mere representation. For him at the time, this object was imbued with life and a container for his feelings. It was the breast. In Hanna Segal's terms it was a 'symbolic equation' (Segal 1981). It was potently, even magically, invested and so potentially it was a 'talisman': and it was a 'lure'.

It was also a balloon covered in flour and water and, at a less conscious level, I think David was also aware of this symbolic dimension. Consequently, he made a split which enabled him to experience the embodied object as the sensuous breast at the same time as knowing that its substance was other than the fantasied flesh. This type of split occurs in the psychoanalytic transference to the therapist as person, as we have seen in Chapter 2. The therapist is experienced as the desired object but, simultaneously, there is an awareness that she is, in reality, not that person. The difference is in the disposal of the art object. The art object continues to exist (unless it is prematurely destroyed). Through it, a slow process of familiarisation, acknowledgement, assimilation and eventually disposal may take place (Schaverien 1991: 106). Consciousness develops as a result of the relationship to the artwork during the process of its creation and subsequently, as a result of its continued existence. In this way the relation to the art object is formative.

The disposal was a gradual and evolutionary process. After some days had elapsed David took his balloon–breast down from the ceiling and left it on a table in the room. It was then left lying around the art room to be moved from one place to another and, as the weeks passed, it physically deteriorated. The milky substance dried, the balloon burst and all that was left was the shell of white papier-mâché, which became brittle. It kept its breast shape but gradually it became chipped and damaged.

This form of disposal was significant in many subtle ways. The breast object was discarded, left carelessly around the art room, to be gradually damaged and to change in its appearance and quality. David did not throw it away, nor did he preserve it carefully. Without consciously owning that this was an attack, it was, I suggest, just that. Its disposal permitted the destructive impulse to be enacted. The art object had been an external embodiment of his internal desires during the process of its creation. This process continued in its disposal. The object which had carried profound significance for the artist changed, its appearance altered through neglect, it became familiar and less important. The affect that had been embodied in it became integrated and David no longer needed the object. In subsequent weeks he created other circular objects in which he unconsciously developed the breast theme.

In psychoanalytic terms we may understand the process of David's enactment as a change from object relating to object use (Winnicott 1971). This is a change from a state of fusion with the mother/breast to differentiation and eventual separateness. We saw earlier in the chapter that this stage is negotiated through a destructive attack on the mother (or breast) who none the less survives. This enables the infant to differentiate itself as an autonomous being in relation to others and to distinguish 'me' from 'not me'.

Further, I am proposing that this was an embodiment of the lure. The desire, the 'looking and longing' (Spitz 1991), constellated in the creation of this art object. The therapist as beholder was lured, too, into a relationship with the artist and the object. Her interest, even desire, became engaged through the visual enactment. She was moved by this enactment of his regressed state, as well as by the innocence and trust which it revealed. There was considerable appeal to respond emotionally and yet, at the same time, an unspoken warning to maintain a distance. It was an invitation to relate but not to interpret. It would have been premature to attempt to express in words the inarticulatable state of the enactment.

The gaze of client and therapist meet and mingle in such an object and yet there are no words that can add to the experience. The therapist is no mere observer, she is woven into the fabric of such an enactment. It is important to respect that such an image, which is a two-way artist–object relating, reveals much but tells nothing. For this reason to ask questions or to probe at too early a stage is to invade a very personal space. Later, it may be possible to refer back to the object or the session but this is not always necessary. The countertransference in such a case is the response to the entire situation, the combined effects of the person and the artwork. The enactment as a whole is affective and the art object cannot be assessed separated from its maker. The enactment is viewed as a symbolic whole. To separate the parts would be to destroy its impact and possibly to rob the artist of the experience.

Was this embodied art object also a reflection of the inner world? Was it a mirror? I suggest that it certainly corresponded with the artist's inner world. It revealed the desired object and stated the need. Perhaps, too, it was an object in which fragmented aspects of the inner world began to cohere (Lacan 1977b). Certainly there was a mirroring function in the breast/object creation. However, this was not a mirror image. I suggest that what was reflected was not only the 'love of self' but the love of 'Other'. By creating an object that embodied the desire he was affirming his own experience – showing himself what he felt. The desire for the Other was embodied in this self-created art object. Thus, a form of separation was beginning through the manifestation of the object.

CONCLUSION

The healing potential of art is significant in this first stage in analytical art psychotherapy. However, there comes a time when the intervention of the therapist is essential in transforming the self-referential state into two-*person* relatedness. It is the therapist who eventually leads the patient out of this state. Without the therapist's interpretations, and engagement, the artist may discover much about himself, but, blinded by his own limitations, will not see beyond the picture. This means that, ultimately, the transference to the person of the therapist must be acknowledged and subsequently analysed.

I stated at the beginning of this chapter that pictures are no mere mirrors of the inner world. What they reveal is not simply a reflection. I have argued that the artist's relationship to the picture is formative. During its making there is a two-way interchange between artist and picture. Although, at this stage, there may be little relating with the therapist, the process does not stop here. The picture in this situation is the first 'Other'; but the viewpoint of an-'Other' *person* is also necessary in order to move from a two-*way* relationship and to introduce a two-*person* relationship. This then becomes a three-way relationship, i.e. artist–picture–therapist.

Chapter 9

The engendered gaze

This chapter is about the effects of the three-way relationship when the points of the triangle, artist–picture–therapist, are equally balanced. This creates a dynamic field within which the pictures are central. They occupy the area in between the people and this leads to a therapeutic interaction which is influenced by the imagery (see Figure 9.1). The lure is the unconscious thread which draws the artist and viewer into the picture. This leads, through the gaze, to a deeper connection with the image. In turn this deepens the connection to the self and leads to an intensification of the interpersonal meeting. The engendered gaze is the gaze that is engendered by viewing the image, but that is not all. This term has a double meaning. It is also the gaze which reflects gender issues in the imagery in many overt and subtle ways.

The centrality of the gaze engendered through the pictures was exemplified, with unusual clarity, by the case study from the last chapter of *The*

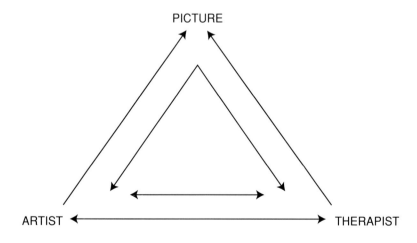

Figure 9.1 Three-way relating – the dynamic field

Revealing Image (Schaverien 1991). Harry created a series of pictures in which a male and a female figure meet and engage in a dance together. They separate and come together in different combinations throughout the series of pictures.

Figures 9.2 and 9.3 are the first of these and echo the very early stages of the meeting. Later a foetus emerges and grows, as we saw in Figures 7.1 and 7.2 (pp. 162 and 163). Unconsciously these pictures came to embody the transference desire. I suggest that they reflected the deeply felt sense of yearning which Harry experienced at this time and they seduced him. We could say that he fell in love with his own image which was embodied in the pictures. They also echoed the interpersonal transference. The therapist was female, and it is likely that his aspirations for relationship became temporarily invested in her. In psychotherapy without pictures, similar images occur in dreams and in the feeling tone of the interaction, but we do not literally *see* the changing nature of these desires.

These pictures, which embodied the patient's desire, evoked a reciprocal desire in the therapist. In Chapter 2 we saw that the intensity of the erotic transference can evoke sexual as well as maternal emotions in the therapist. Here, the dual nature of such a transference was embodied in the series of

Figure 9.2 Harry – Dancers 1

Figure 9.3 Harry – Dancers 2

pictures and the incestuous erotic connection was evoked through them, as well as through the interpersonal relationship. Thus, the erotic transference became manifest in the pictures and we could understand the therapist to have been seduced, in part, through the gaze.

Although these pictures were figurative, this is not always the case. At times abstract pictures influence the relationship just as powerfully as those which depict representational themes. David's object, discussed in the last chapter, was abstract. Its figurative associations were made by the therapist as a response to viewing the enactment as a whole. Viewed together, the combination of person and artwork suggested that the enactment could be representational and so the object took on the aspect of a breast. The aesthetic countertransference was an appreciation of the object and person in relationship.

The pictures by Carlos, which form the main case study in this book, offer an additional view of the centrality of the gaze between client and therapist. This is complex because, at first, apparently little was happening between the people. However, this was belied by the early gift of the picture of the therapist's name (see Plate 1). This indicated an investment in the transference, associating the female therapist with his mother and aunt. There followed a series of pictures which again, apparently, did not

involve the therapist centrally. This may have reflected his fear of intimacy
in the transference. In the early pictures the two-way relating artist–picture
was evident. Through his intense engagement with his own pictures, to
which the therapist was a witness, a change in state began to be effected.

When Carlos became angry with the therapist and the hospital he
expressed this first in his pictures. Through discussion of the pictures his
fury was admitted to the therapist. His engagement in the therapeutic
relationship now became more clearly evident. The pictures were vehicles
for three-way relating. The artist–picture–therapist triangle, which was in
operation obliquely before, became fully activated. In Carlos's process we
see the move from two- to three-way relating. At first the interpersonal
transference was not central for a number of reasons, not least of which was
that there was a real family from which to separate. It was when he began
to confront emotion, which he could not express to his family, that the
triangle artist–picture–therapist led to three-way relating. Eventually he
began to engage in two-*person* relatedness and a form of separation from
the figures of his inner world began. Later in this chapter I will discuss two
of the pictures made by Carlos. These illustrate the effects of the gaze of
the picture in therapy.

It is my intention to discuss the various gazes to which we are subject
and object within the analytic encounter. I would again make the point that
this is intended to be relevant to psychotherapists as well as art psychotherapists, and even to those whose patients do not paint and draw.
The connection through the gaze includes other forms of gaze which, I
suggest, make a picture. The view of another person is one of these and
another is the metaphorical inward reflective gaze.

THE INWARD GAZE

The gazes to which we are subject as well as object within psychotherapy
include a form of inward gaze. The gaze of the imagination could be
understood as the gaze that looks inwards. This is different from the gazes
that look outwards and depend upon what is seen, and taken in, from the
outer world. Clearly what is actually perceived by the eye is an important
part of any activity which involves the making and viewing of visual and
plastic arts. However, I am proposing, following Lacan (1977a), that there
are a multitude of gazes to which we attend, consciously and unconsciously, within therapy. There is the literal gaze, the gaze which sees in
the outer world. This is based on visual perception. Then there are the
numerous ways in which sight is used as metaphor, in our everyday
language and in psychoanalysis in particular. We look inwards and we
look outwards. We have 'insights' in which we 'see' the meaning; we look
at things from the other's viewpoint, etc. My concern in this chapter is less
the metaphorical use of vision than the place of actual seeing. However, I

find that the two are inextricably linked in language and in clinical practice. In the literal sense a look may be felt, it may penetrate, glance off, wander. The analyst may withdraw her gaze from her patient, she may look away in order to look inwards, to take in what is being communicated. She may look away from boredom, to escape a penetrating stare or for numerous other possible reasons. The point is that the intensity or withdrawal of the gaze of the one is felt by the other.

Some recent papers have been written about the gaze and the implication of looks, of various kinds, in psychotherapy. Hobson (1984) writes of therapy with a young woman who initially sat behind his chair and looked at the back of his head. She had to make sure he was there but also to avoid his gaze. Her mother had had dead eyes, she explained, which she sometimes saw in her therapist. That dead look was linked to envy and the fear that she had blinded and killed the mother. He links the eye to the evil that it can sometimes be experienced as embodying. A similar idea is developed by Wheeley (1992) who discusses the role of the eye in child development. Powerful looks can be felt to have the capacity to kill, to damage the other, by communicating the unspeakable horrors which have been seen. The importance of seeing and being seen, in all its facets, is emphasised in relation to case material. She demonstrates the links between eyes and wombs in her retelling of the Oedipus myth. Wharton (1993) discusses patients who use the couch to avoid eye contact with the therapist. Wright (1992) discusses the gaze between mother and baby and the importance of the visual aspect of the relationship. The baby responds to seeing the mother's face and it is this first relationship which leads to the ability to symbolise.

In all forms of human interaction, and this includes psychotherapy, the gaze plays a part. The many gazes which make up these interactions may influence even those whose sight is damaged or whose eyes do not see. The inward gaze is a self-referential gaze. Here I am subject of my own gaze, I look within. Clearly there are aspects of visual art for which sight is a prerequisite. However, the inward gaze, through which I interpret my experience, is relevant even for those without sight. Swearingen (1991) has used the phrases 'sighting in' or 'in-sight' for this inward gaze. This is not really seeing in any physical sense but relies on the idea of vision.

The inward gaze is exemplified by Tustin's (1972: 77–8) description of the development of blind children. She says that development of hand–eye co-ordination hastens a child's awareness of himself as a body in space. The blind child does not have the experience of seeing parts of his body and so realising that they belong to him/her. This means that such a child will remain 'body centred' much longer than is normal. Vivid examples of the way experience is interpreted by such children are given when she quotes Will (1965). He describes comments by two 6-year-old blind children. The first child 'closed the lid of her Braille board saying "I've closed its mouth"'. The second told of a bad dream and then explained that when he awakes from such dreams he always checks in the bed to see if he is 'inside the mouth or not, adding that "under the covers it's a bit like a mouth, isn't it?"' (Will (1965) quoted in Tustin (1972: 78)). The interpretation of the world, in both these cases, is formed through bodily experience in place of vision. Both these children seem to use what could be understood to be an inward gaze to make sense of their own experience. Their interpretation of bodily sensation makes a graphic word picture.

It is perhaps of more than passing interest that Rycroft (1981) reports that people who have once been sighted, but who have lost their sight, report dreaming with visual imagery, whilst those who have never been sighted do not have visual dreams. 'These observations suggest that dreaming is not essentially a visual activity even though to the sighted it appears to be' (Rycroft 1981: 124). This supports the idea that 'dreaming is an imaginative activity as it manifests itself in sleep – the images used by imagination being of necessity those made available to it by sensation and memory' (ibid.). This may have implications for the self-referential gaze that I am suggesting is sometimes externalised in, and through, visual or plastic imagery. Crane (1993) reviews an exhibition of art by blind students and in the widest sense this, too, could be understood to be an externalisation of an inward gaze.

The film-maker Derek Jarman, losing his sight because he was terminally ill with AIDS, asks, 'If I have only half my sight does this mean I have only half my vision?' His film *Blue* (Jarman 1993), from which this is a quote, is a moving testament to the fact that a very visual film can be made without the artist being able to see. His spoken images with sound and the saturation of the colour blue conjure far more complex imagery than if he had drawn his vision literally. His 'vision' is transmitted from his imagination to that of the viewer with minimal use of sight. It is his 'insight' which communicates directly to the spectator by means of the gaze. The colour blue, a vital image, is the only one that is actually seen throughout the film. This is anything but boring. The combination of gazing at the field of unchanging blue and the words, which are spoken throughout, make pictures in the mind's eye. These are more telling and have more impact than would representational forms of the images.

THE AUDIENCE – THE GAZE OF THE BEHOLDER

There are three gazes in the triangular relationship I am discussing. These are the gaze of the artist (linked to the transference), the gaze of the therapist (the countertransference) and there is what I will refer to as the gaze of the picture. This may embody the transference and influence the countertransference.

In order to develop a conscious attitude, to move from the isolation of a so-called 'inward gaze', an 'Other' is required – an audience, a witness, a lover. It is the communication of the inward image to the Other which both affirms and deepens the relationship to the self. Jung and Lacan, in different ways, both indicate that this is essential and by this they mean an 'Other' person. Ultimately an 'Other' person is important and, in most cases, essential. However, as we saw in the last chapter, there are times when the Other is a picture. The 'Other' holds the conscious attitude and so brings to consciousness previously unconscious elements of the psyche. The picture may hold the conscious attitude. It may reveal previously unconscious material and, because it is 'not-self', it is possible for the artist to begin to separate.

Lacan emphasises the complexity of the act of looking at the picture. It brings into focus the artist, the picture and the viewer as all linked and bound by a mutual gaze:

> The function of the picture – in relation to the person to whom the painter, literally, offers his picture to be seen – has a relation with the gaze. . . . I think there is a relation with the gaze of the spectator, but that it is more complex. The painter gives something to the person who must stand in front of his painting. . . . He gives something for the eye to feed on, but he invites the person to whom this picture is presented to lay down his gaze there as one lays down one's weapons.
>
> (Lacan 1977a: 101)

It is this act of 'laying down the gaze' which affects the artist as viewer of her/his own picture and also the therapist as viewer. First, the artist: when an artist makes a picture he/she sees something emerging and very often engages with it from the beginning. The picture here is object of the artist's gaze. When the picture is finished the artist may continue looking, apparently absorbed in the image. I have often observed a participant in an art psychotherapy group take little part in the group discussion after making the picture. He/she merely gazes at his/her picture. The engagement with the image is still live. This is more than just looking with the eye. There is a deep connection which holds the artist/viewer in thrall. It is this type of connection that is, I suggest, a form of 'laying down the gaze'. It can feel intrusive to interrupt this connection because it is evident that there is a process of engagement which needs time and space to develop. It is often said of this stage that the picture is feeding back; it is also said that, in this stage of the process, the picture is mirroring or reflecting the inner world. For the effects of the image to be assimilated, the artist lays down her/his gaze and submits to the effects of the imagery.

It is in the act of laying down the gaze that the therapist, too, viewing pictures in sessions, surrenders her or his gaze. She opens herself to the potential of that particular image and so to the client. Depending on the content of the imagery and also on the quality of the transference and countertransference, she or he may be penetrated, permeated or suffused by the imagery.

In this way the meeting between the artist and the therapist may be focused in the apex of the triangle, the picture. There is a shared gaze through which both are drawn into or seduced by the image. It is sometimes as if the picture is a pool between the pair. The therapist and the client are equally engaged. Both look into the water and what each sees there reflects elements of the self and elements of the other. The gaze of each person is drawn to this centre where the meeting reveals the mix of the unconscious desire of the transference and countertransference. This three-way relationship of artist–picture–viewer engages both people through the mediation of the art object. There is a relationship with the other person, but also a deep engagement in the picture for both artist and therapist. When the gaze of the therapist meets that of the patient in the picture, it illuminates the unconscious relationship between the pair, and so it may arouse strong feelings. Desire may be evoked in connection to the imagery. The imaginal world is brought live into the realms of the visible through the pictures which may well be invested as talismans, and sometimes, by both people.

WHAT IS A PICTURE?

Before discussing the effects of the gaze of the real, actual, pictures in the therapeutic relationship there are other pictures to consider. Lacan poses the question 'What is a picture?' (Lacan 1977a). This deceptively simple question is central to the theme of this chapter. It conveys several potential meanings of the word 'picture' of which art is only one facet. In this way we see that the therapist, in all forms of psychotherapy, makes pictures of the client.

Our perceptions are pictures – we picture each other. If I am object of the gaze of the Other, 'the gaze is outside, I am looked at, that is to say, I am a picture' (Lacan 1977a: 106). If I am a picture, seen and so framed by another, then I am the object of their gaze. But when I see out into the world, the Other is object of my gaze, I frame them. To be the object of another's gaze does not mean that we have to be able to see; we are seen. 'What determines me, at the most profound level, in the visible is the gaze that is outside. It is through the gaze that I enter light' (Lacan 1977a: 106).

Let us consider what it means to be a picture for the other person in the therapeutic interaction. The therapist forms a picture of the patient; the patient is regarded by the therapist and through that gaze the patient enters the 'light'. The therapist, as Other, throws 'light' on the unconscious. However, this is problematic because this is not an objective gaze, untrammelled by the viewpoint of the observer. The viewer will be influenced by all kinds of preconceptions, political and cultural, as well as psychological.

Feminists have pointed out that women, depicted in paintings and film, have been the subject and often, too, victim of the objectifying male gaze (Mulvey 1975; Petersen & Wilson 1976; Parker & Pollock 1981; Rose 1986; Pollock 1988).[1] At its worst the gaze of the therapist may contribute to a form of abuse of the patient. The therapist has more power than the patient and, in this imbalanced situation, her gaze frames the patient who, by revealing the fears and anxieties with which she or he is troubled, empowers the therapist. Gender is one factor in this framing, as we saw in Chapter 2. However, perhaps the greatest potential for abuse is that the therapist has the power to describe the patient's communications as mad. Frequently it is this which the patient beginning therapy fears. The therapist's gaze can then be seen as the objectifying gaze which may assess vulnerability as madness. A 'picture' is formed, of the client, which may be very different from her view of herself.

THE GAZE OF THE THERAPIST: COUNTERTRANSFERENCE

Certainly the client is framed by the gaze of the therapist, from the beginning, and this is characterised by all the therapist knows and all she perceives. However, this is not necessarily abusive. The therapist uses her inward gaze to understand the countertransference. She monitors the effects of this particular client on her and she observes her own responses. This includes 'the picture' in the 'mind's eye' that the therapist forms of this particular person. Thus, the countertransference could be understood to be a form of measured gaze looking both inwards and outwards. This is different from the quality of the gazes in social interactions because behaviour, which would seem impolite in casual interaction, is the essence of the interaction in analytic forms of psychotherapy. In therapy the therapist may look away from the other person, may avoid eye contact, in order to be able to look inwards. The patient may find this rather confusing at first and may attribute this to lack of interest on the part of the therapist. However, this withdrawal of the gaze heralds an attempt to perceive the status of the unconscious communication between the two.

The eye and the gaze are not the same thing. 'This is for us the split which is manifested at the level of the scopic field.' Desire is manifest in the gaze, 'the gaze is the underside of consciousness' (Lacan 1977a: 83). Lacan's distinction between the eye and the gaze is evoked rather than explained: 'something slips, passes, is transmitted, from, stage to stage, and is always to some degree eluded in it – that is what we call the gaze' (Lacan 1977a: 73). This is connected to the scopic drive, the drive to see in all its variations, to see visually and to see – to understand – to perceive. The gaze is indirect and elusive. The eye might be understood as conscious and direct whilst the gaze is the 'underside of consciousness', i.e. unconscious.

In analytical art psychotherapy these interpersonal and self-referential gazes are held in common with other forms of analytical psychotherapy. But there is the additional complexity evoked by the use of art materials and the subsequent effects of the art objects. This involves several subsequent gazes. The therapist's countertransference to the art object is an aesthetic appreciation in which the eye travels around the pictured image. At times this may be a very focused gaze directed to the whole, or to particular facets, of the picture. Inevitably the therapist, as viewer, is first affected by the aesthetic qualities of what she sees. The picture may appear to her as being strikingly pretty, ugly, vitally alive or rather dead. If her interest is aroused, she may be induced to move in closer to look more at a detail or she may recoil in distaste. In this way there may be a physical interaction, a movement towards the picture. She may be attracted to the sensual quality of the paint marks or, alternatively, find the scratchy surface drawing immensely irritating. If the picture is abstract, she may be affected by the organisation of pattern, of marks and relationships within the frame of the picture. She may notice a dominant colour in relation to a less dominant one, or the thin lines or loaded brush marks. The work may be figurative, in which case the relationships between the figures and their ground may contribute to her sense of the picture as a whole. Some figure may stand out or another be hidden or barely observable. She may have to draw closer to make out if this is actually a figure or merely an accidental mark on the paper. In any of these cases she is responding to the aesthetic elements in the work.

Furthermore, the therapist considers the effects of these marks in the picture as a whole and this widens to a consideration of how they relate to her experience of the therapeutic relationship. She looks within to observe her response to both person and picture. Her gaze may glide over the surface of the picture, simultaneously observing the placing of a blob of yellow in the left-hand corner, and the artist who sits before her wearing yellow trousers and speaking of hope. Noticing the connections between these is not a conscious act, it is a subliminal registering of connection. Later, something is said and this wandering gaze becomes focused. A change is registered and a conscious realisation begins to take place. First, this is in the therapist's awareness, which she may or may not communicate to the patient. Thus, an aesthetic countertransference, to person and picture combined, is operating. This is the application of the gaze in its widest, free-floating sense; the whole forms a picture in the mind's eye.

If I see the eye, the gaze is out of focus; if I see the gaze, the eye is not seen (Lacan 1977a). This is like the figure/ground flip – if I look one way, I see the figure but if I alter my gaze, the ground predominates. Sometimes, from the therapist's viewpoint, the figure, in the therapeutic setting, is the patient and the picture is merely the ground. At other times this is reversed and the picture is the figure and the therapeutic relationship becomes the ground. In psychotherapy without pictures, this operates too. The gaze from person to person – from client to therapist – or from therapist to client may be similar. At one time we perceive only the conscious communication, then later, something changes and we hear the other possible meaning of what is said. A gaze may be furtive or indirect or it may be direct and penetrating. What is seen may be what is actually there or it may be distorted by the lens of the transference or the countertransference. Thus what is perceived by the therapist may be monstrous and terrifying or, alternatively, fascinating and seductive. Further, such perceptions do not necessarily depend on visual perception. Thus, the pictures the therapist perceives include the client as a picture. This we saw in my description of David's enactment where the artist and the art object combined to form a picture.

THE GAZE OF THE CLIENT: TRANSFERENCE

The client forms a picture of the therapist and sometimes this corresponds with the therapist's self-perception and so may be seen as the real relationship. However, at other times the perception is distorted by the transference. 'The gaze I encounter . . . is, not seen as a gaze, but a gaze imagined by me in the field of the Other' (Lacan 1977a: 84). The gaze of the transference is thus. The client's view of the therapist is not only a real present gaze but also one that is imagined, courted, feared, attributed to the 'Other'. This 'Other' is the therapist but it is also the unconscious; and this Other, as we have seen, may also be an art object. In the transference the client experiences herself as observed. This may relate to being observed for real, now and in the present, or it may relate to an experience of shame or guilt which is carried from the past. (Lacan's discussion refers to Sartre (1974) who links the gaze to shame.) The client may feel watched, and indeed she is observed, but the feeling may be intensified by the transference.

In the transference the patient forms a 'picture' of the therapist. The therapist is observed and, through the transference, she becomes the object of the patient's gaze. A transference is a view which is more than usually affected by the gaze from within. This gaze can be a true perception of the situation or the state of the therapist, but the colour may be tinted by the transference. Take the comment 'I think I've upset you', made to me by a patient recently. This could be an accurate perception on the part of the patient. His disclosure may have discomforted the therapist in some way in which case his eyes do not deceive him. However, his view may be coloured by the transference and so his perception of outward data is stained by perception from the inward gaze. It may be the case, for example, that he has never disclosed this material before for fear that it would upset his mother. The transference is such that he perceives, in the therapist, the reaction that he had anticipated, and also feared, from his mother. Thus, his present perception is stained by the past and the transference is live in the present. This does not remain fixed and the 'picture' of the therapist is a frequently shifting picture within the frame of the therapeutic setting.

When real pictures – art objects – are involved, there is an added dimension. The artist/client looks at the art object and looks at the therapist and each makes an impression through the gaze. The art object which embodies affect may be experienced as a scapegoat, an object of transference. Subsequently, and as an aspect of the transference, the client may have a countertransference to her/his own image. The aesthetic countertransference in this case is a response to the completed art object. It is his/her own image, familiar and yet not known. When we first step back to regard our own picture, we see something new. This is different from our perception of the emergent image seen in the process of creation. The artist is thus affected by the aesthetic effects of her/his own picture and this, too, has a bearing on the therapeutic interaction. When the client offers her picture to be seen she offers something to herself and also to the therapist. It might be pleasing, horrific or merely interesting. Whatever it holds, offering the picture to the gaze of the therapist will have implications.

THE PICTURE AND THE UNCONSCIOUS

The pictures, art objects, which hold elements of the unconscious may at times be magically empowered by the client and even sometimes by the therapist. This magical investment is one aspect of the influence of the 'life of the picture' (which I have written about elsewhere (Schaverien 1991: 103)). This is the stage after the painting is made and distinct from the 'life in the picture', which is the stage of its creation. Lacan, discussing great works of art viewed in public places, evokes further elements of the unconscious magical investment in pictures:

> Let us go to the great hall of the Doges' Palace in which are painted all kinds of battles, such as the battle of Lepanto, etc . . . Who comes here? Those who form . . . 'les peuples', the audiences. And what do the audiences see in these vast compositions? They see the gaze of those persons who, when the audiences are not there, deliberate in this hall. Behind the picture, it is their gaze that is there.
>
> (Lacan 1977a: 113)

The gaze of those who deliberate in this hall when there is no audience is the gaze of the picture. The figures in the pictures gaze on into the hall unseen but what is this gaze? The background could be the gaze of the culture in which the picture is viewed, and the foreground, the unseen gaze of the absent artist or the viewer. One facet of the gaze of a picture is the viewpoint of the people who figure as subject matter; they gaze on long after they, and the artist who immortalised them, have gone. Moreover, the action continues in the absence of the viewers because the picture has an enduring existence – the picture has 'a life'. Lacan writes of 'the gaze behind':

> You see there are always lots of gazes behind . . . the gaze of the painter, which claims to impose itself as being the only gaze. There is always a gaze behind. But – this is the most subtle point – where does this gaze come from?
>
> (Lacan 1977a: 113)

The gaze behind is clearly complex. This gaze behind is, as I understand it, both that of the picture itself, and also of the figures within it. Further, it is the gaze of the artist who created it which is, in a sense, always there behind the picture. The 'gaze behind' is also the unconscious. It follows that this, too, is related to desire and the lack. Thus, Lacan's discussion raises many questions about 'the life of the picture'. Whether they are viewed within a gallery or a therapy session, pictures have a continued existence; the awareness of this has an effect.

In therapy the talisman picture is magically empowered; it is imbued with life for the artist and sometimes for the spectator. There is a similar quality to the idea of the life which goes on in the gallery in the absence of the viewers. This, too, evokes magical thinking and connects to the picture as talisman.

> The empowering of an object or a painting as a talisman is the result of a magical attitude which animates the object. The status of the object becomes inflated; it is transformed from its material, substantial form and is given an aura which transcends its actual concrete existence.
>
> (Schaverien 1991: 139)

I am suggesting that a similar magical investment is evoked by Lacan's inference of happenings in the absence of the audience. The thought of a gaze which continues in the absence of the viewers taps into the propensity within each of us to regress to the memory of a time when everything was connected, undifferentiated. This is the material of children's story books in which toys come to life when children are in bed. It is evocative of dream life and, too, of the magical investment the artist makes in the talisman picture. The 'life of the picture', attributed to it by the client, continues in the absence of the viewers.

My point is that this gaze behind, the unconscious of the artist, is significant when considering the transference and countertransference affects of pictures. Moreover, the beholder, 'the audiences', parallel the therapist's response to certain imagery. Clearly, a complex set of relation-ships, of relevance to psychotherapists, are implied in these questions regarding art in galleries. The three-way form of relating through the gaze – artist–picture–therapist – is a powerful element in any therapeutic interaction. At times the intended effects of pictures may be malevolent, at others, they may be seductive. The pivotal role of the picture in the triangle is its actual perceived gaze and the gaze imagined by the viewers.

THE GAZE OF THE PICTURE

The apex of the triangle is the picture, it is the focal point, the container for the meeting of the gaze of patient and therapist. Therefore it will be a potent carrier of the transference and the countertransference. Furthermore, the picture's gaze affects the viewers. Clearly, the picture does not have consciousness. However, the idea that the picture itself has a gaze is not new. We have already seen that the gaze of the artist could be understood to be behind the picture (Lacan 1977a; Foucault 1971). The gaze in art has been discussed by Foucault (1971) and Pollock (1988) and in film by Mulvey (1975) and Rose (1986). The first and most obvious gaze of the picture is when there are figures which look out and appear to regard the viewer. This is one facet of the gaze of the picture in therapy too; but it has rather different implications, in the cases which I am considering, than in the portraits of women discussed by Pollock (1988).

We have seen in Chapter 8 that the picture lures the viewer into a relationship. The lure is affected through the aesthetic quality, the surface pattern, the initial impression or the way it is painted. This is influenced by style and technique (Simon 1992) and leads to a deeper relation through the gaze. There is a gaze irrespective of whether or not eyes are portrayed; the affects of the picture communicate 'eye to eye' as Adamson (1986) puts it. This kind of interaction may transcend other forms of communication and at times links directly and at a visceral level. This needs further elaboration and two of the pictures made by Carlos will illustrate the point. The first is the bubble picture, which was Figure 4.4 in Chapter 4. It is shown here as Figure 9.4. This picture could be understood to have allure but this is not an obviously beautiful picture.

This picture is drawn in the faintest of pencil marks. The figure is emaciated and without genitals and the proximity to death by starvation is evident. The atrophied figure is enclosed, and restricted within this bubble/womb. The figure has a terrifying gaze. We see the emaciated death's head staring out at us through eyes which are, hardly eyes at all, more like dark sockets. The mouth is open and lets out a silent cry. If we permit it to touch us, we cannot but be disturbed by this image. I suggest that despite its tragic and rather frightening aspect, this picture has allure.

The viewer is lured into a relationship with this image and, just because

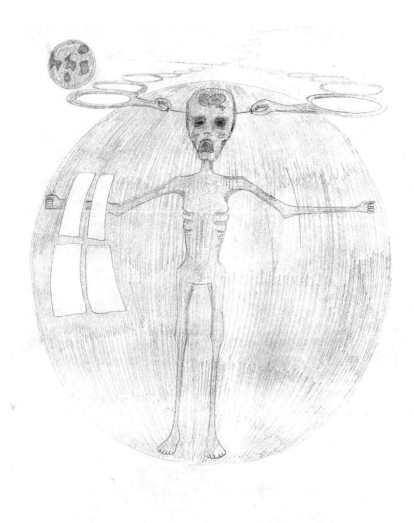

Figure 9.4 The bubble (also shown as Figure 4.4)

it is shocking, it is also fascinating. We are curious and wish to take a closer look, we become interested. If we remember the discussion in Chapter 6 of the injunctions from Kant and Bion regarding the absence of memory and desire, we begin to see what this means. Kant discusses desire as related to interest. When we view a picture such as this, we are interested, we wish to know more. Another element of desire is imagination, and this picture is evocative, so we begin to imagine why or how it has come to be created. It could be said that this picture evokes desire. This desire is clearly not a sexual interest and the lure here is not a positive seduction, but I propose that none the less it has allure. We respond and either want to know more, or are repelled by the surface appearance and so wish to reject it. In either case interest is aroused. This is partly because the artist was visually articulate and so the image 'speaks to us': it appeals to the gaze.

When regarding this drawing, I suggest that we are aware of the gaze behind. We cannot view such an image without wondering about the artist. The gaze of the artist is behind that of the figure which looks out at us, entrapped, within his bubble. The artist's viewpoint is offered to the beholder and, to a greater or lesser degree, we take up his position when we view the picture. So the beholder identifies with the position of the artist. We empathise.

There is a different lure when we regard the image made eight months later, which is Plate 10 in Carlos's series in Chapter 4. Here we feel relief. In contrast to the bubble picture, we see the male figure filled out and triumphant. It is the reverse of the bubble in almost every respect. The lure here is a genuine attraction to the image. It is attractively painted and visually inviting. The figure stands confidently in the centre of the page, his back to the viewer. He appears to be going away, perhaps leaving the place where he has been trapped. He holds a sword aloft, which indicates that he has found his sexuality and faces the future, the sun. Technically this is painted in bright colours and he appears to emerge from the earth. It seems like a rebirth image. There are no eyes in this picture, but none the less the power of the picture projects and so could be understood as having the presence of a gaze. It connects to the eye of the artist and the beholder. The gaze of the viewer contemplates a movement towards a future. No longer trapped, it is a view of freedom. Here the gaze behind is again of interest because, if we are identified with the artist, then as beholders of the image, we celebrate with him. Thus, we begin to see how the aesthetic counter-transference is affected through both – the lure of the image and the subsequent gaze. We then understand a little of how these pictures had the effect of engaging both artist and therapist. It is the gaze behind the picture which affects the deepening of the relationship. The gaze behind, as we have seen, is the artist's gaze behind the picture as well as the unconscious. This deepens the artist's relation to himself and also to the therapist. The first picture reveals a dangerous and fearsome state and the second image is almost like a gift for the beholder, revealing as it does the improved state of the artist. The point is that these pictures, both in their different ways, were a lure and, subsequently, both appealed to the gaze of the viewer. This engagement through the gaze was one significant facet of the therapeutic relationship.

This could be understood to be seduction by the image at a profound level. The lure seduces the artist and the beholder into relationship with the picture and this deepens to engage the gaze. The erotic connection may be a facet of this engagement at first held in the artwork. Later, there is an awareness of the other person and this leads to the three-way two-person engagement of both people and picture.

CONCLUSION

In this chapter I have discussed the three gazes which form the triangle: artist–picture–viewer. These are the gaze of the therapist regarding the client and the picture, but also looking within, and the gaze of the client looking within through the lens of the picture and also looking outwards to the therapist. The third element, the apex of the triangle, is the gaze of the picture. This projects into the in-between space of the therapeutic relationship and engages the gaze of both people. The engendered gaze is the gaze which is engendered through the pictures and sometimes this may embody desire. The unconscious mix of the gazes of client and therapist may profoundly affect the transference and the countertransference. Thus, the transforming potential of pictures in therapy may lead to a move from unconscious to consciousness through the multiple gazes which this triangle creates.

Chapter 10

Conclusion

The purpose of this book has been twofold: it has been to bring the desire of the female therapist out into the light, so to speak, and to open the topic for discussion in all forms of psychotherapy. It has been an exploration of ways in which pictures influence and affect the erotic transference and countertransference. I have discussed some of the ways in which the desire of both female therapist and male patient as beholders are affected by the lure of the imagery. Much of this book has been inspired by my reading of Lacan and particularly his work on the gaze (Lacan 1977a). In his writing Lacan threw down many seeds which remain ready to germinate; some of these have borne fruit in relation to this book.

This work is part of a continuing process and so I do not see it as definitive. It raises many issues for further consideration. In this conclusion I will attempt to point to these as well as to draw some of the threads of the book together. The full impact of the reverberations of the visual image and its correspondence in the psyche offer scope for further examination. The gender of the gaze has not been fully exploited, nor has the distinction between the look and the gaze, to which I alluded in the introductory chapter. In considering Carlos's pictures in Chapter 4, and those of Harry from *The Revealing Image* (Schaverien 1991), we have seen that the gender of the therapist–client pair resonates with the gender of the figures depicted. This affects the therapeutic relationship and is also evoked by it. For example, Carlos's idealised madonna image (Figure 4.9) might have had a different impact if the therapist had been a man. This is not easy to test but it seems likely that the female therapist is more likely to experience a transference connection when gazing on such an image than a male therapist. She is then likely to identify and may respond by rejection of the potential idealisation or else by over-identifying with it.

Similarly the dancers depicted by Harry raise the same question – would a male therapist see himself as one of these dancers or would he be more detached than the female therapist when regarding such imagery? It depends on the atmosphere in the transference but it is likely that the male therapist, although he may be fascinated by such imagery, may not identify so easily with imagery which appears to depict the feminine or anima figure. Thus, I have proposed that the desire of the female therapist may be evoked and, at times, she may be seduced by the image and lured into relationship through the gaze. There is clearly an indication here for future work. To explore the differences in the aesthetic countertransference effects of certain imagery on female and male therapists, respectively.

The erotic transference and countertransference between the female therapist and the female client remains an area for further exploration. (O'Connor & Ryan (1993) in their work on lesbianism and psychoanalysis have begun this.) I am particularly interested to see if the imagery which emerges in this dyad is similar or different from that evoked when female therapists work with male patients. My hypothesis is that there is a perceptible difference. This is hinted at in the case illustration of Elisabeth, whose landscapes seemed to suggest the maternal body in a rather different way than those of Carlos. However, such limited material does not permit any more than a speculative observation and may just be the differences observed between different people rather than reflecting any particular gender difference.

Another area where some further work is planned is the psychotherapeutic engagement when the patient is terminally ill. The countertransference is tested in an unusual way when the patient has not long to live – boundaries are challenged and need to be relaxed a little. When the individuation process leads to a resolution in death rather than life, there is a rather different set of countertransference problems to encounter. This is work in progress.

These are future concerns but for now, and in conclusion, I would make the links between the various chapters. In the second chapter it was my intention to draw attention to the female therapist's erotic arousals in the therapeutic setting. This indicates that, although there is less evidence of sexual abuse of their clients by female therapists, it is not because we are not aroused. Open discussion of these issues makes us conscious and then there is less likely to be unconscious acting out. This, too, merits further exploration and leaves a number of questions which remain unanswered. The current interest in countertransference experience and sexual acting out is evident in several books which are being published at the present time. This is clearly going to receive more attention in the future. Two books which have been published since this manuscript was completed exemplify this trend: *The Wounded Healer: Countertransference from a Jungian Perspective* (Sedgwick 1994), and *Sexual Feelings in Psychotherapy* (Pope *et al.* 1994).

The three chapters which were devoted to discussion of anorexia in a male patient are significant beyond the theme of desire and the gaze. There was an attempt to draw attention to the male anorexic patient and to mark this as a serious, and potentially life-threatening problem for men. Too often anorexia in men is dismissed as an insignificant issue because, as writers continually remind us, only 8 or 10 per cent of sufferers are male. However, we should remember that this small percentage adds up to a great many people. It is clear that their suffering is just as great as that of women although the social roots of eating disorders in men may be understood rather differently. This, too, calls for a great deal more research and particularly into the cultural significance of anorexia in men.

In the case study I demonstrated the ways in which the erotic drive could be understood to be inverted in anorexia. Art came to embody that drive and, in association with the transference, led the way out of the undifferentiated state. This is one significant role of art in this context. Engagement with the art object may lead the way out of the trap which is anorexia. Carlos's own words graphically describe his view of this process. Furthermore, I have proposed that viewing the art object, as a transactional object, may offer a new understanding of its specific significance in the context of anorexia. It externalises internalised aggression and redirects it, giving it an outward form. In this view of the artwork, as a transactional object, I have extended the idea of the scapegoat and the talisman transference (Schaverien 1987b, 1991), and added an additional category. This may have an application beyond the treatment of anorexia. It may offer a way of viewing the role of pictures as treatment in other borderline states and particularly psychosis. Thus, here too, there is potential for future research.

The figure–ground relationship discussed in the book has implications for art therapy and psychotherapy. I have suggested that we might see the picture emerging out of the space where there is silence in other forms of psychotherapy. Pictures exist in the space in-between the people. Sometimes interest in the pictures will have priority over the interpersonal relationship – art is the figure and the therapeutic relationship the ground from which it emerges. However, at other times the interpersonal transference and countertransference is the figure and the pictures the ground. When this occurs the pictures may be like illustrations of the therapeutic transference. A further category would be the type of interaction where the two are interchangeable and the pictures interrelate with the person-to-person transference and countertransference. Neither figure nor ground is dominant; they are of equal status. These different approaches are often arrived at as a response to the needs of the patient and sometimes they are a result of the therapeutic setting (see Schaverien 1994c).

It has been argued that desire is a factor which is present in every therapeutic encounter and, indeed, in every engagement with pictures. We might see the life force, 'libido', as a form of energy which is sometimes channelled into sexuality and sometimes into other forms of desire. We have seen that desire is the move towards the 'Other'. Although it is always present, desire is not always activated in any definite sense. In the therapeutic engagement it may become activated and, very often, this is the aim. It is through eros that consciousness begins to dawn on the unconscious state. We have seen that this is sometimes evoked by a person and sometimes a combination of person and picture. It is in this case that the gaze, engendered through the pictures, evokes desire in the transference and countertransference. When this occurs, a transformation in the relationship in-between the people may begin. This may be the starting point for a transformation in the psychological state of one or sometimes both people.

Notes

3 DESIRE AND THE MALE PATIENT: ANOREXIA

1 It is significant that in the case study in a previous work (Schaverien 1991) the first regressed phase of the work with Harry was when the most pictures were made. This phase, too, lasted for a similar ten months.
2 I have written about the retrospective exhibition in art psychotherapy in Schaverien 1991, 1993.

5 THE TRANSACTIONAL OBJECT: ART PSYCHOTHERAPY IN THE TREATMENT OF ANOREXIA

1 Inpatient admissions are often made because there is concern regarding the physical condition of the patient and, for a time and in some cases, attention to this has to take priority in the overall treatment plan. This means that many professionals become involved and 'things' are done to the patient.
2 This is a term for which I am indebted to my colleague Dr Ragnar Johnson for drawing my attention. In exploring the use of art objects in art therapy with our MA students at the University of Hertfordshire, he pointed out the transactional use of artefacts in anthropological studies.
3 In this chapter I use the pronoun 'she' for convenience. The majority of anorexic patients are female but this is in no way intended to preclude the minority of males who also suffer from anorexia.

7 DESIRE, THE SPACES IN-BETWEEN AND THE IMAGE OF A CHILD

1 An earlier version of this paper, 'The child within', was given in May 1987 at the conference 'Image and Enactment in Childhood' at Hertfordshire College of Art and Design and published in the conference proceedings (Schaverien 1987a).

9 THE ENGENDERED GAZE

1 In film theory the topic of the gaze has been widely explored. It is beyond the scope of this book to enter into discussion of the arguments involved. However, one facet of this discussion is the objectification of women and the various psychological relations of men and women to that situation.

Organisations

Analytical Art Therapy Associates
20 Angus Close
Stamford
PE9 2YU

British Association of Art Therapists
11a Richmond Road
Brighton
Sussex BN2 3RL

Eating Disorders Association
Sackville Place
44–48 Magdalen Street
Norwich
Norfolk NR3 1JU

Prevention of Professional Abuse Network
Flat 1
20 Daleham Gardens
London NW3 5DA

Women's Therapy Centre
6 Manor Gardens
London NW7

Society of Analytical Psychology
1 Daleham Gardens
London NW3

Bibliography

Adamson, E. (1986) *Art as Healing* London: Coventure.

Adler, G. (1948) *Studies in Analytical Psychology* London: Hodder & Stoughton (1966 edition).

Andersen, A. E. (ed.) (1990) *Males with Eating Disorders* New York: Brunner/Mazel.

Barry, M. J., Jr & Johnson, A. M. (1957) 'The incest barrier', paper cited by Searles, H. (1959) in *Collected Papers on Schizophrenia and Related Subjects* London: Maresfield (1986 edition). Given at a meeting of the American Psychoanalytic Association in Chicago.

Baynes, H. G. (1940) *Mythology of the Soul* London: Routledge & Kegan Paul.

Benjamin, J. (1988) *The Bonds of Love* London: Virago.

Benvenuto, B. & Kennedy, R. (1986) *The Works of Jacques Lacan: an Introduction* London: Free Associations.

Bion, W. R. (1970) *Attention and Interpretation* London: Maresfield.

Blum, H. P. (1971) 'On the conception and development of the transference neurosis', *Journal of the American Psychoanalytic Association* vol. 19, pp. 41–53.

—— (1973) 'The concept of eroticized transference', *Journal of the American Psychoanalytic Association* vol. 21, pp. 61–76.

Bollas, C. (1987) 'The transformational object', in *The Shadow of the Object* London: Free Associations.

Brennan, T. (ed.) (1989) *Between Feminism and Psychoanalysis* London and New York: Routledge.

Bruch, H. (1974) *Eating Disorders* London: Routledge & Kegan Paul.

—— (1978) *The Golden Cage: The Enigma of Anorexia* London: Open Books.

Carotenuto, A. (1982) *A Secret Symmetry* New York: Pantheon.

—— (1989) *Eros and Pathos* Toronto: Inner City Books.

Case, C. (1990) 'Reflections and shadows: an exploration of the world of the rejected girl', in Case, C. & Dalley, T. (eds) *Working with Children in Art Therapy* London: Routledge.

—— (1994) 'Art therapy in analysis: advance/retreat in the belly of the spider', London: *Inscape* vol. 1.

Case, C. & Dalley, T. (eds) (1990) *Working with Children in Art Therapy* London: Routledge.

—— (1992) *The Handbook of Art Therapy* London: Routledge.

Cassirer, E. (1955 and 1957) *The Philosophy of Symbolic Forms*, 3 vols, Newhaven, Conn. and London: Yale University Press.

—— (1955a) *Language* vol. 1.

—— (1955b) *Mythical Thought* vol. 2.

———— (1957) *The Phenomenology of Knowledge* vol. 3.

Champernowne, I. (1969) 'Art therapy as an adjunct to psychotherapy', London: *Inscape* vol. 1.

———— (1971) 'Art and therapy: an uneasy partnership', London: *Inscape* vol. 3.

Chasseguet-Smirgel, J. (1984a) *Creativity and Perversion* London: Free Associations.

———— (1984b) 'The femininity of the analyst in professional practice', *International Journal of Psychoanalysis* vol. 65, p. 169.

———— (1986) *Sexuality and Mind* London: Karnac (1989 edition).

Chernin, K. (1981) *Womansize* London: Womens's Press (1983 edition).

———— (1985) *The Hungry Self* London: Virago.

Chesler, P. (1972) *Women and Madness* New York: Avon.

Chodorow, N. (1978) *Reproduction of Mothering; Psychoanalysis and the Sociology of Gender* Berkeley: University of California Press.

———— (1994) *Femininities, Masculinities, Sexualities* London: Free Associations.

Cockburn, C. (1983) *Brothers: Male Dominance and Technological Change* London: Pluto.

———— (1985) *Machinery of Dominance: Women, Men and Technical Know How* London: Pluto.

Cockburn, C. & Ormrod, S. (1993) *Gender and Technology in the Making* London: Sage.

Colman, W. (1993) 'Aspects of anima and animus in oedipal development', paper given to the analytic group of the Society for Analytical Psychology, London, June.

Cooper, J. C. (1978) *An Illustrated Encyclopaedia of Symbols* London: Thames & Hudson

Covington, C. (1993) 'Eros framed; defenses against falling in love', paper given to the conference 'Countertransference and Gender', Association for Group and Individual Psychotherapy (AGIP), London, July.

Coward, R. (1984) *Female Desire* London: Paladin.

Crane, W. (1993) 'Insight versus eyesight', review of 'Look: an exhibition of art by visually impaired young people. Barbican Centre Dec 1992', London: *Inscape*, Summer.

Crisp, A. H. (1980) *Anorexia Nervosa: Let Me Be* London: Grune & Stratton.

Crisp, A. H. & Burns, T. (1990) 'Primary anorexia nervosa in the male and female: a comparison of clinical features and prognosis', in *Males with Eating Disorders*, ed. Andersen, A. E. New York: Brunner/Mazel.

Cunningham Dax, E. (1953) *Experimental Studies in Psychiatric Art* London: Faber & Faber.

Dalley, T. (ed.) (1984) *Art as Therapy* London: Routledge & Kegan Paul.

Dalley, T., Case, C., Schaverien, J., Weir, F., Halliday, D., Nowell Hall, P. & Waller, D. (1987) *Images of Art Therapy* London: Tavistock.

Dalley, T., Rifkind, G. & Terry, K. (1993) *Three Voices of Art Therapy: Image, Client, Therapist* London: Routledge.

Dally, P. & Gomez, J. (1979) *Anorexia Nervosa* London: Heinemann.

Dana, M. & Lawrence, M. (1988) *Women's Secret Disorder: A New Understanding of Bulimia* London: Grafton.

Doane, J. & Hodges, D. (1992) *From Klein to Kristeva: Psychoanalysis and the 'Good Enough' Mother* Ann Arbor: University of Michigan Press.

Edinger, E. F. (1990) *The Living Psyche: A Jungian Analysis in Pictures* Wilmette, Illinois: Chiron Publications.

Eichenbaum, L. & Orbach, S. (1983) *What do Women Want?* London: Michael Joseph.

Ernst, S. & Maguire, M. (eds)(1987) *Living with the Sphinx: Papers from the Women's Therapy Centre* London: Women's Press.

Feldman-Summers, S. & Jones, G. (1984) 'Psychological impacts of sexual contact between therapists or other health care practitioners and their clients', *Journal of Consulting and Clinical Psychology* vol. 52, pp. 1054–61.

Flower MacCannell, J. (1992) 'Desire', entry in *Feminism and Psychoanalysis: A Critical Dictionary* (ed.) Wright, E. Oxford: Blackwell.

Fordham, M. (1963) 'The empirical foundations and theories of the self in Jung's works', in *Analytical Psychology: A Modern Science* London: Heinemann.

———— (1971) *The Self and Autism* Library of Analytical Psychology, vol. 3, London: Heinemann.

———— (ed.) (1973) *Analytical Psychology: A Modern Science* London: Heinemann.

———— (1974) 'Defenses of the self', *Journal of Analytical Psychology* vol. 19, no. 2.

———— (1978) *Jungian Psychotherapy: A Study in Analytical Psychology* Chichester: John Wiley.

Foucault, M. (1971) 'Las Meninas', in *The Order of Things: An Archaeology of Human Sciences* First American edition, New York: Pantheon Books.

Frazer, J. G. (1911) *Taboo and the Perils of the Soul* London: Macmillan.

———— (1913) *The Scapegoat* London: Macmillan.

———— (1922) *The Golden Bough* London: Macmillan.

Freud, S. (1905) 'Three Essays on the Theory of Sexuality', *Standard Edition* vol. VII, London: Hogarth.

———— (1912) 'The dynamics of transference', *Standard Edition* vol. XII, London: Hogarth (1963 edition).

———— (1914) 'On Narcissism', *Standard Edition* vol. XIV, London: Hogarth.

———— (1915) 'Observations on Transference Love', *Standard Edition* vol. XII, London: Hogarth.

———— (1917) 'Transference', *Standard Edition* vol. XVI, London: Hogarth.

———— (1925) 'Some psychical consequences of the anatomical distinction between the sexes', *Standard Edition* vol. XIX, London: Hogarth.

———— (1931) 'Female sexuality', *Standard Edition* vol. XXI, London: Hogarth.

———— (1933) 'Femininity', *Standard Edition* vol. XXII, London: Hogarth.

Gilligan, C. (1982) *In a Different Voice: Psychological Theory and Women's Development* Cambridge, Mass. and London: Harvard University Press (1993 edition).

———— (1993) 'Letter to Readers', in 1993 edition.

Goldberger, M. & Evans, D. (1985) 'On transference manifestations in male patients with female analysts', *International Journal of Psychoanalysis* vol. 66, 295 pp.

Gombrich, E. H. (1963) *Meditations on a Hobby Horse* London: Phaidon.

Gordon, R. (1980) 'Narcissism and the self – who am I that I love?', *Journal of Analytical Psychology* vol. 25, no. 3, pp. 247–62.

Graves, R. (1955) *The Greek Myths I* London: Penguin.

Greenacre, P. (1959) 'Certain technical problems in the transference relationship', *Journal of the American Psychoanalytical Association* vol. 7, pp. 484–502.

Greenson, R. (1967) *The Technique and Practice of Psychoanalysis* London: Hogarth.

———— (1968) 'Dis-identifying from mother; its special importance for the boy', *International Journal of Psychoanalysis* vol. 49, pp. 370–4.

Grosz, E. (1992) 'Phallic mother', entry in *Feminism and Psychoanalysis: A Critical Dictionary* (ed.) Wright, E. Oxford: Blackwell.

Grotstein, J. (1986) *Splitting and Projective Identification* New Jersey: Aronson.

Guttman, H. A. (1984) 'Sexual issues in the transference and countertransference between female therapist and male patient', *Journal of the American Academy of Psychoanalysis* vol. 12, pt 4, pp. 187–97.

Heimann, P. (1950) 'On Countertransference', *International Journal of Psychoanalysis* vol. 31, pp. 81–4.

Henzell, J. (1984) 'Art, psychotherapy and symbol systems', in *Art as Therapy* Dalley, T. (ed.) London: Tavistock.

Hillman, J. (1975) *Loose Ends* Dallas, Texas: Spring (1989 edition).

———— (1977) *The Myth of Analysis* New York: Harper.

Hobson, R. (1984) 'The curse in the dead man's eye', London: *Changes* vol. 2, no. 2.

Hopcke, R. H. (1989) *Jung, Jungians and Homosexuality* Boston and London: Shambala.

Horney, K. (1932) 'The dread of woman', *International Journal of Psychoanalysis* vol. 13, pp. 348–60.

Irigaray, L. (1974) *Speculum of the Other Woman* Translated by Gillian C. Bell New York: Cornell University Press.

Jarman, D. (1993) *Blue*. Film distributor Basilisk Communications, in association with Channel 4/Arts Council of Great Britain/Opal/BBC Radio 3.

———— (1977) *This Sex Which is Not One* Translated by Caterine Porter New York: Cornell University Press (1985 edition).

Jehu, D. (1994) *Patients as Victims* Chichester: John Wiley.

Jukes, A. (1993) *Why do Men Hate Women?* London: Free Associations.

Jung, C. G. (1946) *The Psychology of the Transference* CW 16, Princeton: Bollingen (1954 edition).

———— (1956) *Symbols of Transformation* CW 5, Princeton: Bollingen (1976 edition).

———— (1959a) *'The Transcendent Function'* CW 8, London: Routledge (1960) (1916 edition).

———— (1959b) *The Archetypes and the Collective Unconscious* CW 9, Pt 1, Princeton: Bollingen.

———— (1960) *The Structure and Dynamics of the Psyche* CW 8, London: Routledge.

———— (1963) *Memories, Dreams and Reflections* London: Collins/Fontana.

Kant, I. (1928) *The Critique of Judgement* Oxford: Clarendon Press, translated by James Creed Meredith (1953 edition).

Karme, L. (1979) 'The analysis of a male patient by a female analyst: the problem of the negative oedipal transference', *International Journal of Psychoanalysis* vol. 60, pp. 253–61.

Kavaler-Adler, S. (1992) 'Mourning and the erotic transference', *International Journal of Psychoanalysis* vol. 73, pp. 527–39.

Kay, D. (1985) 'Paternal psychopathology and the emerging ego', in *The Father: Contemporary Jungian Perspectives* Samuels, A. (ed.) London: Free Associations.

Kernberg, O. (1975) *Borderline Conditions and Pathological Narcissism* New York: Aronson (1981 edition).

—— (1993) 'Working with psychotic processes in art therapy', in *Psychoanalytic Psychotherapy* vol. 7, no. 1, pp. 25–38.
Klein, M. (1937) 'Love, guilt and reparation', in *Love, Guilt and Reparation* London: Hogarth Press (1985 edition).
—— (1946) 'Notes on some schizoid mechanisms', in *Envy and Gratitude* London: Hogarth Press.
Kohut, H. (1971) *The Analysis of the Self* New York: International Universities Press.
Kramer, E. (1971) *Art as Therapy with Children* London: Elek.
Kristeva, J. (1983) *Tales of Love* New York: Columbia University Press (1987 edition), Translated by Leon S. Roudiez.
—— (1989) *Black Sun Depression and Melancholia* New York: Columbia University Press. First published editions Gallimard (1987). Translated by Leon S. Roudiez.
Kuhns, R. (1983) *Psychoanalytic Theory of Art* New York: Columbia University Press.
Kulish, N. M. (1984) 'The effect of the sex of the analyst on the transference', *Bulletin of the Meninger Clinic* vol. 48 no. 2.
—— (1986) 'Gender and transference: the screen of the phallic mother', *International Review of Psychoanalysis* vol. 13, p. 393.
Lacan, J. (1949) 'The mirror stage as formative of the function of the I as revealed in psychoanalytic experience', in *Ecrits: a Selection* London: Routledge & Kegan Paul.
—— (1977a) *The Four Fundamental Concepts of Psycho-Analysis* London: Penguin.
—— (1977b) *Ecrits: a Selection* London: Routledge & Kegan Paul. Translated by Sheridan, A. Originally published in French by Editions du Seuil (1966).
Lawrence, M. (1984) *The Anorexic Experience* London: Women's Press.
—— (ed.) (1987) *Fed up and Hungry* London: Women's Press.
Ledermann, R. (1979) 'On the infantile roots of narcissistic personality disorder', *Journal of Analytical Psychology* vol. 24, p. 2.
—— (1982) 'Narcissistic disorder and its treatment', in *Psychopathology: Contemporary Jungian Perspectives* Samuels, A. (ed.) Karnac for Library of Analytical Psychology.
Lester, E. P. (1985) 'The female analyst and the eroticized transference', *International Journal of Psychoanalysis* vol. 66, pp. 283–93.
—— (1990) 'Gender and identity issues in the analytic process', *International Journal of Psychoanalysis* vol. 71, pp. 435–53.
Levens, M. (1987) 'Art therapy with eating disordered patients', *Inscape*, Summer, pp. 2–7.
Little, M. (1950) '"R" – The analyst's total response to his patient's needs', in *Toward Basic Unity* London: Free Associations Press (1986 edition).
MacGregor, S. (1989) 'Attachment behaviour and separation anxiety within the process of art therapy', unpublished MA thesis, Hertfordshire College of Art and Design.
Maclagan, D. (1982) 'Cultivated and wild', London: *Inscape* pp. 10–13.
—— (1989) 'Fantasy and the figurative', in *Pictures at an Exhibition* (eds) Gilroy, A. & Dalley, T. London: Tavistock/Routledge.
Mahler, M., Pine, F. & Bergman, A. (1975) *The Psychological Birth of the Human Infant* New York: Basic Books.
Mann, D. (1990) 'Art as a defense mechanism against creativity', *British Journal of Psychotherapy* vol. 7, no. 1, pp. 5–14.

Mann, D. (1990) 'Art as a defense mechanism against creativity', *British Journal of Psychotherapy* vol. 7, no. 1, pp. 5–14.
——— (1991) 'Some schizoid processes in art psychotherapy', London: *Inscape*, Summer.
McCleod, S. (1981) *The Art of Starvation* London: Virago.
McNamara, E. (1994) *Breakdown: Sex, Suicide and the Harvard Psychiatrist* New York: Pocket Books (Simon & Schuster Inc.).
Meltzer, D. (1967) *The Psychoanalytic Process* Perthshire, Scotland: Clunie.
Milner, M. (1977) *On Not Being Able to Paint* London: Heinemann.
Minuchin, S., Rosman, B. L. & Baker, L. (1978) *Psychosomatic Families: Anorexia Nervosa in Context* Cambridge, Mass.: Harvard University Press.
Mitchell, J. (1974) *Psychoanalysis and Feminism* London: Pelican.
——— (1982) 'Introduction 1', in *Feminine Sexuality: Jacques Lacan and the Ecole Freudienne* Mitchell, J. & Rose, J. (eds) London: Macmillan.
Mulvey, L. (1975) 'Visual pleasure in narrative cinema', *Visual and Other Pleasures* Bloomington: Indiana University Press (1989 edition).
Murphy, J. (1984) 'The use of art therapy in the treatment of anorexia nervosa', in *Art as Therapy: An Introduction to Art as a Therapeutic Technique* Dalley, T. (ed.) London: Tavistock.
Naumberg, M. (1953) *Psychoneurotic Art: Its Function in Psychotherapy* New York: Grune & Stratton.
——— (1966) *Dynamically Orientated Art Therapy* New York: Grune & Stratton.
Neumann, E. (1954) *The Origins and History of Consciousness* Princeton: Bollingen.
——— (1955) *The Great Mother* Princeton: Bollingen.
Newton, K. (1965) 'Mediation of infant–mother togetherness', in *Analytical Psychology: A Modern Science* Fordham, M. *et al.* (eds) London: Heinemann (1973 edition).
Oakley, A. (1972) *Sex Gender and Society* London: Arena & New Society (1985 edition).
O'Connor, N. & Ryan, J. (1993) *Wild Desires and Mistaken Identities: Lesbianism and Psychoanalysis* London: Virago.
Ogden, T. H. (1982) *Projective Identification and Psychotherapeutic Technique* New York: Aronson.
Olivier, C. (1980) *Jocasta's Children: the Imprint of the Mother* Translated by George Craig, reprinted London: Routledge (1989).
Orbach, S. (1978) *Fat is a Feminist Issue* London: Hamlyn.
——— (1986) *Hunger Strike* London: Faber & Faber.
Palazoli, M. S. (1974) *Self Starvation. From the Intrapsychic to the Transpersonal Approach to Anorexia Nervosa* New York and London: Jason Aronson.
Palmer, R. L. (1980) *Anorexia Nervosa* London: Penguin.
Parker, R. & Pollock, G. (1981) *Old Mistresses, Women, Art and Ideology* London: Routledge & Kegan Paul.
Peters, R. (1991) 'The therapist's expectations of the transference', *Journal of Analytical Psychology* vol. 36, no. 1, January.
Petersen, K. & Wilson, J. J. (1976) *Women Artists* London: Women's Press.
Piontelli, A. (1993) *From Fetus to Child: an Observational Study* London: Routledge.
Plaut, A. (1966) 'Reflections on not being able to imagine', in *Analytical Psychology: a Modern Science* Fordham, M. *et al.* (eds) London: Heinemann (1973 edition).
Pollock, G. (1988) *Vision and Difference, Femininity, Feminism and the Histories of Art* London: Routledge.
Pope, K. *et al.* (1994) *Sexual Feelings in Psychotherapy: Explorations for Therapists and Therapists in Training*, American Psychological Association.
Racker, H. (1968) *Transference and Countertransference* London: Hogarth Press.

Rappaport, E. A. (1956) 'The management of an eroticized transference', *Psychoanalytic Quarterly* vol. 25, pp. 515–29.

Rich, A. (1979) *Of Woman Born: Motherhood as Experience and Institution* London: Virago. First published in the USA in 1976.

Rose, J. (1982) 'Introduction – ii', in *Feminine Sexuality: Jacques Lacan and the Ecole Freudienne* Mitchell, J. and Rose, J. (eds) London: Macmillan.

—— (1986) *Sexuality in the Field of Vision* London: Verso.

Rosen, D. H. (1993) *Transforming Depression: A Jungian Approach Using the Creative Arts* New York: Tarcher Putnam.

Rosenfeld, H. (1965) *Psychotic States* New York: International Universities Press.

Russell, J. (1993) *Out of Bounds: Sexual Exploitation in Counselling and Therapy* London: Sage.

Rust, M. J. (1987) 'Images and eating problems', in *Fed Up and Hungry* Lawrence, M. (ed.) London: Women's Press.

—— (1992) 'Art therapy in the treatment of women with eating disorders', in *Art Therapy: A Handbook* Waller, D. & Gilroy, A. (eds) Oxford: Oxford University Press.

Rutter, P. (1989) *Sex in the Forbidden Zone* USA and Glasgow: Mandala and HarperCollins.

Rycroft, C. (1968) *A Critical Dictionary of Psychoanalysis* London: Penguin.

—— (1981) *The Innocence of Dreams* Oxford: Oxford University Press.

Ryle, J. A. (1939) 'Discussion on anorexia nervosa', *Proceedings of the Royal Society of Medicine* vol. 32, p. 735. Quoted in Dally, P. & Gomez, J. *Anorexia Nervosa* London: Heinemann.

Samuels, A. (1985a) 'Symbolic dimensions of Eros in transference–countertransference some clinical uses of Jung's alchemical metaphor', *International Review of Psychoanalysis* vol. 12, p. 199.

—— (1985b) *The Father: Contemporary Jungian Perspectives* London: Free Associations.

—— (1989) *The Plural Psyche Personality, Morality and The Father* London and New York: Routledge.

—— (1991a) 'The parents as messengers', *British Journal of Psychotherapy* vol. 7, no. 4, pp. 341–55.

—— (1991) 'Pluralism and training', *Journal of the British Association of Psychotherapists* no. 22.

—— (1993) *The Political Psyche* London and New York: Routledge.

—— (1995) 'From sexual misconduct to social justice', in *Psychoanalytic Dialogues*, Summer.

Sartre, J-P. (1974) *Being and Nothingness* Harmondsworth: Penguin.

Schaverien, J. (1982) 'Transference as an aspect of art therapy', *Inscape*, September.

—— (1987a) 'The child within', in the proceedings of the conference 'Image and Enactment in Childhood', Hertfordshire: College of Art and Design.

—— (1987b) 'The scapegoat and the talisman: transference in art therapy', in *Images of Art Therapy* Dalley, T. *et al.* London and New York: Tavistock.

—— (1989) 'Transference and the picture: art therapy in the treatment of anorexia', *Inscape*, Spring.

—— (1990) 'Desire alchemy and the picture', London: *Inscape*, Winter.

—— (1991) *The Revealing Image: Analytical Art Psychotherapy in Theory and Practice* London and New York: Routledge.

—— (1993) 'The retrospective review of pictures: data for research in art therapy', in *The Handbook of Inquiry in the Arts Therapies* Payne H. (ed.) London: Jessica Kingsley.

—— (1994a) 'The transactional object; art psychotherapy in the treatment of anorexia', *British Journal of Psychotherapy* vol. 11, no. 1, pp. 46–61.

—— (1994b) 'The picture as transactional object in the treatment of anorexia',

———— (1994a) 'The transactional object; art psychotherapy in the treatment of anorexia', *British Journal of Psychotherapy* vol. 11, no. 1, pp. 46–61.

———— (1994b) 'The picture as transactional object in the treatment of anorexia', in *Arts Therapies with Eating Disorders* Doktor, D. (ed.) London: Jessica Kingsley.

———— (1994c) 'Analytical art psychotherapy: further reflections on theory and practice', London: *Inscape*, Autumn.

Schwartz-Salant, N. (1989) *The Borderline Personality* Wilmette, Illinois: Chiron.

Schwartz-Salant, N. & Stein, M. (1992) *Gender and Soul in Psychotherapy* Wilmette, Illinois: Chiron.

Searles, H. (1959) 'Oedipal love in the countertransference', in *Collected Papers on Schizophrenia and Related Subjects* London: Maresfield (1986 edition).

Sedgwick, D. (1994) *The Wounded Healer: Countertransference from a Jungian Perspective* London, USA, Canada: Routledge.

Segal, H. (1981) 'Notes on symbol formation', in *The Work of Hanna Segal* New York: Aronson.

Segal, L. (1987) *Is the Future Female?* London: Virago.

Segal, N. (1989) 'Echo and Narcissus', in *Between Feminism and Psychoanalysis* Teresa Brennan (ed.) London and New York: Routledge.

Seth-Smith, F. (1987) 'The realm of the mirror', unpublished dissertation for the Post Graduate Diploma in Art Therapy at Hertfordshire College of Art and Design.

Sheridan, A. (1977) 'Translator's note' in *Ecrits* Lacan, J. (1977b) London: Routledge.

Shorter, B. (1985) 'The concealed body language of anorexia nervosa', in *The Father* Samuels, A. (ed.) London: Free Associations.

Simon, R. (1992) *The Symbolism of Style* London and New York: Routledge.

Sinclair, F. (1993) 'The therapeutic couple: does gender matter? Some thoughts on gender in the consulting room in individual psychotherapy', unpublished paper given to the Deparment of Psychotherapy at Edith Cavell Hospital, Peterborough, September.

Sniderman, M. S. (1980) 'A countertransference problem: the sexualising patient', *Canadian Journal of Psychiatry* vol. 25, pp. 303–7.

Spector Person, E. (1983) 'Women in therapy: therapist gender as variable', *International Review of Psychoanalysis* vol. 10, pp. 193–204.

———— 1985) 'The erotic transference in women and in men: differences and consequences', *Journal of the American Academy of Psychoanalysis* vol. 13, no. 2, pp. 159–80.

———— (1986) 'Male sexuality and power', *Journal of Columbia University Center for Psychoanalytic Training and Research Psychoanalytic Inquiry* vol. 6, no. 1, pp. 3–25.

———— (1993) paper presented at the conference 'Contemporary psychoanalysis – contemporary sexualities', organised by the Psychoanalysis Forum in conjunction with the Institute of Romance Studies, University of London, June.

Spignesi, A. (1983) *Starving Women* Dallas: Spring (1985 edition).

Spitz, E. H. (1985) *Art and Psyche* New Haven and London: Yale University Press.

———— (1991) *Image and Insight* New York: Columbia University Press.

Stein, R. (1974) *Incest and Human Love* Baltimore: Penguin.

Stern, D. (1985) *The Interpersonal World of the Human Infant* New York: Basic Books.

Stoller, R. J. (1968) *Sex and Gender* London: Hogarth Press.

———— (1975) *The Transexual Experiment*, vol. 2 of *Sex and Gender*, London: Hogarth.

Swearingen, K. (1991) 'The space to become visible: women's art therapy groups', unpublished Master's thesis, Hertfordshire College of Art and Design of the University of Hatfield.

Tatham, P. (1992) *The Makings of Maleness: Men, Women, and the Flight of Dedalus* London: Karnac for the Society of Analytical Psychology.

Thomson, M. (1989) *On Art and Therapy* London: Virago.

Tower, L. E. (1956) 'Countertransference', *Journal of the American Psychoanalytic Association* no. 4, pp. 224–55.

Tustin, F. (1972) *Autism and Childhood Psychosis* London: Hogarth (1976 edition).

Waller, D. (1991) *Becoming a Profession* London and New York: Routledge.

——— (1993) *Group Interactive Art Therapy* London: Routledge.

Waller, D. & Gilroy, A. (1992) *Art Therapy: a Handbook* Oxford: Oxford University Press.

Warnock, M. (1980) *Imagination* London: Faber & Faber.

Wehr, D. (1987) *Jung and Feminism: Liberating Archetypes* London: Beacon Press (1988 edition); London: Routledge.

Welldon, E. V. (1988) *Mother, Madonna, Whore: The Idealization and Denigration of Motherhood* New York, London: The Guilford Press.

Wetherell, J. M. (1988) 'The bridging function of imagination', unpublished Master's thesis, Hertfordshire College of Art and Design.

Wharton, B. (1993) 'The eye and the I', *Journal of Analytical Psychology* vol. 38, no. 1, pp. 77–85.

Wheeley, S. (1992) 'Looks that kill the capacity for thought', *Journal of Analytical Psychology* vol. 37, no. 2, pp. 187–210.

Whitford, M. (1989) 'Rereading Irigaray', in *Between Feminism and Psychoanalysis* Brennan, T. (ed.) London and New York: Routledge.

——— (ed.)(1991) *The Irigaray Reader* Oxford: Blackwell.

Whytt, R. (1767) *The Work of Robert Whytt* Edinburgh: Beckett, cited in Dally, P. & Gomez, J. *Anorexia Nervosa* London: Heinemann.

Williams, S. (1993) 'Women in search of women: clinical issues that underlie a woman's search for a female therapist', *British Journal of Psychotherapy* vol. 9, no. 3, Spring, pp. 291–300.

Winnicott, D. W. (1967) 'Mirror-role of mother and family in child development', in *Playing and Reality* London: Penguin.

——— (1971) *Playing and Reality* London: Penguin.

Wittgenstein, L. (1958) *Philosophical Investigations* Oxford: Blackwell.

——— (1980) *Remarks on the Philosophy of Psychology* Oxford: Blackwell.

Wollheim, R. (1987) *Painting as an Art* London: Thames & Hudson.

Woodman, M. (1982) *Addiction to Perfection: The Still Unravished Bride* Toronto: Inner City Books.

Woods, S. M. (1976) 'Some dynamics of male chauvinism', *Archives of General Psychiatry* vol. 33, pp. 63–5.

Wright, E. (ed.) (1992) *Feminism and Psychoanalysis: a Critical Dictionary* Oxford: Blackwell.

Wright, K. (1991) *Vision and Separation Between Mother and Baby* London: Free Associations.

Young-Eisendrath, P. (1992) 'Gender, animus and related topics', in *Gender and Soul in Psychotherapy* Schwartz-Salant, N. & Stein, M. (eds) Wilmette, Illinois: Chiron.

Zinkin, L. (1969) 'Flexibility in analytic technique', in *Technique in Jungian Analysis* Fordham, M. *et al.* (eds) Library of Analytical Psychology, London: Karnac (1989 edition).

——— (1983) 'Malignant mirroring', in *Journal of Group Analysis (London)* vol. XVI, no. 2.

Index